Philosophy, Writing, and the Character of Thought

Philosophy, Writing, and the Character of Thought

JOHN T. LYSAKER

The University of Chicago Press
Chicago and London

The University of Chicago Press, Chicago 60637
The University of Chicago Press, Ltd., London
© 2018 by The University of Chicago
Published 2018
Paperback edition 2021
Printed and bound by CPI Group (UK) Ltd, Croydon, CR0 4YY

30 29 28 27 26 25 24 23 22 21   1 2 3 4 5

ISBN-13: 978-0-226-56956-7 (cloth)
ISBN-13: 978-0-226-81585-5 (paper)
ISBN-13: 978-0-226-56973-4 (e-book)
DOI: https://doi.org/10.7208/chicago/9780226569734.001.0001

Library of Congress Cataloging-in-Publication Data

Names: Lysaker, John T., author.
Title: Philosophy, writing, and the character of thought / John T. Lysaker.
Description: Chicago : The University of Chicago Press, 2018. | Includes
bibliographical   references and index.
Identifiers: LCCN 2017050544 | ISBN 9780226569567 (cloth : alk. paper) |
ISBN 9780226569734 (e-book)
Subjects: LCSH: Philosophy —Authorship. | Authorship —Philosophy.
Classification: LCC B52.7 .L97 2018 | DDC 100 — dc23
LC record available at https://lccn.loc.gov/2017050544

♾ This paper meets the requirements of ANSI/NISO Z39.48-1992 (Permanence
of Paper).

For you and me

It is a mischievous notion that we are come late into nature;
that the world was finished a long time ago.
RALPH WALDO EMERSON

Contents

Gambits and Gambles

Motto for Mantras: Philosophy begins in displacement. Wonder, Aristotle's point of no return, is just one transposition.

After Emerson: Philosophy is always running into poetry even as it runs away.

Working Man's Measure: The humanities fail when they command an attention they cannot hold.

Enough Already: For all the praise heaped on Socrates, he is the exception. Philosophy makes its way in writing. Need this be the case? No. But no one thinks from the standpoint of necessity—except by choice.

A Whirl of a Time: "Philosophy"—the concept rattles and rolls as it gathers its instances.

One finds provocative dialogues like Plato's *Crito*. Performatively rich, the dialogue shows Socrates offering Crito, one more time, a lived example of the examined life. But *Crito* is also thematically rich, leading us to consider the range of obligations we owe to institutions of positive law. There are also systematic treatises like Kant's *Critique of Pure Reason*, Heidegger's *Being and Time*, and Habermas's *Theory of Communicative Action*. Each proposes to reorient us within dimensions seemingly integral to the human condition and with claims that should weather any objection by recurring in any effort to contest them. On the other end of a spectrum, at least with regard to magnitude, one finds philosophical miniatures from the likes of François de La Rochefoucauld. Aphorisms offer ungrounded generalizations about topics like human motivation and the probable fates of various character types. To find short forms that leave their thoughts unfinished, turn to Friedrich Schlegel, whose sensibility holds that "a project is the subjective embryo or seed (*Keim*) of a developing object" (1967, 168). Unlike the system, the treatise, or even the aphorism, the fragment courts its own undoing. It fulfills itself in a gesture toward a larger whole that it can only indicate, express, and thereby enlarge. And then there are writings that remind us of no other even as they stir us like no other: Nietzsche's *Genealogy of Morals*, DuBois's *The Souls of Black Folk*, Wittgenstein's *Philosophical Investigations*, and Irigaray's "The Sex Which Is Not One." Signs of a possible philosophy, they struggle to philosophize amid a profound uneasiness with the extant terms of philosophy—good and evil, race, meaning, sexual difference.

I should go on. Philosophy's written character is even wilder than what I've assembled. Think of Montaigne's concentrated essays, which engage personal subject matters such as kidney stones, but in a manner that leads the reader to issues of broad concern, for example, care of the self and addressing one's mortality. Emerson's essays clearly aim toward universality—"History," "Friendship," "The Poet," "Man the Reformer," "Fate," and so forth—and yet, their tone is deeply interpersonal. Or recall Descartes's *Meditations*: full of pauses and recapitulations, reflexive but somewhat impersonal, solitary yet coupled with solicited objections and impassioned replies. And then, more recently, Derrida's performances, which are hyper-reflexive on several fronts even as they follow out numerable digressions—self-absorbed but endlessly responding to texts.

The *Republic* is even more remarkable. It covers an enormous range of philosophy's topography: the soul and the polis, knowledge and justice. It also addresses the ancient quarrel between philosophy and poetry, and in dizzying ways, relying on images (the divided line) and allegory (the cave) while simultaneously undermining the authority of mimetic poetry, questioning, in fact, its right to move freely about a well-ordered city, particularly in the company of those still in the midst of their education. But then, the *Republic* is itself mimetic, although it presents speeches organized around reason-giving rather than actions aimed at our heaving affects. Performatively dizzying, thematically ambitious, the *Republic* is a philosophical and literary masterpiece, with a degree of integration that resists the opposition.

Somewhere between system and the miniature, and outside a republic of letters, lies the professional article and monograph. They usually summarize a current debate among professional philosophers in order to enrich an extant discussion—"add a wrinkle" as some like to say, though sometimes a new direction is proposed or an old one shut down. Such texts are impersonal and minimalist with regard to their literary ambitions. They are written by experts for experts and often employ specialized languages and forms of argumentation, whether symbolized or not.

Returning to the personal, autobiography has also been a scene of philosophy. Depending on one's principal of inclusion, this shelf might include Augustine's *Confessions*, Franklin's *Autobiography*, the *Narrative of the Life of Frederick Douglass*, Emma Goldman's *Living My Life*, and Stanley Cavell's *Little Did I Know*. Autobiographies recount how a life was lived, the situations confronted and the choices made, thereby presenting, perhaps defending, possible paths (including the path of writing, perhaps addressed, inevitably exemplified). It is the genre of a life, of its goods and struggles.[1]

No Instructions for Late Arrivals: "A philosophical problem," Wittgenstein writes, "has the form: 'I don't know my way about'" (2001, 42). Philosophy has been said in many ways. How should we proceed? The professional article has settled into philosophy's default mode, and it now prevails with the inertia of habit. Not without friction, however. Few enter philosophy fired by the dream of authoring professional articles. But we rarely indulge our vexations, at least not in order to work them through. "How should I write philosophy?" The question arises in aversion, but as it turns, an equally gut-based puzzlement follows. What should one consider when one asks: "How should I write philosophy?" I do not have a sufficient feel for the possibilities (and potholes) bound to various modes of philosophical writing. I do not know how to acquire that feel.

For Starters: "I unsettle all things," Emerson announces near the close of "Circles" (1996, 412). The phrase is provocative given the polysemy of "settle." Is he stirring up the stream with which he identifies "Man" in "The Over-Soul," which precedes "Circles" in *Essays: First Series*? Is he unsettling once-settled questions? Or is he taking leave from all things (as opposed to settling among them)? I am drawn to the line because I am, in part, aiming to unsettle how we commit philosophy to writing and thus commit to philosophy. But Emerson's phrase is also a bit grandiose. All things? At once? Would such a gesture be legible? In a garden of genres, bewildered and lured by competing directions, the basic requirements of English grammar remain more or less in play. The meanings of the words I use do not flummox me, although their nuances and histories often surprise. I do not feel the threat of solipsism undermining communication per se. What is in doubt, however, is what I choose when I commit to a manner of writing.

In What Follows: Dry as toast, Thoreau observed that "it is difficult to begin without borrowing" (2008, 31). Several names are germane, each standing for what is not really theirs or mine or yours, though each is ours.

Emerson, who essayed to be better than he had been; *Benjamin*, who wrote in order to be equal to his moment; *Lukács*, for whom form is a way of being historical; *Cavell*, whose proofs move in the just-so of how (and where) he puts the point—

A more general settlement also operates. If "writing" names a differential, disseminating semiotic flow that underwrites and thus overdetermines thought, intersubjectivity, even controlled experimentation—and it does— then, at least on Emerson's terms, which I accept, it functions as a figure of fate. A field of unpenetrated forces whose beginnings and ends elude our reflective, even speculative, grasp, "writing," a metaphor for the metaphorizing that enables conceptualization, envelops us. And yet, that realization (which, in me, has become an observance) does not relieve us of the burden (or glorious task) of finding our way within and through whatever life generates, throws, withholds, unsettles, or destroys.

Our Pragmatics: I present myself, before and to you, as representative of some kind of differential *we* greater than me and "any and all rational agents," a phrase whose address exceeds its semantic scope. And if my writing is so located, moving somewhere between (possibly *jenseits*) transcendence and immanence and toward a kind of representativeness that is neither simply universal nor particular, I take my addressee to be equally elusive.

A Load-Bearing Term: Most of what I have to offer (a subset of what I will give), revolves around *praxis*, which marks philosophical writing as a purposive venture that finds and figures its particular character in its execution even as it tries to reform the situation from which it emerges, for example, ignorance, confusion, broad conformity, collapsing theological orders, or compulsive heterosexuality. I have settled on "praxis" because philosophical writing is purposive, and because it does not merely present idealities discovered beforehand but articulates them in and through its mode of presentation. "Praxis" also recommends itself insofar as it sets philosophical writing into a context of reflective deliberation—asking us how we plan to proceed. Presumably the answer is "I'll write." But note, it is an answer—situations like collapsing theological orders admit of other responses, for example, prayer, nihilistic assaults on houses of worship, a culture war against secular humanism, a life of sensual pleasure now that all is permitted, et cetera.

Moreover, "write" prompts further concerns—to what end, in what manner, where, for (possibly with) whom, and why.

It's Not You, It's Me: "He has a way with words." "Her voice is unmistakable." "The prose is so patient. But elegant too." "Each sentence indicates who is writing—long, reflexive, slightly awkward, even withholding, but measured."

Style aims to name all of these features and more. It concerns those habits and choices—words, topics, constructions, quotations, and so on—that individuate an author's writing, give it a general character against the backdrop of generic operations: oracular, labored, playful, abstract, or concrete. Every path has its way of getting where it's going, and in some cases, a recurring way, which presumably marks a style.

I wish to set the word aside, finding "style" a term for critics, assembled from the third person. Insofar as it becomes one for writers, it usually indicates the effort to individuate, to make room for one's own way of proceeding. It thus connotes, in most cases, an aesthetic goal—to have a style. It says too much, therefore, and in too singular a register. Not that I reject accounting for texts with reference to something like style. But the term is a lump, denoting phenomena as diverse as voice, genre, habitual and invented rhythms, as well as the interplay of syntax and semantics. I wish to consider most of these phenomena, but beyond (without excluding) the goal of literary individuation. In particular, I want to think about how matters like genre and logical-rhetorical operations, chosen or not, have an impact on how thought unfolds. Also, how do these matters open and orient relations between texts and addressees, such that an author might prefer one and not another? And how do a text's manifold dimensions engage a social-historical situation, and again, such that one might prefer a given logical-rhetorical operation or genre? While it does not preclude these questions, "style" seems to displace them, and where it does bear on them, it makes a fresh assay more difficult than it could otherwise be.[2]

Iron Filings

Bear with Me: I rarely feel as if extant debates allow me to situate myself, so permit me a different course (or forgive me). (Or just stop listening. We proceed on your authority.)

Quiet Please: When I think, I listen the hardest.

First, Philosophy: The quest for a first philosophy remains unexamined.

Writing in an Extramoral Sense: Thinking is theft without guilt. A genuine thinker expects thanks from the burgled.

Questions for Answers: Writing is often a fluid affair, even when one struggles. I might fuss with words and syntax. I might labor over paragraphs. But for the literate, set to it and one is writing. Nevertheless, a quick reflection registers the complexity of the matter—words, sentences, and paragraphs, metaphors and examples, logical operators like "therefore," rhetorical operations like irony. All work in concert with varying degrees of friction and fluidity. Writing thus engages a rich and varied ensemble. In writing philosophy, perhaps we should focus on what bears the greatest philosophical weight. Where in my writing (which is a way of asking "how"), does philosophy take place?

Stanley Cavell reads Emerson's philosophy as a particular way of inheriting and transforming (or "finding") language, all the way down to level of the sentence, if not word by word. Cavell's approach is nicely summarized in "The Philosopher in American Life" as he recounts inheriting Emerson and Thoreau: "To write knowing that your words emit a breath of virtue or vice

every moment, that they communicate the means by which you are expressing your desires, know them or not, is to leave your character unguarded"
(2003, 57).

Cavell's view (and practice) is gripping but unusual. Many if not most
philosophers believe that philosophy is principally bound to modes of argumentation, not word-by-word transformations of one's intellectual heritage.
On this view, philosophy unfolds along a path from premise to conclusion,
in how that path is traveled and on where it arrives. Good philosophical writing on this score weaves, without adornment, radiant chains of inference.
"What the philosopher must manage to embody in words," Brand Blanshard
writes, employing, perhaps, the *Republic*'s tripartite account of the soul, "is
not the whole of him, not the impulsive and imaginative part of him, but his
intellectual part, his ideas and their connections" (1954, 27). Chains of inference, each and every word, but what of those texts to which one's work is a
response? What relation should one adopt to texts one quotes or echoes, crit-
icizes or enlists? Does one's philosophy also occur therein? And what about
translation? Is that a matter to be conducted philosophically? Is one's hermeneutic character integral to one's philosophical character? There are parts a
plenty in philosophical writing. How should they be handled?

Writing Reading: "Quote, quote—are you writing or reading?" Could one
credibly essay the former and ignore the latter? For those unsure about how
to proceed, writing proves salient through examples. And examples only become so in the course of being taken as such, that is, by writing. And I know
no way 'round but through, to echo Frost. But more than that, our labors
resound in the texts of others. "This is one of the ways in which it's done,"
each text signals.

The Whole Story: If there are parts, there are wholes—essay, dialogue, aphorism. Pursuing any commits one to a characteristic organization, if only in
a generic manner grounded in (and by) paradigmatic cases. Aphorisms, for
example, are short, aim to be pithy, even memorable, and usually concern
a class of things, as the following show (emphases added): "Both *sleep* and
wakefulness are bad if they exceed their due proportion" (Hippocrates 1950,
209); "Man, the servant and interpreter of Nature, only *does* and *understands*
so much as he shall have observed, in fact or in thought, of the course of Nature; more than this he neither *knows* nor can *do*" (Bacon 1994, 43); "If it be
usual to be strongly impressed by things that are scarce, why are we so little
impressed by *virtue*" (La Bruyére 1929, 45); "*Newspapers* have roughly the
same relationship to life as fortune tellers to metaphysics" (Kraus 1986, 72).

Pursuing a genre thus involves working with its characteristic mode of organization. How should they be handled? But that way of posing the matter may be too instrumental. Hegelian thought seems inextricable from the system, an integrated presentation of *Geist* wherein the whole, or at least its characteristic logic, appears at every point (knowing and doing, works of art and the rule of law), and wherein the activity of the subject (the determinate negations through which *Geist* is explicated and presented) mirrors the object, namely, the substance of *Geist* (a self-sublating, historical totality dynamically unfolding). Emerson's thought is inextricable from the essay. Rather than derive conclusions from unobjectionable or well-established premises, his writings essay various thoughts, that is, he experiments with them, develops and contests them in the company of others. And that way of transmitting thought, usually without resolution, is integral to Emerson's philosophizing, just as Hegelian thought is bound to the system and the labors it requires. Genre and rhetorical wholes may be more immanent to thought than toolbox consultants believe.

Minding Ps & Qs: "Turn to logic if you are concerned with how philosophical writing can and should be organized, whether at the level of elements or with regard to rhetorical wholes." True enough. If the organization of one's thought is logical, that is, valid, one's conclusions will be true presuming one's premises are. De Morgan, introducing his *Formal logic, or, The calculus of inference, necessary and probable,* observes: "The first notion which a reader can form of logic is by viewing it as an examination of that part of reasoning which depends upon the manner in which inferences are formed, and the investigation of general maxims and rules for constructing arguments, so that the conclusion may contain no inaccuracy which was not previously asserted in the premises" (1847, 1). But suppose one's goal is not simply the generation of true statements. Suppose that, like Emerson, one seeks provocation, to initiate a thought that unsettles in a manner the addressee must resolve without final instructions from the author. Or, Socratically, one hopes less to demonstrate a philosophical insight than to draw one out—"do as I do when I say." Or imagine that, like Nietzsche, one desires to invent new modes of valuation by working through and eventually beyond inherited meanings and conceptual dualities like good and evil, discovery and invention, theism and atheism. Or, like Irigaray, one contests the fate of women in philosophy, and in a manner that seeks new futures for women and philosophy, say, by uncovering and displacing the ways in which traditional metaphysics has rendered the feminine mutely material, the masculine loquaciously intelligible. With such goals in mind, how will one proceed? Securing validity will not suffice.

Pardon the Interruption

Start at the Top: I can already hear it: "This inquiry only gets off the ground if we accept that all of these writings involve *philosophy*. Even the sympathetic might wonder, given the range of your examples, whether something like *philosophy* retains its identity at each point in the constellation. Not that it doesn't, but the question is pertinent, and so we need to start again."

If so, two paths come to mind. (*a*) We can assemble some sense of *philosophy* from all that recurs in each text we take to conduct *philosophy* and, then, explore how best to commit that to writing. (*b*) We can begin with some sense of *philosophy* and, on that basis, relegate certain tasks to other fields, say, literature or sociology.

Dodge Ball: But this is what I think. "Philosophy," an open, evolving set (dialogues, essays, aphorisms, professional articles, treatises, letters, and journals) poses less a puzzle of identity than a field of possibilities whose character one should clarify. Given the splendor of each example, I am compelled to ask, "Should I also write this way?" not, "but is all of this really philosophy?"

You may find my shift from the classificatory to the practical unhelpful, perhaps even shallow. Surely I need to demonstrate that each example is in fact a possibility for *philosophy*. But how would such a demonstration proceed? Generalizing from examples begs the question. And if I do not begin with examples, I will have begged the question as well, particularly for those who find philosophy in writings denied courtly influence. My shift into a practical register thus reflects my sense that the classificatory project will never close in a manner that will not reek of special pleading. Also, whether a text proves to be *philosophy*, particularly an odd text, is often resolved after its appearance, and never with simple reference to an ideal type. Most of

Nietzsche's texts are organized in ways that no doubt struck his contemporaries as something other than philosophy, as they might my contemporaries, presuming one could hide the fact that one is reading Nietzsche.[3] And yet, Nietzsche is now a fixture in contemporary philosophical life, and not just among so-called Continental philosophers. This suggests, I think, that with regard to manners of writing, their status qua philosophy is determined retrospectively, and often in contexts of profound disagreement. I thus doubt one could convincingly or fruitfully (or even philosophically) order the set, "philosophy."

There Goes the Neighborhood: "So *everything* is philosophy." Is that what I said? I think I said, more or less, that a manner's philosophical status is initially an open matter (and often remains so for some time, e.g., Montaigne), and one that will not be settled by a general category generated a priori or generalized from a curated series of examples. Faced with odd cases, I'm thus inclined to ask: What here carries the thought, how, and to what end? And then: How does that relate to the work done in other texts that seem less odd? But note, being odd may actually introduce discontinuity into the series and thus change philosophy. Faced with a genre, therefore, or a logical-rhetorical operation, my presumption is that philosophy *might* conduct itself in this manner (as opposed to *may* or *may not*). At the outset, we just do not know. Why then, at the outset, police the field?

My Re-solution: Faced with debates about the spirit of the times, about its defining characteristics, Emerson descends from such heights (or rises from such depths) and announces: "To me, however, the question of the times resolved itself into a practical question of the conduct of life. How shall I live? We are incompetent to solve the times" (Emerson 1996, 769). The thought turns from what we are "incompetent to solve" to what "resolves itself." On Emerson's view, the times are too complex and the character of each variable takes too long to manifest itself. We are thus unable to solve the times, to bring our manifold present into fluid solution, into a homogenous mixture governed by discernible ideas whose operations we can contemplatively survey. But our inability to theoretically grasp our present does not relieve us of the task of living it. And so Emerson insists that the times resolve themselves, meaning, the whole loosens into an assortment of component parts. Faced by the manifold ways in which philosophy has been written, I find myself incompetent to solve the plurality of those modes into a homogenous unity of "philosophy." But an inability to order this surfeit thoroughly does not relieve me of the task of living (or writing) it.

A Rose Is a Rose Is a Rose and I Am None of Them: Spontaneity has a certain allure, at least for those exhausted by the demands of praxis, which cannot forgo either deliberation or commitment. But the gleam of immediacy is just the heat of self-assertion, or the flash of space junk consumed in reentry. Turning back into the currents of life, we needn't cease surveying and mapping what claims, bruises, or compels us. A life of our own requires that we name what we elect to elude and/or transform and that we share some prospective feel for where we seem to be headed. And these tasks require the labor of the concept in the fullness (and opacity) of its occurrence: semantics, syntax, pragmatics, voice, and so much more, including whatever we manage to conduct, gracefully or otherwise.

Content and Form

Slug Bait: As we work to integrate elements within rhetorical wholes, perhaps we should distinguish "the how" from "the what." Doing so would allow us to focus on the play of various logical and rhetorical operations in philosophical writing, as well as typical genres, and independently of any particular doctrine or content. If we focus on features that persist across cases of varying content we might grasp what various manners of philosophical writing entail (i.e., what we take on when we commit to it).

Too easy. What one says, what one finds oneself saying (which does not always square with what one wanted to say), often puts a good deal of pressure on how one says it. Form seems tethered to content in significant ways. For example, in order to avoid self-referential mishaps, one might want to decry universal propositions with something other than universal propositions. Or, suppose one wishes to think about the incalculable interplay of unruly forces that combine to generate categorical thought, but finds oneself trapped in categories like "the Dionysian" and "the Apollonian," to recall Nietzsche's *Birth of Tragedy*. I say "trapped" because this distinction forces one to think the former in the terms of the latter—what, after all, could be more apollonian than the fabulously lined fields of the Dionysian and the Apollonian? The specificity of what is said often shapes how it is said.

Wittgenstein's Example: Philosophical Investigations shows that content exerts pressure at a more general level as well. The *Investigations* considers multiple subjects such as meaning, understanding, the foundation of mathematics, and states of consciousness, discussions that concern one another. For example, a theory of meaning has implications for philosophical psychology. If one thinks meaning is based on ideal contents housed in sounds and marks on paper, one will need a theory of mind that enables extractions (and institutions) of that order. But if one thinks meaning is principally determined by the ways in which words and sentences can be used—as Wittgenstein does, more or less—one will need a theory of mind that focuses on the ways in which we learn to use words and sentences. *Philosophical Investigations* is thus brimming with thoughts that gesture toward one another. Moreover, each topic is approached in ways that suggest the author has a particular way of philosophizing: attention to how words are often (or ordinarily) used, argument by example, and providing space for counter-intuitions in the voice of an imagined interlocutor. Finally, a handful of suggestive concepts, for example, "language game," "form of life," and "rule" recur. While reading the *Investigations*, it is difficult not to suspect that a rich, integrated theory of language and social-subjectivity is lurking in and moving silently between the various discussions.

In his preface, Wittgenstein confesses that he had believed his thoughts "should proceed from one another in a natural order and without breaks" (2001, 9). No such luck: "I should never succeed. The best I could write would never be more than philosophical remarks; my thoughts were soon crippled if I tried to force them on in any single direction against their natural inclination.—And this was, of course, connected with the very nature of the investigation" (9). At one level, these confessions are cryptic. What precisely does it mean to proceed in a natural order and without breaks, that is, what form—his word—did Wittgenstein abandon? And what about the "very nature of the investigation" led him to settle on what he terms an "album" that contains a "number of sketches of landscapes" (9)? I do not wish to pursue these intricacies. But I do want to observe that at no point in the *Investigations* does Wittgenstein uncover a univocal concept or conceptual structure underlying his chief concerns. Instead, each discussion, just like the examples they engage, follows its predecessor without resolving into a unified field of meaning, even when the very idea of "meaning" is interrogated. In fact, Wittgenstein famously suggests that our ability to correctly use a word in multiple contexts only indicates a series of family resemblances, not the presence of an ideal meaning keeping the family together. "Instead of producing something common to all that we call language," he writes, "I am saying these phenomena have no one thing in common which makes us use the same word for all, but they are related to one another in many different ways. And it is because of this relationship, or these relationships, that we call them all 'language'" (2001, 27). Such results are not incidental to the manner in which the book ultimately was organized. Nothing lies behind the landscape Wittgenstein surveys. Nothing like *Geist* or transcendental conditions of possibility emerge from his thought experiments, and so the book has no deep structure that its proceedings should mirror (as with Hegel) or assemble brick by brick (as with Kant). In other words, the *Philosophical Investigations* is an album because that is what the results of those investigations generated.

The Example of Socrates: For the sake of argument, suppose that several of Plato's dialogues aim to instruct through the character of Socrates, through the ways in which he conducts himself while interrogating others (and where and when these interrogations take place and with whom).[4] In this regard, Platonic philosophy would seem to be performative rather than doctrinal, and one might conclude that the possibilities of the dialogue exist independently of any particular subject matter. This may be true of Platonic dialogues up to a point. One finds similar behaviors in many, even as the subject matter changes, for example, exhortations to be courageous, such as what one finds at *Laches* 188b and *Republic* 374e. But those behaviors are highlighted because they exemplify commitments, for example (and again for the sake of argument): (*a*) genuine dialogue requires courage, (*b*) genuine dialogue requires patience, (*c*) genuine learning requires a period of unlearning, and more generally, (*d*) dialogue is a fertile site of moral growth. In other words, performativity is not without content, and that content shapes the performances in question. In fact, it is more than likely that if Plato did not hold those beliefs, his so-called early dialogues would have had a very different character. "The art-seeking eye does not seem to see," writes Jacob Klein, "that the deliberate and elaborate artfulness in the composition of the dialogues is imposed on them by their intent" (1965, 20).[5] Regardless, one could easily write a dialogue organized around very different actions and characters in order to performatively convey different points of view, thus attaching different possibilities to the dialogue form.

Form and Content

Two-Way Street: In entry 269, which closes *Beyond Good and Evil,* Nietzsche laments that his "written and painted thoughts" have lost their "newness," even "novelty" (*Neuheit*), and worse still, "some of you, I fear, are ready to become truths; they already look so immortal, so pathetically decent, so dull" (1966, 236). Though the passage goes on to meditate on the limited nature of what can be captured in writing, Nietzsche's preference for novelty over truth indicates a clear desire to write in such a way that the former is highlighted and the latter postponed. One way to do this is to commit to short elaborations and to eschew systematic connections between terms, observations, even extended discussions, and regardless of terminological and thematic recurrences. And this is precisely how *Beyond Good and Evil* proceeds. It is designed to resist its own drift toward truth, that is, toward a demonstrable universality that seems to call us back to what purportedly lurked beneath our confused notions.[6]

Each entry in *Beyond Good and Evil* is more or less self-contained. It arranges a thought or cluster of thoughts and offers the result to the reader. Several entries are gathered into chapters with thematic titles (e.g., "The Free Spirit," "Natural History of Morals"), but the entries are not presented as a series of premises cumulating in conclusions about these topics. Nor do the chapters relate to each other in that way. Instead, each entry presents a focal concern that, within a section or two, is usually dropped in favor of another, and the same holds true of the chapters. If one wonders why, the beginning of an answer lies in the book's final section—(*a*) by developing thoughts that can stand on their own and (*b*) by leaving them to stand on their own (c) each thought is allowed its own trajectory, particularly when the same term is introduced again in a later section, for example, truth, will to power, value, et cetera. And (*d*) that increases the likelihood of novelty—it allows Nietzsche and the reader to go wherever the writing goes. And (*e*) that likelihood only intensifies if one does not try to square the emerging thought with others that border its concerns.

Contrasting Modes: Syllogistic reasoning requires a univocal use of major, minor, and middle terms. Employ it, and truths are all that one will find, presuming truth was present at the outset. With greater ambition, systematic reasoning works back to necessary presuppositions and articulates them in the guise of phenomena like axioms or transcendental conditions. In thinking that hopes to work its way back in order to proceed from such foundations, entailments that run contrary to one another must be avoided. Commit to systematic thought, therefore, and all lines will converge in mutual congratulation. By avoiding either mode, Nietzsche's thoughts are left to hover in their birthday suits, floating like figures on a canvas, juxtaposed, perhaps repeated, but rarely linked with the connective tissue of deduction or inference, and never amounting to a systematically secured truth. And when such links do appear (as they do in entry 19, for example, where Nietzsche offers four observations in support of the claim that the will is a "unit only as a word"), the gesture acquires a certain novelty as the section recoils on itself (1966, 32). Specifically, the act of "concluding" that the will is a "unit only as a word" appears as an instance of "willing" that is decentered within a manifold and possibly contested process.

Beyond Good and Evil shows how modes of writing can concentrate and / or constrain the kind of thought that arises in the process of writing, and this is as true of syllogistic reasoning as it is of Nietzsche's freestyle prose. And it is also true of the aphorism, at least as conceived by Francis Bacon. By the time he published *Novum Organum* in 1620, Bacon believed that the "whole operation of the mind must be completely re-started, so that from the very beginning it is not left to itself, but is always subject to rule; and the thing accomplished as if by machinery" (1994, 38). According to Bacon, his wayward present had various sources, which he recounted in terms of distorting idols, perhaps to underscore that human thought so often mistakes its own creations for the genuine article. While the origin of each idol varies— human nature, individual character and experience, ordinary language, and the "various dogmas of philosophies"—its effect is the same: "The human understanding is like an uneven mirror that cannot reflect truly the rays from objects, but distorts and corrupts" (1994, 54).

The *Advancement of Learning* explains Bacon's predilection for aphorisms—they keep the inquirer honest. Because "discourse of illustration is cut off; recitals of example are cut off; discourse of connexion and order is cut off; descriptions of examples are cut off; so there remaineth nothing to fill the Aphorisms but some good quantity of observation: and therefore no man can suffice, nor in reason will attempt to write Aphorisms, but he that is sound and grounded" (Bacon 1868, 172). While it is interesting that Nietzsche and Bacon celebrate short forms that eschew "discourse of connexion," and to ends more or less opposite, I am currently drawn to a point of agreement—both believe that different modes of writing inform the content of whatever thoughts are thereby developed.

In the Beginning Was the Deed

Benjamin's Example: Walter Benjamin's *One-Way Street* gathers short entries that range from genuine aphorisms to brief essays to recollections of dreams. Why write like this? "Filling Station," the work's first entry, answers my query (Benjamin 1996, 444). Benjamin elected "inconspicuous forms" in order to avoid the "pretentious, universal gesture of the book" because he took the former to be more effective in "active communities." Benjamin thought short forms were more responsive to contemporary events than scholarly inquiries and results. Rather than survey and present a field of secondary literature in order to situate one's purported contribution, brief and concentrated expressions are free to addresses emerging issues—"Only this prompt language shows itself actively equal to the moment." *One-Way Street* is also suspicious of convictions and the way in which they deaden us. Benjamin thus pursues a discontinuous mode of presentation in order to surprise readers with thoughts they might be less inclined to entertain if central points are forecast. Freed to engage its moment, *One-Way Street* does just that.

An extended entry, "Imperial Panorama," assembles a montage of "stability in decline." Attacking then current slogans like "things can't go on like this," its fourteen subentries work in common to free "this" from a "helpless fixation on notions of security and property" toward phenomena that, on Benjamin's view, have allowed a situation of unintelligibility and alienation to envelop even the wealthiest (1996, 450–55). Turning its back on scholarly conventions, *One-Way Street* engages its moment in a manner that keeps itself to observation, flashes of insight, and arresting images. But they are engagements. From its topics to its dreamlike sequencing, from condensed entries to focal attacks on the slogans of the day, *One-Way Street* takes itself to be (and presents itself as) an intervention. Yes, it is a "book," and yes, it presents various thoughts in a variety of ways. But each ("book," "content," "form") is part and parcel of an effort to redirect the social and psychological currents of the Weimar Republic, and with certain goals in mind: reinvigorating experience, firing disgust with the status quo, and cultivating attentive habits of interpretation.

Benjamin's example casts philosophical writing in terms of purposive action. Even as it leads us to think about the dream logic that holds the book together, and even as it concentrates us on its manifold, it points past itself toward ends it hopes to further. One might find such indications distracting. You might interject: "Ends are possible consequences, are they not? If so, they seem beyond the control of the author and thus external to the writing in question." No. Benjamin's ends inform his choice of subject matter and overall organization. If anything, "the what" and "the how" of Benjamin's writing are rendered even more determinate when one also considers their "why," and this is why Benjamin's example is instructive. Taking philosophical writing in terms of purposive action does not elide issues of form, genre, or content. Neither does it lead us to ignore logical and rhetorical operations, whether *modus ponens* or irony. Rather, it renders each a moment within a larger arc of conduct, contextualizing what is at stake at each point and opening those points to the interrogations of deliberation. In place of the habitual production and publication of an article or book, questions arise concerning the desirability of the goods one purports to realize. Also, the various parts and wholes that determine any mode of writing—punctuation, logical operations, genres, and so forth—enter a deliberative space wherein their ability to facilitate the end(s) in question can be determined.

Suppose I want to communicate an insight *and* cultivate self-reliance in my addressees. Maintaining both commitments presents a conundrum. I want to be communicative (which seems to recommend clarity) and I want to stimulate readers to think for themselves (which recommends a degree of difficulty, perhaps even elusiveness). Can I accomplish both, and if I think I can, for which readership (and note how "readership" already narrows one's addressees to those who can read, and mostly likely read print)? Or suppose I not only want to promote certain thoughts but also interrupt the plausibility of their rivals? I may prove the latter mistaken, but one need not be Benjamin in order to think that convictions are not so easily dislodged. And once one turns that corner, the social psychology of communication becomes a meaningful variable for those committed to writing.

Reworking Making

Life Is Here and Elsewhere: In book 6 of *Nicomachean Ethics,* Aristotle distinguishes "making" (*poesis*), where the end is different from the making, from "action" (*praxis*), where the end sought, say virtue, is part and parcel of the activity as a salient, even determinate, characteristic. Pottery is a case of making because it produces an end different from the making. But if I give someone else money, the end is not the given, here money, but presumably the action itself in terms of the virtue it embodies.

Because writing produces a text, it seems poietic rather than praxical. But how stable is the distinction between poiesis and praxis? My end may be to give money in a virtuous manner, but integral to that end is another end: to provide someone with more money in order that they might do things they otherwise could not do. If I do not desire this consequence (after having reflected on, among other things, the character of the recipient and the nature of his or her need), the end of the action becomes unclear. How does one aim to be generous without simultaneously aiming to benefit another through one's generosity? Giving away money for the sake of giving it away, as if to show that "money means nothing to me," is not a virtue. In fact, it appears foolish, even flamboyant—a kind of histrionic carelessness. And giving in order to appear generous is clearly giving for the wrong reason and thus at odds with virtue.

If my portrayal of generosity is right, the distinction between praxis and poiesis wobbles. The change wrought (and sought) by my gift is not contained in the act but lies with the fate of the one who receives it. It seems, therefore, that integral to giving money in a virtuous manner is the end of transforming the world.

Because the poiesis/praxis distinction is unsettled in the case of certain practical virtues, I disagree with Agamben's claim that praxis "wants only it-self through action; thus it is not productive, and brings only itself into pres-ence" (1999, 76). At least with regard to some of the practical virtues, praxis brings itself into presence by transforming the world, including the character of the one who acts, and these results, to which the agent commits, are not coextensive with any praxical act. Praxis is thus occasionally a matter of con-spiring with the world in order to redetermine its course.

If we take this slippage between praxis and poiesis into account, philo-sophical writing seems more like praxis than poiesis.[7] In writing philosophy, the goal is rarely if ever simply to produce a freestanding essay, aphorism, or dialogue, as if to prove that one could bring into being such a thing, perhaps even in an exquisite manner. Instead, one may want to provoke others to think, to change their minds about some issue, or to transform how they vote, eat, or inhabit language. Or, moving in another direction, one may want to clarify an issue for oneself or work one's way free of distorting conceptual habits. And in these cases, the end is not fully achieved by the artifact. Rather, the artifact is an initial but transitional end that hopefully transforms the world (which includes oneself) toward other ends like those just noted. Be-cause philosophical writing often has these larger albeit elusive goals in mind, it seems more like a gift of money than the production of a pot by a potter. I give the money, but not just to give it. Instead, I give it in order to meliorate conditions of poverty. Analogously, I do not write simply to demonstrate lit-eracy or to publish an article. In the least, I aim to deepen my own thoughts and to transform various conversations.

Rhetoric Anyone? According to Aristotle, a *techne* (technique) is a rational understanding grounded in a *hexis* (standing capacity), which concerns how to produce various states of affairs such as a chair from wood or health in an ill person.[8] The technician is able to produce these states of affairs in a reliable and predictable manner because he or she knows their causes, and knows them so well that she or he is able to teach their proper organization (i.e., the technique). Importantly, such knowledge is a settled matter for the technician; that is, Aristotle does not present *techne* as an ongoing mode of discovery. Rather, it puts discoveries to work: "So of the process of coming-into-being and the motion involved in it, one part should be called thinking and the other producing, the thinking starting from the source and from the form, and the producing starting from the completion of the thinking" (Ar-istotle 2002b, 129).

Take rhetoric for example. In chapter 2, book 1, of the *Rhetoric*, Aristotle presents rhetoric as a technique grounded in a topic-independent capacity (*dynamis*). Someone with this capacity, that is, the rhetor, has the ability, "in each particular case, to see the available means of persuasion (*pisteis*)" conceived in terms of appeals to (*a*) the *ethos* of the speaker (or rivals), (*b*) the *pathos* to which the speaker wishes to lead addresses, or (*c*) various arguments or *logoi* on behalf of the favored view or contra rival views, for example, abbreviated syllogisms, that is, enthymemes, or arguments from examples, that is, *paradigma* (Aristotle 1991, 36–40, I.2, 3–7). The rhetor is thus not unlike a potter who has three or four models for working in clay, although here the material in question involves speeches and the souls of addressees. Importantly, while the rhetor makes use of these modes of persuasion in his or her speeches, she or he does not discover or develop these modes en route. They are rather extant forms of presentation brought to bear on various topics in various situations.

Those who follow Heidegger's reading of Aristotle's *Rhetoric* may object to my characterization of Aristotle's position. "Rhetoriké has no subject area that can be demarcated in any way," writes Heidegger. "Because it does not, it should not be designated as téchne. Rhetoriké is not téchne, though it is téchnikon" (2009, 79). And: "It has a téchnikon, the possibility of providing a knowing-the-way-around, but not about a determinately demarcated region of beings" (81). But possible appeals on behalf of a subject matter, that is, modes of persuasion, are themselves a subject area, particularly since Aristotle focuses on three kinds in particular, and in the context of speech making (as opposed to language in general). I am also unconvinced by Heidegger's argument that since it is an everyday capacity and not a specific trade or occupation, rhetoric is not a *techne*. He claims that the "about-which of rhetoric is the speaking-with-one-another-in-a-deliberative-mode for which there is no téchne. That which occurs to everyone in an everyday and accustomed manner is not specific to a trade or occupation" (92). But not everyone is a rhetor in the sense of one with explicit knowledge of various modes of persuasion and the standing capacity to use them properly. Yes, for political purposes, all citizens might want this knowledge and know-how, but not all have it. In fact, one must be trained in order to acquire it. So yes—"Rhetoric is not a téchne posited by itself, but stands within that of politiké" (Heidegger 2009 91). But this does not mean it isn't a *techne*, and the fact that one must learn how to organize one's speeches in rhetorically powerful ways (and the fact that rhetoric concerns how to organize speeches with certain kinds of appeals) suggests that it is.

(Sort of) against Rhetoric (of a Sort): "The trees have left the forest and formed their own grove—praxis and poiesis, now *techne*, and an occasion

to bicker with Heidegger." But that is my point. In the thick and thin of its occurrence, philosophical writing, particularly when it chases insight, rarely if ever settles to a point where discovery and presentation part company. I could put the matter this way. The discovery of rhetoric, as a topic with a discernible order, involves phenomena that Aristotle's *Rhetoric* sets outside the field of rhetoric itself.

"The mind now thinks; now acts; each fit reproduces the other," Emerson says (1996, 62). The pun is acute. When thought and action fit one another, hand in glove, the thought recurs and the action is initiated. I venture to a museum in the thought that paintings are singular in their address and perusing the galleries intensifies the thought, which in turn entrenches what might become a habit of returning to stand before works that occasionally reorient my sense of . . . well, just my sense. But the occurrence of each is something of a fit; it—say this sentence—appears with a certain suddenness, its arrival is something of surprise. Not wholly unexpected, but neither is a word or a phrase, let alone an entire sentence wholly expected. But when they fit, thought and action mate, and mate well.

Deliberate Writing

Business as Usual: If writing philosophy is a praxis, the question, "How should I write?" becomes deliberate. Deliberations can be routine affairs when one has a good feel for the nature and scope of an action, for example, finding a restaurant or locating a route downtown. In such cases, our purposes are clear, our means are available, and we know our way about. We have a good sense of what we want, why, and how we might pursue it. Other situations are less straightforward. Suppose a friend has died and one wishes to offer condolences. Such tasks are often challenging, but they prove more so when the family has a cultural background different from one's own. Are flowers even appropriate? If so, what kind? And to whom does one communicate one's condolences? Or are "condolences" on point? Perhaps the object of concern should be the deceased, his or her immortal soul, and joy the appropriate affect. What then to do, and for and to whom? Is the nuclear family the principal unit in question, or should one send whatever one sends to the matriarch or patriarch of an extended family? When we do not know what to do, questions arise and intensify if the meaning and significance of our options remains unclear.

How settled is the scene in which philosophical ventures are made? I suspect that for many, writing for publication in a professional venue is the default option and a matter of course. Not that surveying a literature or crafting an argument comes easily. But the larger act of writing for publication moves along a familiar terrain. Planning to submit an article to a professional journal, I usually read the stated editorial principles and submission guidelines and, if the journal is new to me, explore past issues to see what questions are pursued and within what literatures. In either case, I either know my way about or can quickly learn how to navigate the discursive politics of one journal versus another and determine whether my orientation is welcome. But in proceeding in this manner, how reflective and deliberate is my conduct? I have stated aims, namely "publish article X" in order to "contribute to literature Y," but how thoroughly do I know what that entails?

We Somewhat Know What We Do: "In general, the identification of the end prominent in conscious desire and effort with *the* end is part of the technique of avoiding a reasonable survey of consequences" (Dewey 1983, 158–59). This is Dewey.[9] Set in our context, and bracketing the scope of "reasonable," the argument is: (*a*) our desired outcome is rarely, if ever, coextensive with the actual outcomes, (*b*) we are in some sense responsible for some range of the actual outcomes beyond the desired one, and thus (*c*) a genuinely reflective, deliberative approach to praxis anticipates and evaluates a range of likely outcomes for each path under consideration. On Dewey's view we should not simply pursue publication and leave it at that but also explore what publication is likely to bring about. What, for example, are the socioeconomic politics of the venue that will publish one's work, say the cost of the journal to libraries? Or, what are the sociopolitical consequences of one's citation habits? Is one unwittingly entrenching a white-male professoriate? And what is the environmental impact of print versus electronic publication? Such questions go unasked because they are usually regarded as external to the pursuit of philosophy. An analogy suggests the presumption is mistaken.

Many now take their carbon footprint into account, particularly with regard to their cars, and with good reason. "We are driving up the planet's temperature," the Union of Concerned Scientists reports. "Transportation is one of the primary contributors to global warming, generating more than one-third of all U.S. carbon dioxide emissions and 30 percent of America's total global warming emissions" (Union of Concerned Scientists 2014). Many share this position, and it informs how they think about which car to buy, how much to use it, whether to carpool, and so on. And in that regard their deliberative stance is akin to Dewey's. They do not consider their desired ends in isolation from the actual consequences of their actions. Instead, they formulate and reformulate their ends as they learn about the consequences involved in their realization.

We should look at philosophical writing in a similar manner, though not only with regard to ecological consequences. A reflective, deliberative approach to praxis should anticipate and evaluate a wide range of likely consequences. If one does not engage the work of women or people of color, for example, but only cites white-male authors (and it has taken me too long to concretely appreciate this point), one helps establish a discursive community that communicates, through exemplification, "white men are the one's worth reading."[10] Not that such citation habits indicate a wish or desire for that end. A central point of Dewey's position is that desired ends and actual consequences often diverge, which is why we need to keep an eye out for the latter when we pose questions like: "How should I write?" That said, global warming does not puff out of a car's exhaust pipe. It results from numerous factors including how many vehicles are on the road, the character of their engines, what fuels are in use, and so forth. Similarly, citing in a color-blind manner registers different effects if many to most are turning a blind eye toward philosophers of color. A broadly reflective and deliberative approach to philosophical writing requires, therefore, a good feel for the various scenes we enter and impact when we write.

Mistaking Instrumental Reason

Business as Usual? "Praxis, ends . . . does this mean that philosophical writing is instrumental, some tool elected because it takes us where we want to go?" I think I understand the worry. There seems to be something nonphilosophical (in the sense of unquestioning) about pre-given ends and unquestioned techniques. And yet, that state of affairs is inevitable and not quite the prison sentence it seems to be. In writing, one relies on ordinary and technical language, the depth of one's insights, bursts of inspiration, publication media and venues, the capacities of one's readers, and images and examples, and one does so in the hope, confident or otherwise, that each will further one's pursuits or at least not undermine them. But one is never sure. A dialogue might spark participation in the reader, but that depends on how it is executed and taken up, and the latter variable can only be rendered determinate one reading at a time, and by the reader, not the author. More generally, language, rich in historical sediment and pulsing with autosuggestion takes one down paths that occasionally prove surprising and transformative. "Praxis," for example, is such a polyvalent term that its deployment initiates various conversations, which modulate one's use of the term, whether by way of negation or affirmation, partial or wholesale. As a dependent venture, philosophical writing is thus unquestioning in various, vital ways. Said otherwise, and without lamentation, it conspires with the world in order to transform it, and to that degree it remains in the world's thrall. And this is precisely why philosophical writing requires deliberation. "Deliberating is present," Aristotle writes, "in things that happen in a certain way for the most part [i.e., they are ordered as opposed to random], but are unclear as to how they will turn out" (2002a, 42). Assuming a praxical orientation toward philosophical writing is far from "un-philosophical," therefore. If anything, it embraces the tasks contained therein.

But perhaps the chief worry concerns having any end in mind. "Precisely. Philosophy, grounded in wonder, is an open response to the world. If one commences with an end in view that openness is curtailed at the outset." A complex issue circulates in this counter-intuition. Is philosophy, at its inception, ever free of selective emphasis and desire? And can one actually think in wonder, or is thinking always already bound to determinations? For now, the matter can be set aside. Philosophical writing is our concern and that is always a determinate venture. One always writes about something in particular, a question or thesis that has claimed one, say, the good versus the right, and in hermeneutically situated ways, that is, according to terms (and in the conversations) through which such issues arise. Selective emphasis is thus the rule. And even if one begins without a settled position on the topic in question, writing works toward settlement (possibly a temporary one), and irrespective of whether the settlement affirms or undermines a position. Even deconstructive texts settle matters, for example, by demonstrating that the law always appeals to what it can never fully instance, namely, justice, or that a discourse on metaphor will itself make use of metaphor, thus binding the literal to the metaphorical as something other than its opposite.

Propagations: "Settling issues is not the principal worry. Settling issues for some further end is what threatens to turn philosophy into something else, say politics or even propaganda. Philosophy is pursued for its own sake." Set aside the fact that most current philosophical writing is bound in part to careerist goals like professional advancement and reputation. Instead, let us pose the question in a basic manner. Where does the "sake" of philosophy lie? Is it fulfilled in and by the act of writing or does it, in some significant degree, lie outside that act, such that the act is in part a means to some other end?

John Locke's *Two Treatises on Government* opens as follows:

> Reader, thou hast here the beginning and end of a discourse concerning government; what fate has otherwise disposed of the papers that should have filled up the middle, and were more than all the rest, it is not worth while to tell thee. These, which remain, I hope are sufficient to establish the throne of our great restorer, our present King William; to make good his title, in the consent of the people, which being the only one of all lawful governments, he has more fully and clearly, than any prince in Christendom; and to justify to the world the people of England, whose love of their just and natural rights, with their resolution to preserve them, saved the nation when it was on the very brink of slavery and ruin. (1988, 137)

Locke's *Two Treatises* aim to settle issues of the day, for example, whether a sovereign rules by divine right or by consent, whether a sovereign wields absolute power or a power curtailed by natural rights, and whether a sovereign can be deposed should natural rights be violated. And it pursues such settlements in dialogue with others, for instance, Robert Filmer and Thomas Hobbes. But such settlements have other goals in mind as well. Locke is quite explicit that these texts aim to help secure the political standing of William of Orange (1650–1702), who invaded England on November 5, 1688, in order to depose King James II. And Locke aims to secure that standing "in the consent of the people," for only their consent (as opposed to a philosophical justification, which he offers) will legitimate William's rule. Locke's *Two Treatises* thus aim to alter matters that lie outside the arguments he presumably settles in his texts: the de jure standing of William and the convictions of the governed, on which that standing in some sense lies. And in this Locke's texts are quite like the kind of praxis one finds in practical virtues like generosity. The end of what is written is contained neither in the act itself nor in an artifact separable from the act, here the text. Rather, Locke is intervening in currents of his age in order to influence those currents, to lead them toward certain ends. And those ends constitute the sake for which these texts were written.[11]

"What of theoretical philosophy?" one might ask, relying on one of Kant's constitutive distinctions. Consider the *Critique of Pure Reason*. The work's architectonic reflects the fruits of Kant's excavations of the grounds of pure reason. But that excavation has its own purposes.

> But we see it [the value of a "systematic metaphysics, constructed according to the critique of pure reason"] above all when we take account of the way criticism puts an end for all future time to objections against morality and religion in a Socratic way, namely by the clearest proof of the ignorance of the opponent. For there has always been some metaphysics or other to be met with in the world, and there will always continue to be one, and with it a dialectic of pure reason, because dialectic is natural to reason. Hence it is the first and most important occupation of philosophy to deprive dialectic once and for all of all disadvantageous influence, by blocking off the source of the errors. (1998, 117, Bxxxi)

On Kant's view, the application of certain categories of the understanding to things as they are in themselves (as opposed to how they appear to us) leads reason into irresolvable conundrums concerning issues like the existence of a creator or the possibility of moral autonomy. Specifically, and keeping to the latter, if we take "causality" to govern not just those appearances conditioned by human cognition but also the cosmos itself, then humans seem to be unfree, in principle. If so, one's moral commitments (as *one's* commitments) are irrelevant with regard to human motivation and action. Whatever your commitments, the causal series leading up to those beliefs (and the actions they purport to regulate and initiate) predates your birth and thus anything like an act of will or even the particular organism you are. (This also appears to set the origin of our actions outside any meaningful sphere of responsibility—*we* did not do it. In fact, it appears that no *one* did.) Feeling the full gravity of this threat, Kant set out to demonstrate that speculative reason is incapable of insight into things as they are in themselves and, thus, to limit its claims to phenomena, which are empirically real and transcendentally ideal. As he says in one of his most famous phrases: "Thus I had to deny knowledge in order to make room for faith" (1998, 117, Bxxxi).

Whereas Locke tried to arm defenders of popular sovereignty in the wake of revolutionary action, Kant's *Critique of Pure Reason* is a broader intervention designed to beat back pernicious cultural trends. Using the language of his editorial, "What Is Enlightenment?," *The Critique of Pure Reason* is an instance of the "public use of reason"—"the use which a person makes of it *as a scholar* before the entire public of the *world of readers*," a group whose scope is that of the "society of citizens of the world" (1996, 18). Read in this light, *The Critique of Pure Reason* is an intervention in a cosmopolitan discourse with the explicit end of transforming how the terms of metaphysics are understood and used. And such transformations—which name the sake for which critical philosophy proceeds—are not brought about simply through the writing and publication of the book. Rather, such texts must be read, considered, and affirmed or rejected on the basis of reasons, and such texts must be offered on those terms. Otherwise the text will institute precisely the kind of authority-governed immaturity that the age of enlightenment aims to exit according to Kant. It appears, therefore, that even in a canonical text of theoretical reason, philosophy's sake does not lie simply in the writing and publishing of a text. Rather, as with all praxis, it lies in a world the author would have otherwise.

Fits and Starts

We Are Always Doing Things with Words: In his desire to be equal to the moment, Walter Benjamin remained true to (and illuminated) a fundamental undercurrent of philosophical writing. Set to writing, and one conducts one's thought, one's interpersonal and institutional relations, even one's eco-social history.

"But that is true of all writing, no?" It may very well be. But matters in common can also prove decisive, whereas the distinctive may wield marginal influence. (Imagine that the only thing unique to human beings was the ear lobe. Would that render it essential? In the game of basic character, differentia often distract.)

Thought Unfolding: Writing is in part discovery, more an extension of the process of thinking than a mere record of thoughts fashioned beforehand. And while these discoveries are often only implicit in the published version of a text, one should not forget that, most of the time, writing involves a series of visions and revisions and the willingness to erase. In committing to a mode of writing, therefore, one in part elects ways for thought to encounter and develop itself as it unfolds, and one need not believe that "writing" moves across a differential and disseminating semiotic field to agree. Francis Bacon writes: "Neither the bare hand nor the understanding left to itself are of much use. It is by instruments and other aids that the work gets done, and these are needed as much by the understanding as by the hand. *And just as instruments improve or regulate the movement of our hands, so instruments of the mind provide suggestions or cautions to the understanding*" (1994, 43; emphasis added). These remarks, which comprise the second aphorism of *Novum Organum*, are striking. As a labor of discovery, the very act of writing massages and shapes thought. More concretely, the claim is that various modes of writing lead one to entertain or ignore certain kinds of questions, possible challenges, and implications of the would-be insights one is developing.

Freedom From: "The marketplace of ideas—the metaphor's success proves its bankruptcy." Characteristically, the aphorism concerns a single topic, in this case, the concept of a marketplace of ideas. My aphorism charges it with bankruptcy, inverting (and thus exposing) the belief behind the metaphor— the relative quantity of an idea's adherents is a measure of its validity. But an inversion is not an argument. Rather, it presumes that the analogy is a poor one, that economic and epistemic values are quite different. Moreover, it does not even specify the context(s) in which the concept fails. With regard to what ideas? (Is it equally inapplicable to scientific and aesthetic judgments?) Nor does it clarify whether the initial source domain (a demand-side conception of economic value) is cogent in the first place. But that is the nature of aphoristic thought. It calls for a general pronouncement, one that offers a core thought free of justification and disconnected from clearly related issues and the various ways in which they have been pursued. (What exactly did Holmes mean when he deployed the notion?) As a genre, then, the aphorism frees the writer from certain burdens in order that she or he might focus on rendering a specific thought about a singular topic in a particular manner.[12]

Get a Whiff of This: Aphorisms require remarkable concision, slicing off the inessential. They also demand a concentration that gathers the essential. And if one leaves Bacon's concerns (securing a space for unsullied observation), another characteristic appears. Most aphorists offer pungent observations, that is, they hope to capture an insight in an economical and memorable fashion.[13] While this tilts us toward some of the intersubjective dimensions of the aphorism (and thus relations to addressees), we should not make light of the literary demands that aphorisms often place on the author, thus prodding his or her thought, say, toward semantic and syntactic liveliness. One might say that concentration must be textured with suggestiveness, and this requires a patient and delicate touch approaching if not exemplifying wit.

Karl Kraus writes: "Mit einem Blick ein Weltbild erfassen, ist Kunst. Wie viel doch in ein Auge hineingeht." (Seizing a view of the world with a glance, that is art. Amazing how much fits into an eye!" [1965, 91; 2001, 61—translation modified].) This aphorism has both concentration and concision. It says something significant, even deep, about what art can accomplish—with a glance it conveys a conception of the world. But rather than justify the claim, it bathes it in astonishment—*doch*. (One might ask, after all: "Seize"—in what sense? And why a "view of the world" and not just "the world"?) But the aphorism also says more than it states. Two terms, one from each sentence (*Blick*, *Auge*) combine to articulate the flash like temporality (*Augenblick*, "moment," "instant"), which *doch* and *erfassen* connote. The concentration of Kraus's prose thus gestures past its denotative intension with a suggestion that complements and enriches its proclamation.

One might admire the economy of Kraus's effort but regard its wit as a matter of ornament, a clever way of presenting what could otherwise be stated in a series of propositions. (1) Art presents a way of seeing the world. (2) Art does so in an oblique manner (reading "glance" spatially). (3) Art does so in a quick and sudden way. (4) It is amazing that so much can be concentrated in something so partial and fleeting. Suppose that this captures what Kraus's aphorism concentrates. Is our ability to reproduce it propositionally on point? I don't think so. At issue is how certain forms of writing stimulate an author's thoughts, not what a reader can make of the results. My claim is that the requirements (and entitlements) of a genre function as requirements (and entitlements) for thinking and that thinking responds to these limits in generative ways—one arrives at the thoughts one thinks in part through the exercise of the genre. Chancing on *Blick* seems to lead thought to *Augenblick*, for example, that is, certain words carry with them a power of autosuggestion, and a short form like the aphorism, because it focuses thought on each word with an eye for lively language primes thought for autosuggestion, for being responsive to all that a word could mean. This is why first-rate aphorisms have a sculpted feel: everything has been worked into place in a manner responsive to very particular words and sentences.

A Cultivar

Bacon Stretches Out: Thinking develops differently when pursued through the essay. Concision gives way to expansion. This is apparent in Bacon's essays. The 1612 essay "Friendship" is composed of four paragraphs that generalize about friendship in a manner that evidences development. The first paragraph argues that friendship is a cardinal good since it "maketh the yoke of fortune more light" (1996, 301). The second paragraph anticipates resistance to the claim, insisting "he that is all fortune and no nature is an exquisite hireling," suggesting, I suppose, that friendship, indulging our natural sociality, provides a kind of stabilizing loyalty that allows one to stand for more than what proves expedient (1996, 301). A kind of blind loyalty is chastised in the third paragraph, however, and in a manner that does not give way to melancholy, thus rejecting the view (which Cicero champions) that anything short of an identity of wills is friendship in name only. As the fourth paragraph states: "Perfection of friendship is but a speculation" (1996, 301).

Bacon's short essay evidences that the essay, unlike the aphorism, allows thought to orbit its commitments and comment on the entanglements that accrue. Not that anticipated objections to a core commitment underwrite every essayistic expansion. Paragraph three of "Friendship" (1612) not only allows one to "keep a corner of his mind from his friend" but also comments on the difficulties that "great fortune" brings to friendship, announcing that "the higher one goeth, the fewer friends he shall have" (1996, 301). And the other paragraphs offer other generalizations, for example, friendship empowers the understanding and tempers the impact of affect. The expansiveness of the essay is thus somewhat associative—the topic, like a magnet, draws thoughts to itself that the essayist arranges into a whole where they square with some points and prove oblique to others.

The associative expansions of the essay are all the more apparent in Bacon's 1625 version of "Friendship," particularly when set beside the text of 1612. (In fact, tracking how his earlier essays expand in later editions exposes the expansive energies of the essay.) The 1625 publication retains key thoughts from the former but often in an enlarged form—the latter effort runs to ten paragraphs, all of which are longer than any of the four paragraphs of the 1612 discussion. We are again told that friendship clarifies our thoughts, but the point is expanded into something like the following chain: friendship clarifies our thoughts, principally through conversation, though also by way of counsel in matters of manners and business. In other words, the claim from 1612—"friendship will unfold the understanding"—is enlarged with regard to specific activities as well as topics. But that is not all; the rather analytic expansion I've just recounted generates its own subtopics, which Bacon indulges. After praising the virtue of friendly counsel, he offers a brief meditation on counsel itself and whether the counsel of a few friends is superior to the "scattered counsel" of many. Moreover, Bacon marks, directly and indirectly, where his thoughts intersect with various predecessors, mentioning Heraclitus by name and alluding to Plutarch's *Moralia*. The essay thus allows (even encourages) thought to expand on its topic, digress, quote, and allude, only to return, all the while assembling a whole integrated more by contiguity and topical resonance than by analytical amplification or inference.

Montaigne's Founding Essays: In the paragraph that opens "Of Friendship," Montaigne asks (or confesses): "And what are these things of mine, in truth, but grotesques and monstrous bodies, pieced together of divers members, without definite shape, having no order, sequence, or proportion other than accidental?" (1948, 135). The essay is a monstrous genre (if that is even possible), because it proceeds without a secure, conceptual architecture, each expansion following something of its own logic rather than an integrated logic of the whole. (In this sense, it is anti-systematic.) Such a lack is apparent in Montaigne's account of friendship. He takes friendship as a mode of society, terming it the perfection of the class, but never offers a systematic definition of "society," an inventory of the set (though several modes are contrastingly enumerated, e.g., brotherhood, marriage, and "that other, licentious Greek love"). Nor does he provide the criteria by which friendship is accorded the status of perfection. In fact, when Montaigne celebrates his friendship with Étienne de La Boétie (a perfection within this perfection of society), he makes a show of not knowing why they were friends. "Beyond all my understanding," he writes, "beyond what I can say about this in particular" (thus denying himself the fruits of what Kant will later term "determinate and reflective judgment"), "there was I know not what inexplicable and fateful force that was the mediator of this union" (1948 139). Finally, the twenty-nine paragraphs that constitute "Of Friendship" do not relate to one another through a clearly defined concept of "friendship" or systematically tilled terrain of social relations. To use Montaigne's own characterization, we can say that qua parts, their relation is accidental (or un-necessary), though without the anchoring mediations of a substance.[14]

Built En Route: The anti-systematic expansions of the essay are not without epistemic energies, however. As is often noted, the verb "essay" can mean "endeavor" or "experiment," even "to put to a test."[15] Return to Bacon's two essays on friendship. The 1612 version ventures a claim, "friendship will unfold the understanding," which is then tested in several ways in the 1625 edition. The essay is thus a site where thought encounters its own objectivity, and in two senses: it renders itself explicit and, then, interrogates its relative insights. As a genre, therefore, it gathers around an almost Hegelian conception of experience: it posits itself (a thought of friendship is offered) in order to test and possibly surpass itself. One might uncover even more to say about the ways in which "friendship will unfold the understanding" or bump into cases where the opposite seems the case—friends are often too similar and agreeable to locate and challenge our most invisible presumptions.

Rather than championing either position, Emerson's "Nominalist and Realist" experiments with both, finding what seems reasonable and unreasonable in each without a resolving third. The realist trades on the generalized power that comes from universals. "They are our gods," Emerson writes. "They round and ennoble the most partial and sordid way of living" (1996, 578). Each experience is too limited, too partial to underwrite our theoretical and practical projects. No two snowflakes may be alike, but we only recognize and celebrate those differences relative to the category. And so it is across our efforts—energy, matter, and light, or citizen, sister, friend. We rely on conditions for the possibility of each experience that the experience in question does not provide. And yet, universals arise in the course of practices and lives that use them in varying ways, and so they are riddled with partiality. "You are one thing," Emerson observes, "but nature is *one thing and the other thing*, in the same moment" (1996, 581). We lack the view from everywhere and every when, including a view on our own viewing (despite the claims of young, transparent eyeballs). The world, though it answers to us in part, also eludes the terms that orient us, and if we cling to our presumptions, we are confounded, surprised, sometimes punished.

In a systematic treatise, one would try to set this house in order, say, by locating those universals that serve as conditions for the possibility of any (and every) experience. But the essay keeps to its own partialities and thus to the trajectory of its own experiment, testing lines of thought for the ways in which they orient and disorient and offering that test as an acknowledgment of and response to the challenge we face as beings of language. As Emerson says, generalizing about the limits of generalization, and employing the most universal of universals: "But it is not the intention of nature that we should live by general views" (1996, 581). Systematic thought would blanch in the face of such a self-referential snarl. But an essay can leave it be as an acknowledgment of a phenomenon constitutive of its own trajectory. As Emerson says: "There is nothing we cherish and strive to draw to us, but in some hour we turn and rend it" (1996, 586). But drawing a thought, turning it, and rending it, what entails breaking it, disrupting its simplicity ("friendship will unfold the understanding"), such is the work of experimentation, of essaying our thoughts with greater force than aphorisms allow and with greater abandon than systems tolerate.

Quotation beyond Quotas

Thinking With: Thought also unfolds in relation to the texts it engages. Quotation, for example, can add unforeseen complexities, new touchstones for our own articulations. For example, I initially planned to (and for a period did) quote the following in this section: "Quotations in my work are like wayside robbers who leap out, armed, and relieve the idle stroller of his conviction" (Benjamin 1996, 481). What drew me was Benjamin's thought that quotations might relieve us of our convictions and thus redirect our attention. But that is not all he says. Most obviously, he is oriented toward readers, whereas my concern lies with writers. But more importantly, "idle strollers" are the ones he aims to burgle. But that is not my point. Even in the heat of a thought, the words of others echo, and when I record them, carefully, I find I receive more than I bargained for—in Benjamin's case, a question of idleness, of whether quotes conduct thought when one's own is unemployed. Note, I am not claiming that I discovered that Benjamin's remark did not fit my context. It did and it did not. But the way in which it failed me clarified my own point. Even in the heat of its generation, thought can be provoked and clarified through acts of quotation. And that thought leads me—here and now—to disagree with Emerson's strong insistence that "books are for the scholar's idle times" (1996, 58). Quoting, carefully, attending to words has a place in the act of writing. In this sense, explicit quotation provides what Emerson approvingly attributes to cities: collision. More than an appeal to authority, quoting can be a way of thinking along with another, of thinking responsively with and in the language of another. Celan writes: "Quotation marks—to be understood not as goose feet, perhaps, but as rabbit ears, not unanxiously listening out beyond themselves and the words?" (2001, 412).[16]

Shorthand and Shortcuts: Other relations to texts seem immunized against the kinds of redirections just recounted.[17] In *Pragmatism as Post-Postmodernism*, Larry Hickman claims that John Dewey was a postmodernist before post-modernism. Because metaphysics seeks truths that would be free from revision, Dewey rejects it, thus anticipating, Hickman claims, Lyotard's observation that the postmodern involves incredulity in the face of metanarratives, what Hickman terms "master narratives." But Dewey, unlike postmodernism, sidesteps a kind of irrationalism according to Hickman, and precisely by remaining committed to a theory of inquiry, which postmodernism lacks to its detriment: "I have trolled the works of Deleuze and Félix Guattari, Jacques Derrida, Roland Barthes, and even the master postmodernist Lyotard, in search of a comprehensive and coherent theory of inquiry. Nothing I have found approaches the treatment that Dewey gave the subject in his logic books of 1903, 1916, and 1938, and in the numerous published essays that served as sketches for, and clarifications of, those works" (Hickman 2007, 29).

Hickman's claim is provocative, particularly the latter half, since others like Richard Rorty also cast Dewey as a postmodernist *avant la lettre*. And yet, Hickman's path toward those claims remains disengaged from the authors and texts he addresses. In fact, across 294 pages, Lyotard is only mentioned eight times (if one follows the index), but not even a full sentence is quoted. And Derrida and Barthes are only mentioned in the sentence I quoted from page 29. Deleuze is mentioned four times but also never quoted. My point does not concern the principle of charity or whether Hickman has straw manned postmodernism. Rather, when thought concretely engages the language of those it addresses, sympathetically or polemically, one is forced to think through nuances and specificities. And these are opportunities for rich engagements that one misses if one relies on schematizations.

Notice, for example, that Lyotard's text is a "report," a *rapport*, and thus akin to what one might expect from a commission (*Rapport de la commission*), say, one convened around financial matters (*Rapport sur les arrangements financiers*). In fact, it was presented to the Conseil des Universitiés of Quebec, having been commissioned by its president.[18] It is thus not a theory of knowledge or of inquiry but a recounting of "knowledge in the most highly developed societies" or, less Eurocentrically, "knowledge in advanced industrial societies" (Lyotard 1984, xxv; 13). Its claims are thus, to some degree, empirical, for example: "We may thus expect a thorough exteriorization of knowledge with respect to the 'knower,' at whatever point he or she may occupy the knowledge process" (Lyotard 1984, 4). And, at a more general level, they concern processes by which various claims come to count as knowledge, but again, assessed from an empirical standpoint, not with regard to such processes per se.

I pause before the "report" dimension of Lyotard's notorious work because it cautions me when I comb its hundred or so pages for something like "a comprehensive and coherent theory of inquiry." Is Lyotard simply refusing or unable to offer such a theory to the scene he describes, or is he refraining from such an account in order to assume the burden of confronting inquiry in its historical facticity, say, in a move away from modern tropes of totality (inquiry per se), toward postmodern discourses—itself a variant of the modern—that track and respond to the dispersion of practices that once seemed centered, unified, and universal? This question opens a provocative scene of encounter for those inspired by pragmatism and wary of French theory. And even if one is averse to the Kantian idiom that Lyotard maintains, one should consider what range of empirical material a "comprehensive theory of inquiry" must review. And within that review, one can ask: Is inquiry a univocal thing, or is it a historically evolving, diversifying set of practices whose general character can only be found in the diversity of its practices? Is a "comprehensive theory of inquiry" a metanarrative? It seems to me that Lyotard's text posed that question in 1979, and in a manner that should give us pause if we are tempted to dehistoricize inquiry in the effort to theorize it.[19]

Do You Speak English? The issues discussed around quotation only intensify when the text in question has been written in a language other than one's native tongue and/or emerged in a historical period at a qualitative distance from one's own. But in a general way, they are similar. How one engages translated texts (or translates them oneself) opens and closes passages for thought. For example, Lyotard's title, *The Postmodern Condition: A Report on Knowledge,* concerns knowledge in the manner of *savoir,* "knowing-how," as opposed to "knowing-that," *connaissance,* the former opening up what Lyotard aligns with the pragmatics of narrative and scientific knowledge, which involve the prescriptions (or meta-prescriptions) that govern how scientific statements should be formed such that they can be candidates for evaluation (Lyotard 1984, 18–27). Because Hickman defends Dewey's notion of an "operational a priori" (fruits of previous inquiries that function as the presumptive starting points of present inquiry), quoting in order to think with Lyotard might have helped clarify whether such presumptions, particularly at the level of logical form, operate as kinds of know-how (and with what consequences), or whether we should maintain such a distinction.

For Examples

Finding the Matter at Hand: Whereas modes of quotation establish a relation between one's thought and the texts one engages, examples orient thought toward subject matter, that range of phenomena about which one seeks to be insightful, for example, the nature(s) of judgment, works of art, the limits of dichotomies, or the differences between organic and inorganic nature. And while examples have obvious pedagogical value, here I want to consider *thinking through examples* (much like I considered *thinking with quotations*).

While examples can be merely mentioned, they also can initiate detailed considerations. I worry that the commodity form continues to absorb works of art, overdetermining, even colonizing their character. Even if one hasn't read Adorno, one still may worry about how the global art market affects the range of artworks traded there—films, paintings, novels, and the like. (Such a list merely mentions, by the way.) But what does the existence of art markets actually indicate? It indicates that works are bought and sold, but that fact leaves the relation between "artwork" and "commodity" rather abstract.

One film quickly comes to mind—*Fatal Attraction,* which was nominated for six Academy Awards, including Best Picture. The film portrays a woman's obsession when a weekend fling with a successful lawyer leads nowhere. She stalks and harasses him and his family, such that the film is little more than a deployment of the misogynist figure of the fury that hell knows not. For all that, perhaps because of that, it is a creepy, intense film, and it did very well at the box office. However, initial test audiences did not like the original ending, and so a new ending was shot and edited into the official release, and this is why the film comes to mind; it exposes the inner logic of commodified art. Whereas one might expect to find artistic reasons for the ending of the film—reasons immanent to the development of the narrative, for example—anticipated consumer response proved more decisive in this instance. And that concretizes what the commodification of art decomplishes. Various aesthetic elements and the logic of their integration reflect less the immanent integrity of the work than the demands of the consumer. Commodification is not simply a fate that artworks undergo when they enter the market, therefore—in some instances, it determines crucial features of their character.

"One film does not prove that film in general, let alone artworks as a class, are being commodified." Indeed. But I am not suggesting that an extended example, in virtue of being extended, somehow proves representative, thereby establishing an empirical claim. Rather, examples concretize claims, for author and reader.

Wittgenstein, for Example: "Consider, for example, the proceedings that we call 'games.' I mean board-games, card-games, ball-games, Olympic games, and so on. What is common to them all?—Don't say: 'There *must* be something in common, or they would not be called "games"'—but *look and see* whether there is anything common to all.—For if you look at them you will not see something that is common to *all*, but similarities, relationships, and a whole series of them at that. To repeat: don't think, but look!" (Wittgenstein 2001, 27).

Why the imperative? Wittgenstein fears that a certain habit of thought with regard to universals—that they are based on an implicit recognition of shared essences—might set thought down a path of seeking necessary and sufficient conditions. But tarrying with concrete examples, thinking through them—"board-games, card-games, ball-games, Olympic games, and so on"—can interrupt the inertia of that presumption and confront thought with phenomena that require another look. Examples need not only further a thought, therefore. By introducing phenomena not wholly immanent to the claim, they can prompt redirection.

Excessive Cases: Because examples are selected in the course of writing, they do not function like raw data clamoring for interpretation. Nor are they experimental results confounding an initial hypothesis—the conditions under which one begins to write "for example" do not evidence experimental control. But nor should one assume that an example will serve as a mere placeholder. As Derrida has observed, an example is codified through what it purportedly exemplifies—and thus not sui generis. But it is also nonidentical to the other members of its class—and so not a simple instance. "The example itself, as such, overflows its singularity as much as its identity" (1995, 17).

And that suggests that examples are always more (or less) than team players, if our writing is up to the occasion. Irene Harvey observes: "Examples always exceed whatever frame one seeks to place around them, or whatever cage one strives to capture them within. Such is the necessary danger of the use of exemplarity" (2002, ix).[20]

We Gotta Remain in This Space: While seeking an entry point into the origin of the work of art—the event that allows the artwork to work as *art*—an inevitable circularity dogs Heidegger's heels.[21] If he begins with examples, he presumes their appropriateness and thus a certain conception of art, which they exemplify. But neither can one derive one's concept of art from some more general concept—for example, poesis, mythos, *Geist,* or beauty—without presuming that art can be characterized in this manner. In trying to characterize a class of phenomena, therefore, one seems haunted by special pleading. Such a realization does not lead Heidegger to abandon his inquiry, however. Rather, he believes we must try to complete the circle (1993). But what could this mean? Given that the essay proceeds by way of examples (a painting by van Gogh, a poem by C. F. Meyer, and a hypothetical Greek temple), I take it we should assay generalizations from example to example, following their indications until the lines of thought they open circle back into our point of departure, leaving us with a reflective equilibrium among our general conceptions and the examples that come our way. Yes, the circle may never close. Each example might prove discontinuous with our presumptions, thus transforming the point at which we find the next example. But we'll only reach that conclusion (and that new beginning) if we carry out the analysis that Heidegger champions.

But even that kind of reading may prove self-congratulatory if our initial selections are too in keeping with our presumptions. Reading Celan, Gadamer claims, "one must begin to interpret at the point where the poem sounds peculiar" (1997, 101). And Derrida reports, also reflecting on Celan, though speaking about poetry more generally: "I try therefore to make myself listen for something that I cannot hear or understand, attentive to marking the limits of my reading in my reading" (2005, 166). While a profoundly different feel for Celan and for textuality in general distinguish the meaning of these two statements, they nevertheless agree insofar as both advocate seeking out the strange and discontinuous rather than the complementary.

One path toward the strange runs through potential counterexamples. Suppose one takes artworks to solicit our attention on behalf of something to which they bear witness such as their own exquisiteness, those no longer able to bear witness for themselves, or an ethical way of inhabiting language.

With such a thought in tow, and with examples able to justify and concretize the generalization, one might turn to works that seem to counter the claim, for example, minimalist sculpture and ambient music. What then results? Perhaps they are not actually counterexamples. Or, maybe they are the kind of exceptions that prove a rule. Or, in their discontinuity, they might lead one to rethink what it means to generalize across a class of historically evolving works or even to think categorically.

In Nuce

Sublime Self-Knowledge: What is most our own did not begin so. Nor will it end in our hands.

Good Posture: The patterns of propositional logic are pruning devices, threshers of thought. Does this premise entail this conclusion? With certainty? Something less? Has the scope of the conclusion been properly limited, and is one's evidence suitable to that kind of claim? Can I really claim "all," or should I venture "most," or "many," or just "some" (that is, at least one), and draw the category thinly enough to include an exception that would support the rule? Good manners alone require that we not re-gift broken inferences.

To Be Continued: What does the footnote or endnote enable and frustrate? Sometimes they are placeholders for thoughts that eventually return to the main body of the text. Other times they are mini extensions of budding ideas. Often they are just moves in a scholarly arena. But notes need not be merely ornamental, and they rarely are in the course of writing. Sometimes thought just won't quit.

Wise Up: Straight talk always belies an angle.

A German Sense of Humor: The a priori tries to arrive ahead of time, which is why it is a species of comedy.

Irony

In All Sincerity: Irony lurks in several exemplary texts, particularly Platonic dialogues. In fact, Socrates is identified with irony, both by other characters in the dialogues and later readers, including Cicero and Quintilian, Schlegel and Kierkegaard. More recently, "irony" has been a cardinal term for proponents of deconstruction, notably Paul de Man, and Richard Rorty's pragmatism favors an ironic approach to the questions and answers of metaphysics.

Unsurprisingly, the concept of "irony" covers so much ground that the term less gathers diverse instances than marks an ongoing contestation over its proper meaning and use. As a category, therefore (or a "universal" in the scholastic sense), the term always says one thing while also meaning something else: deceit and sincere provocation, a rhetorical act and the semiotic play on which rhetorical acts are parasitic.[22]

Ironic Being: Cosmic and tragic ironies cannot be the final word for writers. Such ironies befall agents despite (or even because of) their purposive strivings. For example, and keeping things closer to home than Oedipus, a war designed to deter terrorism might intensify the conditions that gave rise to it. Or, a scholarly defense of the nature and value of historical research might lead a know-nothing legislature to cut even more funding for higher education. As a dependent practice, philosophy is not free from such snarls. Praxis conspires with opaque forces. But even if cosmic and tragic ironies underwrite philosophy, one will wonder whether and how to write about it.

The ironies that animate deconstruction are more or less cosmic. Self-knowledge, for example, is temporal and thus transpires through a language that must be iterable, that is, general and abstract. "Self" allows a speaker to posit and recognize itself as the one speaking, the one spoken about, and the one spoken to, each a distinct if not isolated moment, even in the course of this sentence. But "self" applies to all speakers, and to oneself regardless of one's changing character. A condition of the possibility of self-knowledge thus prevents one from ever encountering oneself in one's singularity, as Paul de Man has noted in a now famous passage.

> The ironic, twofold self that the writer or philosopher constitutes by his language seems able to come into being only at the expense of his empirical self, falling (or rising) from a stage of mystified adjustment into the knowledge of his mystification. The ironic language splits the subject into an empirical self that exists in a state of inauthenticity and a self that exists only in the form of a language that asserts the knowledge of this inauthenticity. This does not, however, make it into an authentic language, for to know inauthenticity is not the same as to be authentic. (1983, 214)

This "irony" proves cosmic because it concerns the structure of symbolic self-consciousness per se, at least on de Man's terms. As he says: "Irony possesses an inherent tendency to gain momentum and not stop until it has run its full course; . . . it soon reaches the dimensions of the absolute" (1983, 215).[23]

But that isn't the final word. Given de Man's account, one might rethink aims like self-transparency and authenticity and ask: What else might self-knowledge mean? Or, one might lament the deformations wrought by categorical thought and aspire to a mystical language or work to uncover some kind of "intellectual intuition." Whatever one does, if one continues to write, limited ironies will remain writerly options.

Having Something Other in Mind: Faced with noncosmic ironies, custom turns to Quintilian. Irony asks to be "understood in a sense other than that of the actual words," he says, even the opposite (2001, 3:53). It works either as a trope (namely, through a reliance on a contrary word or two) or by way of a whole figure of speech, which might include an entire passage or, in Socrates's case, a life.[24]

Irony might seem an odd fit for philosophy. While its character varies with time, place, and temperament, philosophy often employs overt definition and clear (at times symbolic) argument for whatever is affirmed and negated. But irony negates the applicability of an overt meaning and often supplies a covert meaning supported only by the negation, without argument, of what is ostensibly said.

About two-thirds through his revision of philosophy, that is, *Walden*, Thoreau recounts a war between ant colonies, one red, one black. "It was the only battle which I have ever witnessed," he writes, "the only battle-field I ever trod while the battle was raging; internecine war; the red republicans on the one hand, the black imperialists on the other" (2008, 155). Throughout his portrayal, which grips with the drama of the observed and his observing, Thoreau analogizes these fierce biters with human battles, remarking: "The battle which I witnessed took place in the Presidency of Polk, five years before the passage of Webster's Fugitive-Slave Bill" (2008, 157).

Presuming that Thoreau's report is accurate about who was in office during this battle, and given the first two-thirds of the book, which chart the universe for aspiring cosmopolitans, it seems odd to suggest that these reds and blacks met and fought on U.S. soil. And sensing that, I am led to think that these lines of political geography are precisely what Thoreau would erase. Yes, there may be continuities between ant and human bellicosity, but this war between colonies pays no heed to the purported commander in chief of the United States, nor did they take or even seek his leave to make war in Massachusetts. Instead, they gathered on a land below the geography of nation states. And this land, in its seasons, with its inhabitants and ponds, is the *terra infirma* toward which *Walden* turns, chapter after chapter, politically anarchic if bound to higher laws. In other words, I cannot help but find in the overt meaning of the section's final sentence a meaning quite contrary—in the circulations of nature, freed from the myopia of commerce and its institutions, one does not find a presidency, but what Thoreau finds in his small cabin—a site "in such a withdrawn, but forever new and unprofaned part of the universe" (2008, 63).

I take this irony from *Walden* to be paradigmatic in the sense of lying close to the center of a radial category. By way of an overt meaning that it negates, the passage conveys a covert meaning that becomes increasingly available when read in the fuller context of the chapter and the work as a whole.[25] But neither claim—Polk's presidency does not extend to ants and nature operates beyond the political geography of nation states—is supported with clear premises marshaled into a tried-and-true inferential pattern. Instead, irony and the flush of its discovery constitute, in part, the persuasive power of the passage. But is this proper for philosophy? Should philosophy present something covertly and negate something without explicit argument?

Catch-23: The ironies that befall us still bear our names.

Socrates as Example: Thrasymachus asserts that Socrates would "do anything rather than answer if someone asked you something" (337a).[26] More specifically, he seems to suggest that Socrates hides behind the speeches of others in order to refute them.[27] This amounts to a kind of *eironeia* (which connotes deception and the wearing of masks), because, or so Thrasymachus insists,

Socrates only appears to dialogue with others. Worse still, he pretends to do so from a "love of honor" that he perversely gratifies by appearing smarter than everyone else (337a). And this is not a one-time affair. Thrasymachus speaks of Socrates's "habitual irony" and how it leads Socrates to not "answer yourself and say what you assert the just to be" (336c).

The charge of "habitual irony" suggests that Thrasymachus is less interested in particular Socratic tropes, for example, proclaiming a kind of ignorance, than in Socrates as an ironic figure whose entire conduct may be deceptive (to keep Quintilian's distinction). Note, this is not just any charge, particularly if we recall that the Socrates in question is a character in a Platonic dialogue (as is the Thrasymachus who presses the question). Across the Platonic corpus, Socrates is almost always a figure of philosophical inquiry, of its aspirations, procedures, and limits, particularly as it contrasts with sophists (Gorgias), poets (Homer), rhapsodes (Ion), generals (Laches), prophets (Euthyphro), and agents of commerce (Cephalus).[28] The charge thus concerns the activity of philosophy itself, and whether its conduct, at least as characterized by Socrates, is in good faith.[29] But given that Socrates is Plato's character, and Plato's chief character, Thrasymachus's charge concerns, first and foremost, Platonic writing and the roles that Socrates plays within it, including his ironic tropes—their tones of mockery are, in part, what lead Thrasymachus to accuse Socrates of disingenuously pursuing notoriety.[30]

Presumably, Plato leaves it to us to work through the charges of Thrasymachus.[31] Characteristically, he stages a problem rather than resolves it, and thus even in the matter of irony, Plato does anything but state a view, let alone his own. But I would stress that the problem of irony is nevertheless very much Plato's own. How does Socrates's conduct, qua character, help realize the aims of genuine dialogue about matters of justice, courage, love and the like? Quintilian may be correct when he says that Socrates "was called *eiron* because he played the part of the ignoramus who marveled at the supposed wisdom of others" (2001, 4:61). But that characterization is insufficient to wave off Thrasymachus's suspicions, and I take it that Plato is asking, through Thrasymachus, for a richer account than Quintilian provides hundreds of years later. More precisely, Plato has prompted his readers to think irony teleologically, as part and parcel of a practice we will not understand unless we have a feel for its goal.

I have tarried with Thrasymachus's accusation, if only briefly, because it offers *a* way of thinking about the role of irony in philosophy—as an act, described more or less well by Quintilian, that helps further an end that would be less well realized by an ensemble of completely direct presentations. I realize this leaves me ridiculous in the eyes of Kierkegaard, who thought that

Socrates was ironic across his "whole existence" and who regarded "expressions and turns of speech" as "trivialities" (Lear 2011, 5). It also localizes my interest, contracting it from phenomena like an ironic attitude or ethos.[32] But this is because I am considering the kind of choices one makes while writing, and irrespective of whether one's general attitude toward existence is ironic. Or, said more strongly, even one whose existence is ironic still must deliberate about when to rely on ironic tropes (and which ones to employ).[33]

Ironic Settlements: In most discussions, critics focus on what irony demands from readers, and in some cases, with what effects, and those seem to provide irony with its usual why. At this point, however, I would like to remain with the possible effects irony might have on thought in the course of writing. Recall Thoreau's ant war vignette, which functions nicely as a case of what Booth termed "stable irony." Its covert meaning seems intended and we can more or less articulate the point it makes about a finite class of phenomena — life and land circulates outside the de jure reach of nation states. "Settled" is a good term in this context because Thoreau's thought seems settled in the construction of the irony. The reader may have to do a double take or two to catch on, and that may unsettle one enough to rethink the terms of one's settlement with land and law, but for the one writing, settled ironies are for thoughts whose trajectories have arced and landed.

A Road So Crooked I Met Myself Coming Back: There was a time when I suspected that only settled thoughts could be presented ironically. One needs a firm grip on the gap between the overt and covert to write ironically. In terms of thought's self-relation, therefore, irony seems to be an operation of self-preservation, even if it promises readers more. (Such are cases of *pedagogical irony*, I would say. Their principal purpose lies with reorienting an addressee.) But my conversations with Lynne Huffer about Foucault's unsettled narrative voice slowed me down. What kind of historian is speaking here, she helped me ask, and with what kind of authority? At least in the first volume of his *History of Sexuality*, Foucault experiments with free, indirect discourse, which refuses to present as a reliable narrator of historical fact. Rather, it pursues a "desubjectivating, rhetorical practice" (one is not sure of the nature and purpose of the subject recounting the history), which might "free thought from what it silently thinks, and so enable it to think differently" (Huffer 2012, 39). And Jonathan Lear has suggested that irony includes a capacity exercised "in the service of helping oneself and one's readers to move in the direction of virtue" (2011, xi). I thus wonder whether my initial take on irony (my pretense, even) was well founded.

At stake is the kind of experience afforded the writer in his or her execution of irony. Lear believes that ironic experiences occur when one encounters a "gap between pretense and aspiration" (Lear 2011, 24). Say you are committed to self-knowledge. (This is one's aspiration.) And suppose you believe that requires a rational interrogation of your affects. (This is your pretense.) But one day, relentlessly interrogating your recurring anger, it dawns on you that a deep desire propels your interrogation. Affect(s) thus orient and impel their supposed other. You thus find a lack of self-knowledge (and thus irony) in the distinction (reason/affect) that had structured your pursuit of self-knowledge.

Huffer and Lear and would have us be ready for such uncanny encounters, and I share their sensibility, as should be evident from my explorations of the example and quotation. But through what does such a sensibility operate? Can one proactively write one's way into such experiences? Can there be what we might term "transfigurative irony"?

This Thought Has No Substance: Consider Nietzsche's provocative term "will to power" and its valences in *Beyond Good and Evil*.[34] Section 13 states: "Above all, a living thing must *vent* its strength — life itself is will to power —: self-preservation is only one of its indirect and most frequent *results*" (1966, 21). And in section 36, he claims: "The world seen from the inside, the world described and determined according to its 'intelligible character' — it would be will to power and nothing else" (1966, 51). The claim, as I understand it, is that all life pursues conditions conducive to its growth. But that is not my present concern. Rather, I am drawn to the kind of claim Nietzsche offers. In speaking of "life itself," Nietzsche is invoking, rhetorically, the site of substance — that which, at base, determines the existential character of a diverse range of derivative phenomena. For example, perception, imagination, and discursive judgment stem from mind; all created things arise from a divine creator that is the ground of being; or, all things are variously intensified configurations of an energy that relentlessly morphs without ever being created or destroyed. I say this because, on Nietzsche's view, human affects are modalities of a "primitive form of the world of affects," a "*pre-form of life,*" one in which all the affects lie unified until they "branch-off and organize themselves in organic processes" (Nietzsche 1966, 50–51). "Will to power" thus names the ground to which the rest of organic life stands as consequent. We should be unsurprised, therefore, if, in section 259, Nietzsche orders us to "gründlich auf den Grund denken" (think completely from the ground), and just before he insists, again, that "life is just will to power" (1966, 217–18).

Given Nietzsche's assault on the "prejudices of the philosophers," it is difficult not to look for irony in concepts that retain the aura of substance. In section 4, we are told that untruth is the condition of life. In section 12, which precedes the section introducing will to power, Nietzsche declares war on the "atomistic need," and he names "*Stoff*," the substance of materialists, as one product of this need. Then in section 19, we read: "Willing appears to me above all as something *complicated*, something, which is a unity only as a word" (1966, 26). And if we turn to such words, Nietzsche proclaims: "It is *we* alone that fabricated [*erdichten*] cause, succession, for-one-another, relativity, force, number, law, freedom, reason or ground [*Grund*], and purpose; and if we write [*hineindichten*] and mix into things this sign-world as an 'in itself,' then we sprout [*treiben*] yet one more time as we have always sprouted—*mythologically*" (1966, 30). What then are we to make of a concept that purports to "think completely from the ground" and marks willing as a seamless, unified phenomenon lying at the heart of a diverse array of affects?[35]

Meaning to Mean Something Else: If irony is operative in Nietzsche's concept of will to power, we should doubt either the scope of his generalization (life itself) or what he generalizes (that all life seeks conditions conducive to its growth). Both are part of the overt meaning of his sentences. And yet, why reiterate a claim (in the first and final sections) and argue on its behalf if the reader should suspend the heart of its sense? That might be the ploy, but if so, it is a tedious one, and I am at a loss as to why Nietzsche would do so.

As I read them, the scope and content of Nietzsche's generalizations are in earnest and the concept of will to power is integral to the new psychology Nietzsche inaugurates in section 12. ("Will to power" is first generalized to life itself in section 13, and it characterizes the "soul as a social structure of drives and affects" [1966, 20].) But this is not to deny that will to power, qua concept, operates in part through irony. What is deployed but ironically negated is the conceptual-rhetorical frame of "substance" that each invokes, a frame that purports to secure (*a*) a kind of identity among the consequents because it (*b*) names what lies outside mythology and rests among things as they are in themselves. One might think that Nietzsche's remarks are contributions to substance metaphysics, but that discourse (that pretense, in Lear's terms) is being ironically displaced, which, once one hears it, prevents "will to power" from settling into an axiom or *arché*.

And yet, Nietzsche is also at pains *not* to allow his sense of the mythological to deny him claims about life itself, and thus his irony is only partial in this instance. And what is left over, the scope and content of Nietzsche's uses of will to power, is transfigured by this displacement of substance metaphysics. Taken from the frame of substance and released into the cluster of terms that gather around without disappearing into it, will to power inflects inter-pretation, violence, valuation, appropriation, mythology, injury, drive, and so forth, with a variable, because varying, sense of purposiveness. Concretely, this means that "all" does not mean "always in the selfsame way" but analogi-cally, perhaps, or in a similar manner. And so tuned, "all" now requires com-parative operations that acknowledge, formally, differences among what is thereby designated, as well as the place and perspective of whoever is making the comparison. Second, the "itself" of life comes to mean something other than what lies behind a veil of appearance. Instead, it directs us to life in its multiple facticity, including the facticity of our own regard for whatever we find in our way. And, given the fate of "all," "life itself" also begins to recall life in the very multiplicity that a substance metaphysics threatens to subdue.

Something other than the settled thoughts of pedagogical irony circulate in Nietzsche's concept of will to power, therefore. Its irony initiates a trans-figuration whose ends it cannot foresee. Not that it is unintentional. I take it that Nietzsche's use of "will to power" is proactively displacing substance metaphysics not unlike he is making war on the atomistic need. But what is intended is an ironic inauguration of semiotic relations and transformations whose eventual shapes are not intended but seeded and left to the rumina-tions of future interpreters.

Message in a Bottle

Celan: Shifts in genre, turns of phrase, and the nested rooms of irony, example, and quotation have an impact on thought in its unfolding. But writing, like all remarks, also has an addressee: "A poem, because it is a manifestation of language and thus essentially dialogical, can be a message in a bottle, posted with the—not always strongly hopeful—belief that it can somewhere and sometime wash ashore, on heartland perhaps" (Celan 1986, 183). What Celan says of poetry is true of everything written or spoken. Every text is addressed to another. Even a journal is addressed to one's future self, and this address marks an ineliminable performative or illocutionary dimension of its language.

Who Is You? One might ask: "Why deliberate about a formal condition?" But this formal "you" is not the actual addressee of any speech act. Even a vague "Hey, you!" has someone particular in mind. If the wrong person turns around, we usually do not accuse them of misunderstanding us. Instead, we further specify whom we meant. And even a cry for help ("Can anybody hear me?") still seeks someone who can and will help. But most cases are clear-cut. One speaks with oneself, friends, colleagues, love interests, aggressive strangers, customers, nonnative speakers, native speakers as a nonnative speaker, and so on. And shifts in addressee usually lead to shifts in presentation. Even in conversation, I will discuss a text differently when speaking with colleagues, undergraduate students, folks at a bar, or editors when pitching a volume. And this is as it should be. If I address another, I should seek successful ways to do so, and this requires responsiveness to addressees in their concrete particularity.

Between You and You: While sites of conversation often call to mind singular interlocutors, it is not uncommon for one's addressees to be multiple, and in writing, this is usually the case. Even among family, differences arise: children, siblings, parents, cousins, nieces, in-laws, et cetera. As a placeholder, "addressee" often involves various relationships among diverse, even conflicting demands, many of which can be in force simultaneously. And this holds true for philosophical writing as well: fellow experts, students, researchers in other disciplines, perhaps even that mysterious creature, the "general reader."

Osip Mandelstam, whom Celan translated, reminds us that an addressee also can (and probably will) be unknown. "And so, although individual poems, such as epistles or dedications, may be addressed to concrete persons, poetry as a whole," Mandelstam wrote in 1913, "is always directed towards a more or less distant, unknown [or 'secret,' as he terms it elsewhere] addressee" (1979, 73). Mandelstam, who appreciates the performative dimension of poetry, also grasps the temporality of its address—poems remain open, greeting all who chance on them. But not just poems. Because texts usually do not dissipate in their occurrence, breath returning to wind, the formality of their performativity lingers, opening them to whoever happens by. True, they might not be "meant" for everyone's eyes or ears, and so one might hide one's love away. But left alone, texts remain quite inviting, which is why one hides them in the first place.

Philosopher-Solicitor: A philosophical address does not simply greet others in order to greet them. It draws their attention to its thought, to the thinking concretized and underway in the interactions of its genre (should there be one) and the various rhetorical-logical operations it employs. Each bit of writing thus arrives on the heels of something like: "Consider this." Of course, *this* varies, but in the least, one is invited to follow along, to experiment with an essay, concentrate with an aphorism, think along with a quotation, or follow the steps in a formalized inference—to do a good bit of whatever that text is doing, though one may decline or respond in unsought ways.

It's How You Said It: Because one is invited to philosophize along, various commitments contribute to the character of the resulting engagement. In this sense, writing is not unlike conversation, where diction and tone and sentence length shape the kind of relationship one has with one's addressees. Condescend, and one's addressee may ironically play the fool or tune out. Witticisms may spark a kind of alertness, though they also may prove distracting. And a monotone voice makes one difficult to follow.

This brings to mind Aristotle's remarks on informal conversation, the kind of banter that accompanies relaxation. For such activities he identifies an excess, buffoonery, a deficiency, boorishness, and a mean, charm. He claims that "there seems to be a harmonious way of associating with people—sorts of things that one ought to say, and a way of saying, and likewise a way of taking what is said. And the sort of people among whom one is speaking or to whom one is listening will also make a difference. And it is clear that in connection with these things too there is an excess and a deficiency with respect to the mean" (2002a, 76–77, 1128a). When writing philosophy, different ends are in view, including a kind of thematic inventiveness, and so harmony among text and addressee may not be a principal good. But the more general terrain of Aristotle's observation is pertinent.

The Hour of the Wolf

Motto for Militarists: War is hell by all means.

Rare, Please: A polemic is an attack aimed at discrediting and/or refuting another's point of view. (One should be unsurprised to discover the word's etymological ties to warfare.) Walter Benjamin writes: "Genuine polemics approach a book as lovingly as a cannibal spices a baby" (1996, 460). The analogy is apt. The polemicist aims to end the life of a thought or position. And it proceeds with eyes oblivious to the many things that life might yet become. In fact, a polemic only takes into account what will enable the refutation. "Polemics mean to destroy a book using only a few of its sentences," Benjamin adds. "The less it has been studied, the better" (1996, 460).

You May Be Seated: In *Philosophical Discourse of Modernity*, Habermas interprets Heidegger as yet another variation on the philosophy of the subject who also attributes to philosophical categories a decisive importance in the development of culture. Despite Heidegger's concerted effort to think past modern subjectivism, whether of the head (Descartes, Leibniz, Kant, and Husserl), heart (Pascal, Nietzsche, Rilke), or hand (Marx) (and this is my trio of categories), Habermas believes that Heidegger only manages an indeterminate negation of the subject, thus remaining bound to its orbit: "Heidegger passes beyond the horizon of the philosophy of consciousness only to stay in its shadows" (Habermas 1987, 139). And beyond those negations, Habermas only finds empty invocations of an archaic origin imbued with quasi-sacred authority. Because these gestures abandon the gains of modernity, including its differentiated sense of validity and its delimitation of philosophy's reach, Heidegger is regressive on Habermas's terms: "To make his claims of necessity, of a special knowledge, that is, of a privileged access to truth, plausible, even if only superficially, Heidegger has to level the differentiated develop- ments of the sciences and of philosophy *after* Hegel in a bewildering manner" (Habermas 1987, 136).

En route to this critique, Habermas seasons Heidegger in various ways. First, he reads Heidegger through figures he takes to be arch-subjectivists, namely, Nietzsche (by way of Dionysus) and Husserl (by way of intuition), without really considering how and where Heidegger differs from or trans- forms these obvious influences, or how Heidegger, more generally, engages the history of philosophy. Second, Habermas pays no attention to any devel- opment within Heidegger's own thought, particularly around the question of the subjectivism that Heidegger himself found at work in *Being and Time*. Third, where Heidegger seems to depart from figures like Nietzsche and Hus- serl, Habermas interprets him as feebly on the way toward Habermas's own position or that of Habermas's pragmatist forbears. Consider, for example, Habermas's take on Heidegger's cardinal thought, the disclosure of beings through an event of being. Heidegger insists that this event follows a logic that cannot be found in the occurrence of any being—subject or object, di- vine or mortal. But Habermas casts the thought of disclosure as a mystified recounting of the power of assertions—to indicate and grasp the appear- ing of beings. In Heidegger's texts, Habermas claims, "the luminous force of world-disclosing language is hypostatized" (1987, 154). Fourth, Habermas takes the point at which Heidegger is at his most radical, particularly when read back into Habermas, and renders its origin nonphilosophical. As Hei- degger has it, there is an originary sense of truth, as an event of disclosure, which precedes and enables not only assertions but also all communicative acts. Habermas denies that this step toward truth as disclosure, even though it marks Heidegger's famous "turn" or *Kehre*, reflects any internal develop- ment in Heidegger's thought. Instead, he attributes its emergence to Heideg- ger's catastrophic engagement with National Socialism: "This step is so bereft of plausibility that it cannot be satisfactorily explained in terms of internal motifs discussed up to this point" (1987, 155). And: "As a matter of fact, the re- versal is the result of his historical experience with National Socialism" (1987, 156). Finally, if only in a footnote, Habermas dismisses William Richardson's observation that Heidegger had already begun to work out this turn toward originary truth in 1930: "In my view, this text—first published in 1943 and based on the text of a lecture from 1930, which was 'revised several times'— does not permit any clear interpretation in the sense of Heidegger's later thought" (1987, 404).

The polemical aspects of Habermas's reading do not evidence the cogency of Heidegger's position, but their disagreement is not my current concern. I want to show how a polemic engages those it would refute or dissuade. First, a position is aligned with presumably outmoded models. Second, its remainder is translated into terms designed to convince all readers that the polemicized thought moves within the polemicist's register, much as Christian missionaries and theologians presumed that others had a rival God or gods, irrespective of whether theism even applied to their beliefs, rituals, and institutions. Such translations are worrisome because they wax totalitarian. They imply, very much on the sly, that whoever holds such a view has not propounded it as well as the polemicist. And this allows the championed view to appear as if it redeems what is worthwhile in the polemicized. In short, the polemicist allows his or her terms to reify, thereby rhetorically instituting them as *the* terms for any and all possible discussion of the matter.

But sealing off the terms of discourse is not the polemicist's only goal. Or rather, to insure it, war must be waged against one who might threaten that order, that is, an example must be made of the example. Polemics seek out the weakest points in a thought and exploit them, often without attending to whatever complexities underlie them. And wherever such complexities prove unavoidable, as when Habermas wrongly times Heidegger's turn toward originary truth, the import of the problem is minimized or dismissed. The opponent must remain an opponent, and a defeated one.

Polemics are, in part, an amalgamation of quotes, examples, modes of argumentation, and so forth. But across the whole, a more general tone and posture are apparent. The invitation, delivered from a lectern reads: "true believers welcome." Because the target is subject to a clear narrowing of point and purpose, the polemicist appears uninterested in an open learning process that might lead to the kind of redirection we have considered at various points, most recently in Nietzsche's ironical deployment of will to power. The polemicist is trying to win an argument in a zero-sum manner rather than pursue the conflict in a transformative way. A spirit (or tone) of self-preservation thus runs through the text's address. And it only intensifies when one catches how the narrowing is effected through a translation that casts the target in terms favoring the polemicist. The assault's backdrop is thus a banner depicting a catechism, the curriculum of a school in which genuine dialogue is rhetorically foreclosed.

Habermas's reading of Heidegger is doctrinal and dismissive, even derisive at points. One sympathetic with Heidegger has to go to extra lengths even to finish the chapter let alone engage it (though it repays doing so). Second, disciples receive little provocation to be more than children of their *Doktor Vater*. Set in a context of rival schools, what might occasion a potentially transformative engagement gives way to an exhibition of school colors at the level of hermeneutic approach and unchallenged presuppositions. And those new to the discussion, if swayed by Habermas, should think Heidegger a waste of time. The polemic is thus also a gesture of exile toward those who would not be true believers and a clear communiqué to the undecided: this is the curriculum—take it or leave it.[36]

It's the Gesture That Counts

Interrupt the Cliché: Philosophy is a game of show and tell. The goal? To be transformed while handling the ordinary with due amazement.

As You Know . . . In "Punctuation Marks," Adorno reflects on the significance of phenomena like the ellipsis, quotation marks, and exclamation points. An ellipsis, he claims, is "a favorite way of leaving sentences meaningfully open" in order to suggest an "infinitude of thoughts and associations, something the hack journalist does not have; he must depend on typography to simulate them" (1991, 94). The worry, I take it, is that an ellipsis is something of a promissory note within a confidence game—I could go on, but the point is made. But for how long? Has it been made? The bravado of the ellipsis is unbecoming.

Called to Task: "I think." "I argue." Neither proves the existence of the philosopher. Nor "I doubt."

After Butler, Following Cavarero: One's writing should answer a question one's reader should ask: Who are you? As Wallace Stevens has it in "The Creations of Sound":

> We say ourselves in syllables that rise
> From the floor, rising in speech we do not speak.
> (1 9 7 1 ,   2 5 1)

Even Good Advice Goes Bad: Short is sweet. But are my aims confections?

Mixed Media: Music allows one rests, repeats, rhythm too. Written to be played, it acknowledges breath and the body's savoir. Written to be heard, and more than once, it leads by example. Moving, it paces itself and those in tow. Might concepts, in their intake and expression, also have mercy, particularly given English rhythm?

Achtung! When philosophy exclaims, it borders on the prophetic, which brooks no disagreement. "Hear me, you heavens! Listen, earth! For the lord has spoken" (Isaiah 1:1). Socrates did not hector Euthyphro, though he, too, addressed heaven.

Furnishing the Space of Reasons

Bedside Manner: In a conversation, one's manner influences how well things go. Tone of voice, posture, how we move our hands and lips, how our foreheads lean or turn—each contributes to the resulting exchange. Roll your eyes while another is speaking and the possibility of a fruitful exchange (generous, imaginative, interactive) diminishes. Utter a barely audible "I forgive you" and you suggest otherwise. A material semiotic underwrites conversation. But not only the meaning of utterances is inflected by how they are delivered. Our manner also indicates some of what we expect from the exchange.

Someone yells, fists clenched: "Do you understand me?" Is a reply even sought? Is it even a question? Not that replies are impossible. But room for them has been curtailed. "It is in large part according to the sound people make that we judge them sane or insane, male or female, good, evil, trustworthy, depressive, marriageable, moribund, likely or unlikely to make war on us, little better than animals, inspired by God. These judgments happen fast and can be brutal" (Carson 1995, 119). Anne Carson's claim is empirical. But that is the scene of deliberate writing, and prospectively so.

We should not be misled by stark examples, however. In most exchanges, one's manner is more of a nudge toward certain results, like when we ask, "How are you?" to a passing friend but avoid eye contact. (And there are other variables. Did we slow down, stop altogether, barely break our stride?) Acquiring a feel for what our manner suggests, in the sense of "to indicate" as well as "to call forth," is crucial. Our manner rarely rises to the level of a sufficient antecedent to a desired result. Probabilities are thus the phenomena on which our sights are set, both with regard to (*a*) what we will be taken as saying and (*b*) what possible replies are likely to seem live or even valuable to our addressee. But this is what one should expect with praxis. The steps it takes toward the future are not determinate enough to allow for technical production. Deliberation in the thick of praxis conspires with fluctuating variables in order to bend our condition toward ends worth pursuing.

What Is My Way? Lysaker is a suburb of Oslo. I thus address you as a Norwegian American. Or do I? I wasn't raised in a culturally literate, let alone self-identifying, set of "Norwegian Americans." My mother's lineage, through her mother, is Jewish in some part, though a part of that part converted to Catholicism well before emigrating in the nineteenth century. But again, I wasn't raised in a culturally literate, let alone self-identifying, set of no-longer-Jewish Catholics. Not that such a lineage could never matter. The year 1933 proves otherwise. But in this context, and in the broader context of a philosophical address, what context do those phrases add?

What about American? I find that difficult to say. "American" is wildly contested by all who claim (and resist) the name. What do I acknowledge, therefore, if I present as "American"? You can meet a boo for every cheer and never leave the shore. Moreover, many "Americans'" are resolutely anti-intellectual and regard the radical reflexivity of philosophy, which cannot accept tradition *simpliciter*, as anti-American. I thus resist setting my philosophy along an American grain. And don't tell me that's quintessentially American. It's not, as American exceptionalism makes plain.[37]

Skin Tone: "We can hear race around a corner, before we even see it. Race is as much, if not more, in the voice than in the skin color" (Mendieta 2014b, 112). Eduardo Mendieta is remarking on the sonic ways in which racialization situates persons in patterns of recognition and misrecognition and thereby subjects them to asymmetrical fates. How does ethnolinguistic identity announce itself in philosophy, and with what effects? "They all sound alike" also offends in philosophy. Because members of any group will endorse a wide range of views, one should be wary of too closely aligning commitments and ethnolinguistic identities, even if they are one's own. But what if the matter is manner? What topics are worth our attention? What examples does one imagine and use to concretize one's generalizations? If one uses foreign words or idioms or a dialect, from where and how? Whose counterexamples come to mind? Where does the accent fall? I'm still finding my way through these issues, even among friends.

A Provocative Site: "Moral reform is the effort to throw off sleep," Thoreau writes (2008, 64). The line helps explains *Walden*'s epigraph: "I do not propose to write an ode to dejection, but to brag as lustily as chanticleer in the morning, standing on his roots, if only to wake my neighbors up" (2008, 5). And could *Walden* be prouder? It is weighed down with condescension at points, for example, in its second paragraph, where Thoreau suggests that no one near him has lived sincerely. At other points, Thoreau is positively smug with self-congratulation. The second paragraph closes with the claim that no reader would stretch the seams of *Walden*, which Thoreau offers as a coat, though it may serve whomever it fits. And note, we are not even out of the second paragraph. As a work of reform, therefore, *Walden* sometimes— and only sometimes—misses the mark with histrionics that divert the reader from a scene of reformation to Thoreau's own self-regard.

Emerson terms the mark in question "cheer," whose nineteenth-century resonances are remarkably precise: (*a*) a shout of praise or encouragement that is able (*b*) to dispel gloom and (*c*) infuse life, in the case of philosophy, with provocations, exemplifications, and disclosures. And please, do not think cheer a matter of optimism. One can cheer through honest courage even as one's thought pauses us with pain, even tragedy. "But I want to talk about the blues," James Baldwin says, "not only because they speak of this particular experience of life and this state of being, but because they contain the toughness that manages to make this experience articulate" (2010, 70). I also recall Baldwin's thought because it underscores that tone is not a matter of reason containing affect, but, in the case of cheer, of not being undone in the surge of all one is called on to feel, think, and say.

Differences in the Grains of America: Baldwin and Thoreau are inheritors of what Eddie Glaude has called "Ralph Waldo Emerson's call upon us" (2017). Glaude too. And Anna Julia Cooper, who quotes Emerson at the close of her "Womanhood: A Vital Element in the Regeneration and Progress of a Race," and with Emersonian tact, introducing the line by asking: "Will you allow these words of Ralph Waldo Emerson?" (2016, 19). And me, which makes us something of a "we" finding something of ourselves in his pages. But a difference courses through our inheritances, one of manner, of how that call is heard and to what ends we find ourselves thereby directed. Arguing with William F. Buckley, Glaude writes that Baldwin "insists on a sense of perspective"—"How the question of who we are gets handled, managed, and pursued under adverse conditions matters" (Glaude 2017). For example, note the restraint in "adverse conditions." Or, consider what might count as a sufficient acknowledgement of the place of race in Emerson's corpus. Do we ignore it as a misfortunate artifact of nineteenth-century American letters? Do we expose it, name it, and move on to what might preserve us, say, the phrase that Cooper invokes—"the measure of our sincerity and therefore of the respect of men is the amount of health and wealth we will hazard in defense of our right" (2016, 19)? Or do we follow out what it means to say, as Emerson does in "Fate"—"We know in history what weight belongs to race" (1996, 776)? And follow it out like one follows out his puns and persistent revisions of biblical verse? I once thought the middle path sufficient. But given how "race" persists, and as a trope of social life (and death), that settlement seems inadequate, which in turn must be acknowledged in a manner that proves one's sincerity.

What We Bear: Cavell asks: "For what is writing responsible?" He replies, beautifully: "Not to hearten pointlessly; but not to dishearten expansively" (2005, 279). He is led to this remark by Benjamin's claim that "there is no document of civilization which is not at the same time a document of barbarism" (2003, 393). Benjamin's line haunts, and in doing so, orients—one's ears turn toward echoes of violence and injustice and what they ravage: succor, resistance, recognition, life. But the "very power of the perception," Cavell warns, "disguises the fact that it is as much phantasm as insight"—too many differences are blurred, erased. And everything else that civilization announces— cooperation, ingenuity, perseverance—seems eclipsed by the condemnation, which risks a "frenzied invitation to a madness of misanthropy" (2005, 279).

I am unsettled on this point. It makes me pause in a way I had not previously, and before a line, Benjamin's, that has become part and parcel of my thought. But I am also unsettled because I'm not sure how to locate, let alone weigh, evidence, given I disagree with Cavell's assessment. But maybe one can disagree, and effectively, without covering up the issue, which involves Benjamin's claim and whose evidence counts, and how.

My initial resistance lies with how Cavell receives the claim, namely, as an inductive generalization about a class of objects. But this eclipses its expressive dimension, which conveys shame and desperation, a sense of being buried alive. My initial disagreement, then, amounts to: Benjamin's remark may look that way but it doesn't sound that way. I say this because Benjamin acknowledges that his thought requires an extreme dissociation, and of oneself, and that acknowledges that other relations to these "documents" are not only possible but extant. (To render the dissociation assertoric, one could say: *X* can be a document of barbarism as well as other things. I presume, for example, that many qualifications underwrite sincere pledges of allegiance.) Second, what is expressed in this dissociation is something of a mood that Benjamin believes he requires to read history against the grain, which echoes, as Cavell knows, Emerson's insistence that we rake language to open cases that have yet to be tried. The intensity of Benjamin's line is thus bound to his effort to intensify experience and thus move readers past themselves, per-haps like Thoreau's crowing. Benjamin's line is *schwer*, as one might say in German, "real, real heavy," which gives us a sense of what culture bears. And that is not born, in turn, without pain. But Cavell's charge of misanthropy loses this, and how Benjamin's heaviness nevertheless carries some love for humanity, particularly those crushed, but also those addressed.

A second line of disagreement takes its leave from a larger context sur-rounding Benjamin's charge of barbarism: "The themes which monastic dis-cipline assigned to friars for meditation were designed to turn them away from the world and its affairs. The thoughts which we are developing here originate from similar considerations" (2003, 393). This suggests that Ben-jamin's remark is bound to the kind of meditative praxis that accompanies the phrases that Evagrius Ponticus assembled for desert fathers in the fourth century. Benjamin aims to redemptively tune readers toward the affairs of the world, what in his case revolves around fascism, but also the broad complicity of so many others who play along in part because a "stubborn faith in prog-ress" keeps them dully amazed that such things remain possible. I thus find Benjamin's line resounding with the kind of blues sensibility that Baldwin admires: "Now I am trying to suggest that the triumph here—which is a very un-American triumph—is that the person to whom these things happened watched them with eyes wide open, saw it happen" (2010, 72). In Baldwin, dissociation becomes a "passionate detachment" that tries to say history as it is, in the same key, even, but in the saying not be undone, in part because one has the power to say (and hear) such things.

A Struggle with Ourselves

Desert Flowers: Crito, Euthyphro, Alcibiades—what did they learn? Every sentence carries a wager, usually lost.

Welcome the Interruption: A particular logical-rhetorical operation counters the polemic, at least in a general way. Anticipating objections situates one's writing in a scene of disagreement, which suggests that disagreement is possible, and reasoned disagreement, presuming one anticipates a thoughtful interruption. It also indicates that disagreement is something philosophers welcome, even solicit, and occasionally generate in the absence of an immediate other. Anticipating objections thus stages a scene of reception. In fact, it even models the kind of response desired. Not that there need to be winners and losers. What Cavell seeks for a democratic public can be admirable in philosophy as well: "The conversation over how good [our] justice is must take place and must also not have a victor . . . not because agreement can or should always be reached, but because disagreement, and separateness of position, is to be allowed its satisfactions, reached and expressed in particular ways" (1991, 24–25). But only to a point. Losing gracefully is a virtue on the basis of what it acknowledges—truth (or insight) trumps pride. Inversely, some appeals to incommensurability are little more than gestures of self-preservation, a way to escape a schooling. But also, new paths might emerge over a course of justification, even when we think we know what awaits. I can't say I've hit bedrock often enough to know that it was my spade that has turned.

Wittgenstein, for Example: In its very first entry, *Philosophical Investigations* unleashes an interlocutor who contributes significantly to the philosophizing

carried on throughout the book. After imagining how a shopkeeper understands a note marked "five red apples" (in this case, by finding what each
word indicates), a voice interjects: "But how does he know where and how he
is to look up the word 'red' and what he is to do with the word 'five'?" (2001,
2e). The interjection bears a counter-intuition. Mustn't the shopkeeper already know what "red" means to make use of a book that correlates it with a
particular color? Or does the shopkeeper only need to know how the word is
used? The interlocutor is unsatisfied. "But what is the meaning of the word
'five'?" "No such thing was in question here," Wittgenstein replies, "only how
the word was used" (2001, 2e). Admittedly, the reply is perplexing, initiating
a discussion rather than concluding one. Also, I'm not sure what "here" indicates. Centuries of thoughts are in play. But my concern lies with the effects of
performing such an interruption in this particular way, namely, in the voice
of another.

As noted, explicitly introducing counter-intuitions acknowledges and
invites them. Texts that never entertain them seem monological, even suffo-
cating. Every reader has one or two counter-intuitions, and when an author
leaves them unaddressed, it begins to seem like positive avoidance. And that
in turn dulls the reader to most everything but those points where his or her
questions seem begged.

But note, acknowledging counter-intuitions exposes them and thus allows for their contestation. Anticipating objections is thus a gesture of inclusion that also seduces one's addressees into positions of vulnerability. It may
prove, over time, that certain questions dear to one's readers, questions that
seem to demand an answer, arise from presumptions that stand in need of
redress, as might be the case with a "particular picture of the essence of human language" that presumes meanings must be grasped by a self-conscious
mind in order to be understood, even learned.

Not that staged queries can't misfire. Are they deep objections? Are they
taken seriously? Or are they tackling dummies? Anticipating genuine objections, that is, problems that are immanent to one's position, invites readers
to test where and how those problems are eventually met. In section 1 of the
Philosophical Investigations, this requires that the interlocutor's dissatisfaction
is not simply an expression of slowness. (If the interjections keep tripping
over Platonism, situation comedy ensues, one laced with the passive sadism
that accompanies laughter at the expense of another.) The alternative is a site
of resolute exposure, and that leaves readers between author and interlocutor, caught in a seat of judgment.

Catching Ourselves in the Act: My predilection for rhetorically self-conscious texts may give the impression that a stance toward addressees only arises among the stylistically ambitious. Not so. Every remark has a performative cast: interruption, question, demonstration, proof, assertion, promise, taunt, insult, provocation, invitation, and so on. And relations between speaker and addressee are determined by that cast, and to varying degrees and with varying effects. Some are clear and direct: insults are designed to hurt. They may fail, but their object is usually clear, though several are possible: weakening the self-esteem of the insulted, winning the admiration of a bystander, returning a hurt, et cetera. Others, like anticipating objections, are less like sticks and stones. They require a kind of uptake in order to come to fruition. (I need to take up the invitation slipped my way in the first section of *Philosophical Investigations.*) Still others operate at a more atmospheric level. (How do you convey welcome?)

Who's on First

Dear "Your Name Here": *Zarathustra* presents itself as a book for everyone and no one, which conveys a pun in English that the German more or less lacks. (The book is for *Alle und Keinen*, "all and none.") Many are drawn to "everyone and no one" because its meaning is more easily gleaned: a book for everyone but no one in particular. And that tunes the reader. This work is for me, though not in the full cast of my particularity. It addresses me in a more general way that I share with others and may have to discover along the way. Not that this renders the book democratic. We all may share the condition of being between beast and overman, but that is all, and among that set, only a few may have the wherewithal and luck to overcome themselves and greet a less pathetic future. Or suppose that "everyone" involves "all those living at the time of publication," who are hereby put on notice. "You are all destined to close out your days among last men who aspire to expire, and with the equanimity of sleepwalkers." And the *Keinen*? The true addressees are to come, that is, not yet among those who are likely to or even can read the book. And such as these may never arrive. No one may acquire the escape velocity to break free of the orbit of man. At present, the book is thus for none, and it may remain so.

So Tell Me, Who Are You? The addressee is marked by the pronoun "you," a term bound to the "I" who speaks. "You" are presumed to be another "I" who might speak in return, to me (your you), and who, in the least, could speak in turn, even when doing so out of turn. Between us, writing always occurs in the space of a we, one diminished by the question, Who is your audience? Who are we, destined to meet in the course of this exchange? The rhetor and those about to be persuaded is one answer, but only one.

Each concrete addressee, as well as the speaking I, meets within a more general we, one marked by the term "generalized other," the one for whom language means and works proximally and for the most part, as Heidegger would put it in *Being and Time*, or ordinarily, as Cavell would have it. The standpoint of the generalized other belongs to neither the speaker nor the addressee but underwrites them both, which authorizes another we at play when we write—the "we" who live in the company of these words and phrases, their grammar and stock performances. The understanding operative here, which knows how and knows that, underwrites more local communities, whether rationalized or folklike, as well as all ego acts, including the formation of writerly intentions. Strictly speaking, writing is always a rewriting of this semiotic field (or wave).

I Am You, You Are Me, and We Are All Together: In *Giving an Account of One-self,* Judith Butler argues that language gives us to ourselves only to whisk . . . it, I suppose . . . away: "It is only in dispossession that I can and do give any account of myself" (2005, 37). She has two movements in mind. The first is semantic, and de Manian. That which renders me legible leaves me substitutable: husband, friend, professor, son, self, even I. Each term individuates and distributes. The second movement is structural in a pragmatic sense. "The address," she writes, "establishes the account as an account, and so the account is completed only on the occasion when it is effectively exported and expropriated from the domain of what is my own" (2005, 36–37). Hear me speak and watch me go, you and I together, in the company of us.

Extra care is in order here. Accounting for oneself is integral to philosophy. (Defend the unexamined life and you'll see why.) And as Butler reiterates, the call of conscience, whatever its measures, seeks an account of what we stand for, what we do, what we forgo. And I agree. But some of Butler's terms give me pause. "Oneself" is an awful shorthand for beliefs, actions, character, and consequences, an ensemble or multiplicity that is not "one's" in any clear sense of possession. Autopoesis marks thought's occurrence, and the script of one's thought is already in the hands of a generalized other before one adds one's name. My intelligibility to myself is already bound, in part, to my intelligibility to another, and at points of genesis and destination. (This is Mead rather than de Man.) But if my own is already in some sense less then exclusively yours or mine but ours (to accept, contest, ignore, celebrate, transform), it seems off to say the scene of address dispossesses me. It rather disposes me to myself in the company of others. And that is less my dispossession than my genesis. And even if some range of possibilities are thereby foreclosed (as with all genesis), others arise; if the semantic displaces, it also reconfigures, and with a capacity to contest—say, with words like "dis-possession" or "opacity" or "mine" and "yours," each of which is ours.

To be sure, a concrete other might expropriate what I offer, whether an insight or a stumble. But the scene of address that seeks and thereby helps generate accounts is not limited to the dialectic of self and other made fa-mous by Sartre in his analysis of the gaze, which now reads like the look of desperate (even horny) men. Among the ever-proliferating roots of address, expropriation occurs when an address is received but ignored or when recog-nition is either withheld or denied. In these cases, something has been given but not returned (which remains a reply). Or, what has been given has been mishandled to the degree that we neither re-cognize ourselves nor find new possibility in whatever returns. But even then, I usually am not dispossessed but irritated, maybe hurt, possibly harmed if the illocutionary conditions are right. And each effect evidences that I am not wholly dispossessed. I would thus prefer to say that the scene in which we remain in situ is one of you and I together in the company of us.

Where Are We? Consider a revision of John 1:1 that seems to thicken Goethe's famous rendering—in the beginning was the deed.[38] Martin Buber writes: "Im Anfang ist die Beziehuung" (In the beginning is the relationship [or the connection]) (1970, 69). Wittgenstein makes much the same point, albeit less directly. In a notebook from 1937, he writes: "The origin and primitive form of the language game is a *reaction*; only from this can more complicated forms develop" (1980, 31e). I have emphasized the word "reaction" because it indicates that speech acts (and the games within which we offer them), are responses, reactions to established scenes in which the speaker is already en-meshed. In Buber's terms, in order for there to be an "I" addressing a "you," you and I must already be related in some manner or other; we must already be connected.

One might conclude from Buber's provocative reading (it is much more than a translation), that the relation is prior to the deed. That may be Buber's point, but if so, I'm not inclined to share it. If we prioritize relation at the expense of deed, we cast it as inactive copresence, a kind of being-alongside one another that is either static or moving through inertia. But why not take relation to involve interaction, and at a primary level, particularly since it is difficult to conceive of how either stasis or inertial movement give birth to action?

Wittgenstein's entry from 1937 continues: "Language—I want to say—is a refinement [*Verfeinerung*], 'in the beginning was the deed'" (1980, 31e). Deeds are also refinements—they rework a situation toward a new outcome, which is what allows relations to be richer and more dynamic than two points along a line, or two lines lumbering along in parallel.[39]

For No One: As far as I know, philosophical writing bears toward more than one addressee. Its "you" is plural and diverse. An essay cannot be for everyone and for every one. Whether anticipating objections or waging a polemic, the "you" of our "we" is not univocal. Too many differences are in play in you, from ranges of literacy to background knowledge to available time and degrees of interest, and that is to assume exchanges within a single language between native speakers. The "general reader" is an abstraction, perhaps a dream image for wistful populists, or a term of art that stands for an amorphous market share without a clear demographic.

You Are Going to Read This: And yet we write. One group that often comes to mind involves the concrete others within one's epistemic-practico field, whether other experts, workers of the world, or one's fellow citizens. Presuming a shared horizon of understanding and concern, one contributes to a common project, whether the generation of academic knowledge or revolution. The professional article is a paradigmatic example. It proposes a "contribution" to a conversation among experts whose terms it presumes even when it proposes to modify them. When puzzling over how much to explain and what degree of jargon is in order, the fellow expert comes to mind, and one can ask, fruitfully: What would I need in this case? The "we" of the professional article is thus fairly univocal, and that makes possible the genre's topical focus and relative complexity. These are my people, it says, this is one of our problems, and here is a go at a solution.

One should not charge professional articles with elitism. "Elitism" in discursive fields involves the arbitrary exclusion of interlocutors from conversations in which they could otherwise participate. It would be elitist to require debates about ethics to be conducted in Latin, for example, or to limit aesthetics to discussions of works readily available to the wealthy but outside the general purview of others with genuine interest in and talent for the field. But the professional article is for professionals, for experts. It thus can presume all kinds of things (terms, names, and texts) that the group holds in common. In evaluating how a bridge was built, one needs to know how bridges are built. This holds true for professional articles in epistemology as well.

Professional articles seem to be an enlightenment genre par excellence, each a chapter in a perpetually revised encyclopedia. Because the goal is a contribution to an evolving field of peers, clarity seems an overriding virtue. One needs to be clear about what precisely is broken and how one, qua author, proposes to fix it. This allows one's fellow experts to see what is at stake and to evaluate the proposition. The strictest measures of inferential reasoning also seem advantageous. If one wishes to make an advance, logical validity seems like a minimal goal. One's information may be fraught, and there will always be presuppositions, but one should avoid confounding one's crew by wringing the false from the true.[40]

For Your Eyes Only: Even outside of expert cultures, not every sentence is for every reader. Given a plural set of addressees, this seems like a prudent maxim. An author might occasionally dip into or even work up to issues and discussions that demand a great deal and so abandon some or even most readers at one turn or other, even if she or he begins and closes a unit with a hospitable staging of the problem or a recapitulation of findings. And in this sense, writing is not unlike teaching, where one modulates levels of difficulty, sometimes casting a wide net, sometimes giving the brightest set something thick to chew. Not that anything is hidden or secret or esoteric in such ventures. Rather, even within expert cultures, one struggles to meet everyone one greets along the way.

Not that one might never elect to proceed esoterically, that is, following Arthur Melzer's conception, by indirectly or secretly communicating one's core commitments while simultaneously concealing them (or rendering them obscure) with distracting arguments and claims, which in turn may add up to a distinct, exoteric doctrine that one may but needn't hold.[41] But why be deliberately esoteric? Presumably a set of hostile circumstances surrounds the publication and reception of one's text. Again, one's addressee is a formally open category—whoever can read is welcome. If one fears repercussions from likely readers, it may prove prudent to distract them. Or, if one fears that the little knowledge one has will prove a dangerous thing in the minds and mouths of others, one might try to fixate them on less explosive fare.[42]

Importantly, indirect communication need not be esoteric. Nor does difficulty evidence an overt effort to ditch the hoi polloi. In fact, only those doctrines otherwise accessible to writer and reader alike require an esoteric cast. (There is no need to hide what cannot be seen.) This suggests that esoteric writing, like pedagogical irony, is an activity of self-possession, even self-preservation. And that gives me pause, as does all cryptography.

Every One Is Everybody

One Foot Never Leaves the Bank: No matter how technical philosophy becomes, it circulates in the currents of language: grammar, etymological histories, and the sociocultural histories of expert communities. Cavell has argued that deconstruction must make use of ordinary language to demonstrate the instabilities it locates, to speak, therefore, as Derrida does, of a letter and a graphic difference that "reminds us that, contrary to a widespread prejudice, there is no phonetic writing." Or, as Derrida's next sentence has it: "There is no purely and rigorously phonetic writing" (1982, 5). (As I hear it, the thought is that one needs a whole lot of decidable to mark the undecidable.)

Donald Davidson, impatient with exaggerated claims concerning incommensurability, argued that a general translatability underwrites our capacity to recognize differences between languages (1984). For example (mine), *gemütlich* isn't quite the same as "cozy," but where both words converge, we are talking about a quality of domestic space, and that commonality renders the terminological difference knowable. (The more general point, already in Hegel, is that if another language were utterly incommensurable, we would lack access to the differences that would vindicate anyone purporting to know the abyss lying between. In fact, we might not even recognize such behavior as linguistic in the first place.)

My claim rides piggyback on these arguments, but to different ends. What interlocutors have decidedly in common marks a matter that a writer might not only presume but interrogate. In other words, one may also address various kinds of *doxa*. They are more generalized and disparate than the concrete others of one's peer group, but they still operate in one's communities, expert or otherwise. Aristotle's *Nicomachean Ethics* is strewn with the views of his day, and he entertains them alongside more focused discussions with the likes of Plato. (One of the most fascinating is the thought that the final chapter of one's flourishing may not be written until one's death. It ain't over 'til after it's over.) Wittgenstein's interlocutor in *Philosophical Investigations* often presents as a committed Platonist, a figure standing for more than particular rivals within then-current debates. The interlocutor thus seems like a stand-in for a common conception, and one can imagine personifying various common presumptions in order to let them pose objections.

At Sea: Quotidian is an extraordinary word.

Talk behind Your Back: Interest in a more general addressee recalls Hegel's *Phenomenology*, that "path of despair" for natural consciousness. Hegel aims to ferret out what operates behind the back of consciousness—for example, that knowing is an instance of pure, immediate objectivity or that freedom is preserved by controlling how we erotically and discursively respond to the world of appearances. Now, in general (and in Hegel, the general carries the show), such commitments have analogues in the history of philosophy, particularly the latter, which Hegel forthrightly names "stoicism." But they also had and retain roots in broader cultural locales. The chapter titled "Sense-Certainty" captures a presumption more or less still operative: knowledge requires objectivity, and objectivity increases as the contributions of the subject decrease. One cannot make any progress in Hegel (or in epistemology) until one is free of this presumption. Knowledge is a subjective achievement.

Hegel's example is telling. Philosophical writing may require a kind of diagnostics that runs beneath the explicit give-and-take of propositions, one capable of finding the hinges on which various positions swing, hinges assembled by and for a generalized other more than by the concrete others of one's epistemic-practico community.

Thick Unlike a Brick: It is less that I think Nietzsche holds (following Emerson) than thought comes to us. But the insight is attenuated if we only note the lyric cast of thinking. Other, determinate forces accompany the muse.

Our opacity to ourselves is one of Butler's chief concerns in *Giving an Account of Oneself*. Something like an individuated, social-historical unconscious courses through (*a*) whatever we would recount (our experiences, lives, motivations, commitments, deeds, and desires) as well as (*b*) the terms of our accounting (from their norms to the names and syntax we employ, many of which operate as institutionalized codes). Acknowledging such fates is not enough, however. The language of "opacity" already arises in an act of self-knowledge that proves paradoxical if it allows such terms to have the final say. Acknowledgment of our opacity is thus a turn in a larger arc of learning, and one that requires concretion. When, where, and with whom does our thought go strange or clumsy, with regard to what? And not just according to my own lights, but yours as well. Philosophically, one cannot simply stop trying to learn more. And yet, acknowledging that there is always more to learn may temper the pursuit with greater patience and generosity, with ourselves and others, as Butler herself suggests.

Against Slogans! "The liberal subject," "Cartesianism," "postmodernism," "dualism," "capitalism," "socialism," et cetera—one hears the crinkle of straw men (or the crackle of talk radio) in these terms and phrases. "Not me," they declare, "and I mean that in a bad way"—at least that is often the clearest message being sent. In reaching behind the back of one's interlocutors, one needs genuinely operative presumptions, and that requires citation, quotation, and analysis. What really drives this thought? Slogans are sometimes used in the affirmative, but when used diagnostically, they bluster more than muster. Analytic, continental, feminism, deconstruction, post-structuralism, positivism, pragmatism, Eurocentrism, enlightenment, and so on. Liberal, conservative, communism, socialism, capitalism, neoliberalism, anarchy, flimflamarchy, . . .

For Examples: A mountaintop chill pervades texts that forgo examples, which do more than concretize. Examples also open testing grounds on which readers can stand and, more importantly, evaluate. In the we of our address, the example is posed by the author for the reader, and with a certain degree of what purports to be evidential force. "This claim makes sense with regard to phenomena like this, doesn't it?" Several replies are possible. "No, it doesn't. Here is a dimension of the example not covered by the claim." Or: "It does, but this is an irregular case." Finally, examples breed in the mind, and so tug and seduce readers into to the task at hand.

A Bad Reading Award: In 1998, the journal *Philosophy and Literature* awarded Judith Butler first prize in its Bad Writing Contest. A brouhaha ensued. Heady days.

Writers "won" the prize for sentences deemed "stylistically lamentable." But the true bone of contention was specialized, technical language in humanistic writing. Generalizing the point of the prize in the *Wall Street Journal*, Denis Dutton ridiculed "vatic tone and phony technicality" and declared that Butler "beats readers into submission and instructs them that they are in the presence of a great and deep mind. Actual communication has nothing to do with it" (1999). I'm not sure how one could know this. And once the "emperor's clothing" cliché appeared, the scene of argument constricted. (That isolated sentences were the target suggests it never arrived.)

Butler replied in the *New York Times*. (Like I said, heady days.) Rightly, she suggested that "bad writing" was a smoke screen for intellectual disagreements about the relative value of postmodern theory, which then wielded real influence. I would add that only within the context of such disagreements can one assess the merits of a writer. Wonderful sentences without insight are not in fact wonderful sentences, at least not in philosophy. One cannot take writing seriously without assessing its validity. In this regard, Martha Nussbaum's polemic, "The Professor of Parody" (1999), is more on point, even though it repeats some of Dutton's accusations and erroneously glosses the offending sentence. For Nussbaum, the real issues are Butler's purported (*a*) turn away from material conditions toward the discursive and symbolic, and (*b*) her refusal to provide a normative frame for the transgressions she celebrates, which (*c*) leaves her institutional politics hovering between legal quietism and radical libertarianism, which (*d*) symbolic transgression cannot save. Whether this gets Butler right is a different issue, and a serious one. But in this context, my concern is setting an author's prose into her or his larger project and assessing it within that project. As Michael Warner observes: "Any way of writing that could be said to fit necessity cannot be simply called bad" (2002, 136–37).

To what, if anything, might difficult and technical prose contribute? Amid the slings, arrows, and chortle, Butler found this question. (Is there a prize for that?) How might one challenge what passes for common sense, a concern as old as philosophy? With that end in mind, Butler defended the use of complex concepts such as hegemony. Their density says several things at once, in this case, power, operating invisibly, often unintentionally, and in ways that subordinate certain lives while privileging others. And that might prod readers to interrogate what usually passes as necessity or valid tradition. Even if it directs readers toward the author and her or his panache, more centrally, theoretical jargon tries to interrupt certain habits and indicate phenomena obscured by those habits. (Call that its double duty, or triple duty if jargon does and aims to confer authority on the speaker.) More generally, difficult, technical language tries to cultivate a kind of attention that often wanes in the comfort of ordinary language, as Jonathan Culler has observed in his contribution to the fracas.[43] Of course, jargon threatens to eventually dull that attention if uttered with fervor, particularly when the writer fails to concretize whatever is being indicated. ("Hegemony" names how social power functions without specifying its character or effects, and those seem

the principal concern. No one would resist the hegemony of genuine justice.)
But any string of words can fail to land.

Dutton believed that Butler had abandoned her addressees. I don't think
so. Communication was not beside the point, but neither was it the only
point. Powerful, technical language engages readers as one might engage an
engine, and that might enable readers to better receive whatever is on offer.

Knowing That I Don't Know: If Socrates is an exemplar, acknowledging ignorance seems integral to philosophy. But more than that, and for one's public,
one should not be afraid to learn in public.

The Secret Addressee

On Behalf of No One: We address more than our peers and the everybody assembled as the general addressee. Most people also write for an internal audience of teachers, formative influences, and friends, an intersubjective set far narrower than the concrete addressees of one's epistemic-practical community. I imagine this assemblage focuses our efforts more than the others—these are the ones we aim to impress, convince, provoke, and engage.

Then there are those whom some write against; or, the enemies are easier to pick out—the purported scourge of deconstruction, the nonsense of the nothing, or still, after all these years, the flattened grave of the Cartesian subject, the ghost in the machine long departed. Reading these texts, one feels like a bystander, rubbernecking. One is called to witness the beatdown, though skirmishes sometimes prompt others to join the fray, perhaps as a "just defender" or just to add a kick for good measure.

Still others find the generalized other sunk in concrete, and to the point that they despair of being heard. The loneliness of such texts is palpable. Some diaries, say Kierkegaard's, read as if written for a posterity he knows will find him. Benjamin's *Theses on the Philosophy of History* read like echoes in an empty room.

The most curious addressees are neither concrete nor general, at least not in prototypical ways. One does not know them, and that distance is integral to the relation and what it requires. But neither is the addressee someone who arrives without any of the same generalized meanings and conventions—that condition precludes an address altogether.

Anticipating an unknown reader, one imagines them having to look back, receiving one's prose in a manner denied current and foreseeable interlocutors, including oneself—for everyone, from no one.

Seeing around the Corner: In 1913 Mandelstam compared poems to messages in a bottle: "The message, just like the poem, was addressed to no one in particular. And yet both have addressees: the message is addressed to the person who happened across the bottle in the sand; the poem is addressed to 'the reader in posterity'" (1979, 69).

At one level, all writing, insofar as some unknown, unintended reader finds it, has a secret addressee. This is a "you" one can neither elect nor disavow. But I am interested—and here I follow Mandelstam—in writing that takes this chance to heart and prepares itself such that it might be ready.

When philosophical writing orients itself toward a secret addressee, it leaves the confines of the professional article and experiments with a thought whose legibility is uncertain within the "we" convened and presumed. Mandelstam observes: "In addressing someone known, we can speak only of what is already known" (1979, 70). Denying the consequent, I add: in venturing something unknown, we address someone unknown. Known and unknown are matters of degree, of course, but when philosophy assumes the burden of thinking anew, it needs something new from its addressee, and they might be a long time coming. "Each poet creates an expatriate space," Alice Fulton writes, "a slightly skewed domain where things are freshly felt because they are freshly said" (1999, 3). Philosophical writing that aims toward invention and/or reformation seems similar. In struggling to say something just so, one reaches out toward a reader who can hear it just so. And that vulnerable but cheering gesture (which does not leave the world as it is) lines a new settlement.

Avant-garde art expatriates when it strives to mean according to its own example. This is why romantic texts, at least in part, have to educate readers about their own trajectories. Ambitious philosophical writing pursues a similar effect, and inherits a similar burden, but through a repatriation of the overlooked (performativity), the lost (the question of being), even the despised (the body, desire, the dickless). Not that new terms aren't required, for example, "transcendental conditions," "being-in-the-world," "the sex that is not one," "nonjuridical power," "a double consciousness," "an extramoral sense," and so on. And not that familiar terms are not recharged, for example, "the ordinary," "sexual difference," "ambiguity," *vita activa*. But in each case, such terms bear us back toward where we have always been, or, depending on your logic, been unfolding.

Hey You! Mandelstam claims that a secret addressee finds her- or himself hailed by name. This isn't quite right, and it can't be on Mandelstam's own terms. He requires poems to astonish with their originality: "The fresh air

of poetry is the element of surprise" (1979, 70). But if I am genuinely surprised, it is not only that another has a thought that I, too, hear, but also, I
now better hear what before had only whispered and teased. If so, the name I
find is the one I discover in the course of a reading, in response to a surprising solicitation, one that seems the inverse of the uncanny—the admittedly
strange strikes me as intimately familiar. This adjustment bears notice because it indicates that one's contemporaries can prove secret addressees. The
future is now.

Neither Here nor There: Writing for a secret addressee recognizes how one's
words are accompanied by an open invitation to whoever might chance on
them, that, like it or not, each unit of meaning involves a hand outstretched
in a gesture of welcome. This is part of the vulnerability of writing. But it also
awakens the vulnerability of response in all who take up the offer—as the
writer unfolds in a venture, so, too, the reader, opening toward what might
broach another name for what had seemed intimate and settled.

I find the vulnerability of writer and secret addressee utopian. Not in
the strict sense of nowhere. That "utopia" is a cry of despair. "Anywhere but
here. Anyone but me." But when a writer ventures the incipient for a secret
addressee who in turn welcomes it, something neither here nor there transpires but nevertheless arises, and from nowhere else but what the relation
(or encounter) affords. Writing is thus always a sign of hope, even when it is
pessimistic.

Impudence: Mandelstam recalls a poem by Konstantin Balmont and accuses
it of insolence. It pursues the individuality of its saying at the expense of its
addressee. Because it is the charge that intrigues me, and because Russian
is beyond me, I will not (and cannot) address the poem or the reading in
the manner it deserves. But I can tarry with the suggestion in a general way.
Elitism narrows the secret addressee by unnecessarily coding itself in an ornamental cloak. Insolence (or is it insecurity?) exhausts itself in securing its
own presentation—"I am a sudden crack / I am a thunderclap breaking," we
find in Balmont (in translation). For certain? One may announce one's plan
to remake the conscience of one's race in the smithy of one's soul. But can
one announce that one has finished the job? If so, no one else need register
and gauge, praise or blame what takes place. Not that the reader is prevented
from replying—but again, we are in variable affairs. The matter is one of
tone, though one could also say bearing, as when one or another is haughty
or noble or anxious. An insolent bearing—which I hear in the phrases "of
course," "as is well known," or in dismissive references toward rival views—

falls short of the hopeful venture that risks itself and so, in turn, needs someone at risk in return.

WTF: The stark racism of Kant and Hegel is now well known if too often ignored. Their remarks are destructive in a variety of ways. One is particularly
salient in this context. Even when they do not explicitly venture conditions of
possibility for human emancipation, texts extend an offer, utopian in promise, whose acceptance requires the reader to bear with the text, that is, to engage it, even in its incipience. Thinking with Kant, thinking with Hegel, elud-
ing dogmatism, finding content in form—that's hard but often exhilarating
work. Imagine being in the thick of it. One feels the power of a transcendental
argument, the insight of immanent critique. And then one chances on Kant's
estimation of Native Americans and those of African descent: "Too weak for
hard labor, too indifferent for diligent [labor], and incapable of any culture,"
he concludes that they are "despite the proximity of example and ample
encouragement—far below the Negro, who undoubtedly holds the lowest of
all remaining levels that we have designated as racial differences" (Mikkelsen
2013, 186–87). Once found, it is difficult not to hear the echo of this contempt
throughout Kant—you are too weak for this, you are incapable of this—and
precisely because it retracts the invitation that arrives with every sentence.[44]
Or, moving from the illocutionary to the perlocutionary, and following a
remark from Paul Taylor, the sexism and racism of philosophy often wearies
those who are required to read past the ways in which their existence is only
acknowledged in remarks that exclude them from the philosophical. Why
not close the book and walk away?[45]

Nostalgia Isn't What It Used to Be: The secret addressee is not the universal
subject of universal reason. The terms in which writer and secret addressee
meet arise only in the reading encounter, and so they are not sufficiently
accounted for by referring to a universal faculty or some *sensus communis.*
(That future never was, nor could it be.) The subject of writerly liaisons is an
aspirational phenomenon, the object of a hope or a longing. But it is also one
partially written into existence through the ways in which the writer renders
the incipient legible. This is why the message in the bottle is such an apt
image. Such gestures may be lost at sea. Or they may arrive and fail. "It is a
delicate matter," Emerson writes, "—this offering to stand deputy for the human race, & writing all one's secret history colossally out as philosophy. Very
agreeable is it in those who succeed: odious in all others" (1969, 387).

When We Undo Things with Words

Even Stop Signs Say "We": When I entered graduate school in 1989 it was clear to many that language was war by other means, to revise a famous revision of a notorious vision. On the one hand, it was a mobile army of metaphors on truth-functional plots, for example, "army," "plot" and "metaphor," troops carrying terms from one zone to another, source domain to target, marking fields where snow could fall in its whiteness. But also, and more importantly, the central plots in the history of language were drawn up as plots against the particular, the historically unrepresented, and the unrepresentable. Rootless in the gathering snow, plots without headstones, they were less than leaves to be raked, not even dry grass for wind. Less than secret addressees, many were, paradoxically, explicitly ignored.

Those fates—gays, women, people of color, a more than human world, those that had once been a class but had lost even that—they provided marching orders. The limits of language *must* be traced and exposed, the measured plains unsettled, particularly at the margins. Marching armies *must* be met en route.

Some imagined great conflicts where villains would be overcome—great dualisms, ontotheologies, centrisms of all stripes. Others pursued little wars. Saboteurs, guerillas, the interventions were strategic—halting the onslaught with an indigestible term or repossessing dispossessing gestures.

The Might of "Might": Sticks and stones, but words . . . Poor advice. Words can hurt, like slaps or gut punches, particularly when said by those with institutional power or by those one took to be allies (or at least not enemies). Such effects are perlocutionary, though a kind of illocutionary disenfranchisement may also occur if time and place, speaker and addressees (and not just the abused) line up. "Whites only," like Being, can be said in many ways. So too, "women need not apply."

In turn, one seeks to undo a certain kind of language by way of more language, say, a request, an insistence, perhaps even a command or rule. Consider the scene in which such corrections arise and to which they respond, a scene at once intersubjective and institutional, conscious and unconscious, and in its venture, thoroughly hypothetical, recalling that "hypothesis" not only names a presumption designed to be tested but also a line of thought taken as a ground for action.

The effort to correct offensive and harmful speech involves an action that moves in an ideal field, "ideal" as in "imagined." One hears an offensive word or phrase and responds in the turn of an "as if," as if the relation could be more than bellicose, as if the speaker were something other than an object behaving in an unpredictable fashion. Instead, here is one who could have acted otherwise and might act otherwise. And in responding with an eye on a future that sometimes accompanies the subjunctive, the hearer proceeds as if they both shared a site of moral standing and accountability, say, a hill in Tennessee, each with a hand on a jar of tea, each expecting the other to behave in a manner that can justify its conduct (and, if asked, will).

Writing to Resist: Certain terms persist like tumors, which grow at the expense of their host languages and languagers. Like Anthony Appiah, one might seek to redress them, exposing the word "race," for example, as a false universal, noting that it says nothing in a biological register beyond what is said by the morphological terms it purportedly gathers in an explanatory manner (1992). And one might go on to argue, as Naomi Zack has, that the term lingers, despite its obvious vacuity, because it sustains a subject-social position that allows one to act as if another were less intelligent, hard working, or sexy, perhaps just an unpredictable object whose movements may require one to stand one's ground (2005). Not that biological registers demarcate all there is to say about this. I would insist that in the first and second person, "race" names a way of regarding oneself through the regard of others, as well as a way of regarding others. And from the third person, geographies and institutions, bridges and borders bear the traces of actions and reactions moved, in part, by a sense of race. And one might argue that we'll prove to be poor psychologists and sociologists if we jettison the concept of race even if, in a biological register, its uses are vicious.

In redressing "race" along such lines, one proceeds as if speaker and addressee shared a site of epistemic standing and accountability. Here, too, the attitudes are reactive, the speaker presuming that her or his hearers could believe otherwise, and on the basis of reasons. And each sentence re-lines that site, which two or more might share. That is, not only is a shared space thereby imagined, but also, in raising questions and offering reasons, one is already traveling toward another. And one expects, less empirically than morally, that others will also walk the talk.

Imagine What Follows: We are here, with all that means and does not mean, at least not yet. When we undo things with words we imagine and step into determinate sites, terrains not yet traced in Wallace Stevens's "Anecdote of the Jar," with its solitary "I" gathering the tame and untamed to itself, or rather, to the jar set on a hill in Tennessee.

The future is now. Not that these sites of proactive imagination open the whole terrain on which we meet. We have already met by the time we approach unpredictable objects or address another as if you and me in the company of us might yet act or think differently. And to render that meeting explicit, we could undo other things with words—namely, the metaphysics of presence, which thinks of our being-in-common in terms of co-present beings. As Jean-Luc Nancy has it, beings already share a site of compearing by the time they meet or part or pass, oblivious to what might have been (1991). Not that such a site can be named, except perhaps as a "condition for the possibility of naming," though even then, "condition" is an "exscription" as opposed to an inscription, which focuses on what is to be named rather than the events of compearance or exposure that enable naming (Nancy 1993).

Early in his career, Nancy aligned such exscriptions with the phrase "literary communism," an activity that draws language back to the scene of our compearance, one where singularities arise, together because apart. The term "singularity" was chosen because it draws us away from the determinations of language, from its campaigns, its inscriptions, and toward a shared site of exposure. Singularity is thus not a concept of determinate or even reflective judgment. Instead, it is an invitation to begin again, to look again, to listen again, a beckoning even to return, after the leaves have fallen, to a plain *Sinn* of things, as if we had come to the end of the imagination's "as if," "Inanimate in an inert savoir," as Wallace Stevens puts it in "The Plain Sense of Things."

But as literary communism turns us toward a scene of mutual exposure (encounter, relation), it also imagines that absence of imagination, as Stevens puts it in the selfsame poem. In reimagining scenes of originary exposure, literary communism, in its animated even earnest *savoir*, repeats the "as if" of those who would politically correct hurtful speech and/or critically recast (or cast off) deforming language. Beckonings and invitations are more than plain arrangements of and steps within the shared space of compearance.

They are already attempts to render it habitable, that is, more than the absence of the imagination is being imagined in sentences intent on exposure, encounter, relation.

We have always imagined more than we have known, and perhaps this might complement the imagination Eddie Glaude has championed: "Imagination then is that feature of deliberation or inquiry that guides our attention beyond the immediately experienced so that we can take heed of those lessons of the past as well as take in those as yet realized possibilities that attend any problematic situation" (2011, 116). In its idealized variations, the imagination finds possibilities buried in what came before, including "the imagination." And so I wonder where my address points, as if it were Whitman's beard in Ginsberg's supermarket, and whether we might someday meet under that roof.

Unknown Friends

Dear Dear: In 1848, Emerson exclaims: "Happy is he who looks only into his work to know if it will succeed, never into the times or the public opinion; and who writes from the love of imparting certain thoughts and not from the necessity of sale[,] who writes always to the unknown friend" (1973, 315). Like Mandelstam's secret addressee, "the unknown friend" underscores that writing moves in a *we*—friendship requires no less than two who meet in a kind of mutual recognition. (If only I think we're friends, we're not.) And this we also has a more determinate character than the formal, structural relation of speaker and addressee. I can play both roles as writer; I cannot play both roles as friend. But whereas "secret" and "unknown" carry similar valences, "friend" indicates something more.

Handle with Care: In presenting as an unknown friend, one's writing needs to be available, which need not be the same as clear, though it needn't preclude it either, particularly unnecessarily. (That seems contemptuous.) But more than clarity, availability calls for a kind of individuation. "It's there in the writing, such as it is. It may be wrong. The matter is more complex than I have fathomed. But I'm not holding things back." This is a kind of sincerity with regard to what is objectified, and with regard to the task of objectification, and a kind of tenderness for another you.

A certain kind of clarity might move to a contrary end—in its ease of appearance, whatever is at stake might go missing. Richard Rorty's prose is often so lucid that readers sometimes fail to register its full implications (or complexity): "Europe did not *decide* to accept the idiom of Romantic poetry, or of socialist politics, or of Galilean mechanics. That sort of shift was no more an act of will than it was a result of argument. Rather, Europe gradually lost the habit of using certain words and gradually acquired the habit of using others" (1989, 6).

The displacements are clear and exact. "Decisions" give way to "shift" and "gradual" change (loss, acquisition), and "will" is replaced" by "habit." Simple enough, and by 1989, there had been at least a hundred years of such remarks from the likes of Dewey and other pragmatists. What this simplicity obscures, however, is how the thought recoils on the event of its own acceptance and rejection, terms that seem to drag us back into the will and its decisions. Not that I'm a continent or culture. But neither is Europe a person, and thus I wonder if we should talk about "habit" in such contexts. Finally, if Rorty is right, then Romantic poetry and Galilean mechanics were adopted according to terms at odds with their own self-understanding, which leads me to wonder if they were in fact adopted. (Can I agree with you if I do not share your reasons for believing what you believe?) Rorty's prose shimmers with ease, even when it's doing yeoman's work. That's not coy dissimulation, which runs counter to friendship's presumption of sincerity. Nor is Rorty simply leaving room for the reader to continue thinking, which a friendly address requires—spelling out every entailment is pedantic, even insulting, a version of impudence. But the ease of virtuosity can lead another in over his or her head. If Rorty had made us work harder by exposing more of his own hard work, we might have arrived with greater dexterity at those points where his thought proves most rebellious.

More or Less Nothing More or Less: A second-order availability also seems requisite for those who would address unknown friends. One should account for one's accounting, make it legible, even if one fears that it is whim, as Emerson does in "Self-Reliance," or just another interpretation, as Nietzsche announces in *Beyond Good and Evil.* Not just to cover one's rear. That's for those who write for unknown enemies. Fearing an ambush (or the shame of failure), one pursues justifications for almost unthinkable interlocutors and battles counterexamples so counterfactual that a reader might wonder, justifiably: "What planet are you on?" A writer who aspires to be impregnable has no friends—only enemy combatants and those who surrender. Not that philosophical writing lies outside agonistics. But writing to the unknown friend calls for a different manner of address.

One's recounting may also be performative. The presentation may be elaborated, foregrounded, even belabored. And those reflexive remarks may entail a confession: nothing but these words support what I have ventured, but also, and this is equally important, nothing less. Kant finds grounds for

the judgments of theoretical reason, which can inform, unfailingly, his future. His gesture of critique thus radiates with a certain kind of responsibility. Others are thrown back on the poverty and power of their judgments in
the just-so of their occurrence (and recurrence), which means each thought
must be earned and renewed time and again, its purchase reestablished. It
would be a mistake to regard writers like Stanley Cavell as any less circumspect than modernity's princes of reflexivity, Descartes and Kant.

Show Yourself: Melody Edwards, a colleague at Emory, told me in an email: "I
find much of Emerson's writing has a way of reaching into the soul of a person." That has been my experience as well. And when one asks why, a common reply is: it's as if he is speaking to me in particular. Emerson's prose has
a very particular voice—earnest, cajoling, at times, aflame. One would never
mistake it for another's, say, Hegel's, who has a voice of his own, one uninterested, as the dialectic turns, in my name. (Emerson will settle for nothing
less.) And this is integral to their effects. Emerson favors a certain kind of
provocation, Hegel, the demonstration of conceptual self-possession. When
prose accentuates provocation, awakening another to genuine thought,
it should earn the reader's trust. Having a sense of who is prodding and
poking—that they stand behind their words, if not wholly in them—helps
establish intimacy, which in turn fans a mood of abandon wherein a reader is
ready to risk new names.

"We need to lose the world, to lose a world," Cixous writes, "and to discover that there is more than one world and that the world isn't what we
think it is" (1993, 10). And that, on her view, requires exposure to loss. That
also has been my experience. But certain gains facilitate such losses, say, an
unknown friend with whom to share the world wherein we realize the world
isn't what we think it is. "We annihilate the world with a book," she says a
bit later, thinking of the writer (1993, 19). But only through venturing—and
thus preserving, as its pre-image—a certain way of being there, receiving,
responding.

There is more to us than we think: "Let us agree," Ed Casey writes, "that
finding your own voice in philosophy is not something of strictly personal
significance; nor is it something so abstractly true as to leave the actual self
who is doing the thinking altogether behind" (2010, 31). I think we must
agree. Recounting the idiosyncratic, or just naming what occurs clings to
the thinnest positivity. Philosophy ventures something representative, even
when, especially when, one grows skeptical about the universal, the necessary, and the ahistorical.

Easy Come, Easy Go: Richard Rorty and Daniel Dennet have easy, carefree voices that delight in their skepsis, as if to say: "It isn't so hard to let go of these terms: truth, self-knowledge, God the creator of heaven and earth. I did it, and look at me now: unburdened, vibrant." Addressing the idea of a God whose creative vision secures human meaning, Dennett writes: "There is no future in sacred myth. Why not? Because of our curiosity. . . . Whatever we hold precious, we cannot protect it from our curiosity, because being who we are, one of the things we deem precious is the truth" (1995, 22). Nietzsche wondered through his madman what gave us the power to wipe away an entire horizon. Curiosity, Dennett replies; this is where it leads. Simple as that; just follow its lead. No pain, and gain to boot. With an even more radical feel for our origins, Rorty writes: "To sum up, poetic, artistic, philosophical, scientific, or political progress results from the accidental coincidence of a private obsession with a public need" (1989, 37). Again, the tone is brisk and easy. Genius occurs when someone's idiosyncrasies "just happen to catch on with other people—happen because of the contingencies of some historical situation, some particular need which a given community happens to have at a given time" (1989, 37). "To sum up . . . ," "coincidence," "just happen," matter of fact events accompanied by a matter of fact tone. And since Rorty in particular tends to underplay his brilliance, his prose also conveys: "I did it, and you can too." And that solicits a certain kind of reply. The reader finds him- or herself, as friends do, in what is now a joint project.

Beneath Contempt: In some cases, friends also need enemies, and thus an address to an unknown friend can rally the troops by rhetorically establishing another no one really wants to be. Nietzsche gleefully plays this card, and we share in his delight—who rallies to defend the herd, the last man, the ascetic priest? Dennett also plays the bully from time to time: "This book, then, is for those who agree that the only meaning of life worth caring about is one that can withstand our best efforts to examine it. Others are advised to close the book now and tiptoe away" (1995, 22). Unless you believe that the meek will inherit the earth or that cowardice is the new cool, you're likely to take the bait, and feel the better for it as you leave behind those who cower. Of course, if you make yourself known and run afoul of the program, you're likely to be next for the stick. Ritualistic sacrifice, even of the rhetorical sort, is risky business.

A Note Toward a (Less Than) Supreme Friction: To prove less clumsy in the presence of music, Barthes posits: "Rather than trying to change directly the language on music, it would be better to change the musical object itself, as it presents itself to discourse, better to alter its level of intellection, to displace the fringe of contact between music and language" (1977, 180–81). To this end, Barthes offers us the grain of a voice, one he distances from any pheno-song, namely, "everything in the performance which is in the service of communication," taking the set from Julia Kristeva, as well as its contrary, the geno-song, "where the melody really works at the language—not at what it says, but the voluptuousness of its sound-signifiers, of its letters" (1977, 182). Geno-song names the direction in which the grain of voice runs. Does philosophy have something of this? A way or manner of speaking, of raising questions (say, like children or scolding schoolmasters), of objecting (say, generously, or not), of reading, of inhabiting the myriad speech acts that make up the pheno-song of philosophy? And does it matter, philosophically speaking?

How I commit or execute any of those deeds that seem integral to philosophy will indicate other commitments, model them, and thus model philosophy like some kinetic sculpture twirling in discursive space, churning the very currents that turn it. Barthes locates the grain of the voice in the "very friction between music and something else, which something else is the particular language (and nowise the message)" (1977 185). Might I, too, lodge a friction, even as, particularly as, I decline the invitation to imagine language but nowise the message? (To be irreducible to X is not necessarily to be free of it, and I don't see how my voice can be pried from the topics that claim it, orient it, compel it speak. I could address other issues, but at the cost of being me. But perhaps my resistance arises because here the analogy between music and philosophy begins to break.)

On Not Being a Snowflake: My willingness to follow Barthes (and given the point at which we part, whose explicitness marks a way of remaining abreast) recalls me to Adriana Cavarero's worry that "grain" neglects voice, at least in its originary register, that unique sonority we each convey simply through the sound of our voices. "Indeed," she writes, "in Barthes' writing, the voice and body are still presented as general categories of a depersonalized pleasure in which the embodied uniqueness of each existent (something that Barthes never thematizes) is simply dissolved along with the general categories of the subject and the individual" (2005, 15). The voice I seek resounds on the other side of this ancient picture. I imagine voice rising with and through language as it gathers itself among syntax, semantics, logical-rhetorical operations, even genre, and only finding-offering itself through these circulations. But Cavarero writes toward the other side of the picture, its underside on her view.

I recall Cavarero's reflections for the difference they introduce, and because the difference that drives them, that between the sensible and the intelligible, troubles me in this context. I worry about her almost phrenological belief that the uniqueness of a voice is somehow the uniqueness of whoever is speaking, that a series of tones somehow contains and thus conveys him or her. Cavarero insists that the "human condition of uniqueness resounds in the register of the voice" (2005, 8). But unique in what sense, and regarding what? Humanness? I don't see how. A baby's coo resounds in a relation underwritten by attunements selected for across a sublime, evolutionary history that primes more than parents. I don't see how the sensible and intelligible can be distinguished in such cases. You recognize the voice of your beloved entering a room. What precisely do you hear? "The uniqueness of the voice is an incontrovertible given of experience, technologically proven by digital machines that can trace it; this is not a problem" (Cavarero 2005, 8). But the problem concerns what those machines register, and what that uniqueness concerns. An almost purely sensible if relational uniqueness leads Cavarero to posit a "different way of thinking the relation between politics and speech. In a certain sense, it is simply a matter of focusing on speech from its vocal site" (2005, 200). But the spatialized terms already indicate that this different way of thinking is working with something, namely, speech, against which a part, "the vocal site," comes into focus. If I am right, the uniqueness conveyed by a voice is the uniqueness of something more than the resounding "acoustic, empirical, material relationality of singular voices" (Cavarero 2005, 13). Our currents are waves in a larger stream. Voice, as it concerns me, conveys this more, and without erasing differences, whether Cavell's, DuBois's, Emerson's, Hegel's, or Cavarero's, to the degree hers resonates in English translation (which I doubt). I regret, now more than ever, how limited I let my ear remain.

Dancing Cheek to Cheek: Too one-sidedly for my liking, Emerson requires one to establish the self to be shared. (Friends work this out together, I think.) Regardless, "voice" is one way to imagine the result in the context of writing. An intense individuation helps establish conditions of intimacy with a reader who might respond in kind. This is not quite Cavell's point in *Conditions Handsome and Unhandsome*, where Emerson stands as another self that you yet might be (1990). Instead, I have something closer to philosophical charisma in mind. But the thought is far from foreign to Cavell's prose, which I first found self-absorbed. He always recalls past texts. His sentences are long, their rhythms laborious. He proves prodigal when it comes to enumerating possible terms. "Look at me," I kept hearing, and: "Don't think this is my first rodeo." Thinking of deconstruction, whether it dissolves saying into quoting—as if I were only ever an iteration, rather than a being whose character lies in part in the task of perpetually refinding and reformulating our, you and me, iterability. Cavell writes:

> This sense of philosophy's opposite possibilities is, at any rate, why I am drawn (and take the likes of Emerson and Wittgenstein to be drawn) not to undermine but to underline such distinctions as that between quoting and saying. I can imagine that this might be said of deconstruction too. Then style and its obligations become the issue—what I might call the address of language, or the assumption of it, perhaps the stake in it. I have most consecutively followed the consequences of (something like) the distinction between saying and quoting in my *The Sense of Walden*, which can as a whole be taken as a meditation on Thoreau's distinction between what he calls the mother tongue and the father tongue (see *Senses* pp. 14–16). (This is something like—and nothing like—the distinction between speaking and writing. In *The Claim of Reason* it is at one point registered as the difference between what I call the first and second inheritance of language. (1988, 133)

It would take time to mark and track every play: (*a*) "consecutively" instead of "thoroughly" and "consistently," though saying both by way of avoidance, (*b*) "something like and nothing like," or (*c*) the three ways of thinking "style and its obligations," which move from the object (the address of language) to the subject (the assumption of it) to some odd middle term (the stake in it), which demands that one fathom what is at stake in an address that temporarily settles on the word "stake." Even the graphemes are multiple, and he cites two previous works. Fresh from my undergraduate years, I read these lines in 1988—or tried to read them. I was unable to assume its address or find the stakes in it. But now I hear something quite different in these very same presentations. "I'm here in every word," they say. "Are you?"

You Asked for It: "I wasn't talking to you." Does this pass in philosophy?

And You? In *Dialectic of Enlightenment*, Horkehimer and Adorno recall a scene in which Beethoven discards a novel by Walter Scott, shouting: "The fellow writes for money!" (2002, 127). Whether from virtue or limited opportunity, philosophers rarely write for money, at least not directly, and particularly not their own. But many write for advancement, that is, the dictates of the profession suffuse the professional article and overwhelm the genre, which purports to be the currency of expert cultures. Why this topic? Why this cite? Haven't I heard this paper before? "Career advancement" is the road more traveled, meaning, it functions as a principle of selection. Not that insights are impossible therein. But unknown friends (and far too many trees) disappear when the end is a vita line; one is curating one's future more than addressing another. I suppose a friend of use might reply, but she or he is not integral to the address, and the return one seeks is not discursive. And this seems all the more evident when an article or piece closes with an empty wave toward "political" or "ethical" implications, as if to say—here is where I really stand.

Friendship involves goodwill. One not only wishes the other well, but also, one is committed to helping him or her be well, and not just reactively. Friendship is a relation of proactive beneficence. So, too, a text written for an unknown friend. Something is brought to term that needed to be said, something that one might have in common with another, some good in which we two might meet. Nothing ventured no one gained.

Dear Writer: Living is more frightening than dying. We're always starting over.

Resoundingly Reticent

Patience Is a Virtue until It's Not: The confusing—not always confused. The convinced—often unconvincing. A certain kind of incoherence may be valor.

A Knowledge Broken: Our "you" is manifold, and one way to reach out to all (not, reach all) is to individuate, to not rely on lines of thought that presume they know their addressees in advance. But even the most individuated address proves generic at points.

In the *Advancement of Learning*, Francis Bacon suggests that "writing in Aphorisms hath many excellent virtues, whereto the writing in Method doth not approach" (1996, 234). Method in this sense concerns how knowledge is delivered or presented, whereas syllogistic reasoning governs its generation or invention. (Rhetoric anyone?) And within method, certain deliveries are magisterial, suited to dogmas that need to be learned and accepted. Other deliveries concern contestable matters, however, which calls for a method of probation. For those who wish to write deliberately, such matters are germane. Our inner audience, concrete others like fellow experts, the generalized other, the secret addressee, even the unknown friend, how will they be affected by decisions at the level of genre and logical-rhetorical structure?

Bacon is drawn to aphorisms in matters of probation. On his view: "Methods are more fit to win consent or belief, but less fit to point to action, for they carry a kind of demonstration in orb or circle, one part illuminating another, and thereby satisfy" (1996, 235). In other words, methods draw the matter at hand into their orbit and account for it according to established terms. If I already know that the cosmos, as a whole, manifests the will of God, my task with every particular case is to show how the divine will is thereby manifest.

To the degree there is a puzzle, the puzzle is fathoming God's mysterious ways. But when particulars are the issue, Bacon is drawn to probations less burdened by the weight of the whole—"but particulars," he notes, "being dispersed, do best agree with dispersed directions" (1996, 235). Concretely, this means that when we evaluate contestable claims about particulars (sun or earth, which revolves around which?), they should be addressed from diverse (or dispersed) directions, something that methods circumvent. The aphorism, however, limits itself to a single direction, the writer's, and without coming full circle—that is, aphorisms eschew systematicity. It is thus a better prompt for action, the reader's, than for indoctrination.

The thought is that aphorisms initiate a certain kind of activity in readers—probation, and, at least as I see it, in no less than three directions. One might approach the subject from one's own direction. Delivered without justification, let alone systematic defense, the aphorism is an individuated assertion. "What would you assert about the matter?" it thereby asks. One also might wonder how such a claim squares with other claims about related particulars (e.g., the movement of the moon). Third, one might work back into one's overall conception and mull over the implications of this particular thought, presuming the observation is potent enough (does one's conception of God revolve around heliotropism?). "Aphorisms," Bacon writes, "being a knowledge broken, do invite men to enquire farther; whereas Methods, carrying the shew of a total, do secure men, as if they were furthest," that is, at the close of the matter as opposed to somewhere in the thick of it (1996, 235).

Genius: If it leaves us all feeling like secret addressees in our own way . . .

Chew on This: "There is a single root cause of nearly all the evils in the sciences, namely, that while we wrongly admire and extol the powers of the human mind, we fail to look for true ways of helping it" (Bacon 1994, 45).

This is aphorism number 9 in Bacon's *Novum Organum*. It attempts to identify in one, concentrated thought, a single force undermining the sciences. In part, the thought is provocative because it's slippery. The purported single root is actually double—we wrongly admire *and* we neglect remedies. A fourth prod thus accompanies aphorisms. They call for rumination. What precisely is being claimed? (The effect only intensifies when the aphorism employs a pun or some other vehicle of wit.) And by prompting rumination, an aphorism primes the reader for the interrogations noted above. Are there other evils? And what precisely is an "evil in the sciences"—is it moral in any significant way? Also, is it true that we have failed to look for constructive intellectual aids, or simply failed to find them? And doesn't nature like to hide, as Heraclitus had it? Is science only undone by its own missteps? The aphorism leaves room for the reader without leaving him or her empty-handed. It is a genre of inception.

Swallow This: Axiomatic presentations or definitional statements establish a different climate. Like the aphorism, they do not recount their derivation. But unlike the aphorism, they bury the particularity of their genesis in a haze of self-evidence. And so they do not invite the reader to think backwards, that is, through their terms and the assertion at hand. Instead, they direct readers to what presumably follows forthwith, which enables probation with regard to their results but not with regard to their inception.

At the beginning of his *Ethics*, Spinoza declares in definition 6 that "God" is an "absolutely infinite being." I'm not sure what that really means and so I struggle to proceed. In moments of impatience, I turn to diagnostics and think that "absolute infinity" is actually a negation of indefinite infinity on both ends of the stick and, thus, more a move in apologetics than a conceptualization rising to recount a genuine phenomenon. With more sympathy, and after instruction by friends, we might imagine the fullest and fiercest intensification of existence—perfect in its kind, beyond the terror we're able to withstand and, thus, awful instead of beautiful. But that seems beyond being, which is unthinkable without limits, without change, without you and me unfolding in the grammar of the flying imperfect. And so another diagnosis: "absolute infinity" seems to flee being rather than consummate it.

No one should be persuaded by these vents. The questions are difficult. But by beginning axiomatically, Spinoza positively discourages his readers from beginning at (as opposed to with) this beginning. And so, too, in his first axiom, which declares: "All things that are, are either in themselves or in something else." The either/or seems to preclude the possibility of codependent origination. "Accident or substance; choose one, please."

Perhaps such questions are impertinent at the start of the *Ethics*, and perhaps that is for the best, at least for Spiniozists. For now, just note how differently, qua addressee, one enters texts that appeal to axioms and definitions, and how one begins with a knowledge broken.

Provocation / Demonstration

Disputing Taste: Fifty thousand Elvis fans can be wrong.

A Zero-Sum Proposition: Nothing leaves the world as it is.

If and Only If: Demonstrations account for a certain range of phenomena, for example, the nature of artworks or truth, or the basis of judgments about the really real, that is, metaphysics. In philosophical writing, they usually culminate in and rely on validity claims and thus each doctrine presents itself as adequately accounting for the phenomena in question. The result is a knowing that or *connaissance*, which is demonstrated as such.

With demonstration, the principle intent is to evince the validity of a position and, thereby, answer a question and/or resolve a dispute, for example: Does god exist? Or: Can metaphysical judgments be made on a rigorous, systematic basis? The addressee is a fellow member of one's epistemic community, and she or he is being shown the reasons for adopting the view. Multiple kinds of evidence may be presented en route: transcendental arguments, dialectically immanent critiques, phenomenological intuitions, necessary and sufficient definitions, and so forth. But the goal of the praxis is to demonstrate. Demonstrations do not underscore the nature of their performance. Instead, they employ what they take to be an acceptable mode of demonstration through which they develop and defend their view. Kant employs transcendental arguments, but such arguments are not offered as exemplifications of philosophizing in the way in which the elenchus is offered by Plato as a way of philosophizing, even political life.[46]

But the demonstration is not incidental to the praxis. Within a given epistemic community (whether a gnostic cult or the cosmic family of any and all rational agents), demonstration exemplifies how knowledge is produced, and performing properly is essential to the result. If the mode strays too far from established ones, or if those modes fall into crisis, the results may not be accorded the status of knowledge. In fact, "modes of demonstration" may become the phenomena in question, as they are in Descartes's *Meditations* (appeals to the senses, appeals to the senses under ideal conditions, appeals to self-evidence) and Peirce's "The Fixation of Belief" (the method of tenacity, authority, the a priori method, and the genuine method of scientific investigation).

Proofs for the existence of god are paradigmatic examples of philosophical demonstration. They try to show that god exists on the basis of commitments that most presumably share. ("It stands to reason" underwrites their address.) Descartes, for example, argues that the content of the idea of god — its objective reality — requires, as its cause, a ground of equal formal (or what might think of as existential) reality. (It is as if he'd found a huge light and needed to locate an energy source that could power it.) Given our objective reality is paltry compared to the formal reality of "God," the cause of our idea of god must lie outside us and in something . . . well, something not just godlike, but just like "God." Philosophy that aims at demonstration more or less follows this pattern. Relying on the unforced force of reason, it aims to lead its addressee to a conclusion that all should share if the reasoning is valid and sound.

Relative to demonstration qua praxis, transcendental arguments institute a similar relation to their addressees. In exposing conditions for the possibility for various phenomena, such as the experience of empirical objects (Kant), the appearance of melody in a sequence of notes (Husserl), or assessing whether judgments correspond to their objects (Heidegger), transcendental arguments demonstrate the existence of those conditions (though not the ontological character of their existence). Space, for example, is a condition for the possibility of our experience of objects because it cannot be derived from such experiences. Try to locate space in a world of objects and it is always already there in the locale of the locating. Even dialectical thought, again qua praxis, inclines toward demonstration. Hegel's *Phenomenology* evinces time and again that would-be patterns of knowing fail on their own terms. It doesn't report but shows this. Sense certainty, for example, presents as the immediate and rich knowledge of sensuous singularities. But in presenting as knowledge, in adding to its sensations the reflexive claim "and *this* is true," it loses hold of its sensuous singularity and dissolves into a succession of empty universals (this, here, and now), which mediate every truth claim it ventures.

And Now for Something Somewhat Different: Emerson writes: "Truly speaking, it is not instruction, but provocation that I can receive from another soul" (1996, 79). I take provocation to contrast with demonstration (what Emerson terms "instruction").[47] The contrast lies with the end of the praxis. With provocation, the goal is less to demonstrate that some state of affairs is the case than to bring about a state of affairs in one's addressee. We might say that provocation aims to initiate a thought process that unsettles the addressee in a manner that he or she must then resolve without any final instructions from the author.

Ambiguity is one path toward provocation. "In self-trust, all the virtues are comprehended," Emerson writes (1996, 65). What does this ask of the reader? It is part exhortation—it aims to rally us to self-trust, as if to prepare us for the task it also sets. I say "task" because the line drops a puzzle. How are the virtues thereby comprehended, that is, what is the meaning of *in*? In knowing self-trust, do I know all the other virtues? Or does comprehending a given virtue require self-trust? I prefer the latter, but the specifics of the claim and my reason for preferring it are left to me.

Puns, like irony and all double-talk, including self-referential snarls, are other ways to play provocateur. Emerson's last great text, *The Conduct of Life*, is built on a triple pun. Human conduct, that is, action, conducts life, that is, conveys it, and to a certain degree, the book, in orienting us toward issues like fate, power, wealth, and so on, aspires to conduct the times, as in direct them. However, the provocation is not just to hear and think these senses of "conduct" as we read. Tensions lurk within, thus provoking further thought, namely, what kind of life is conducted by a conduct that follows a conductor or aspires to conduct others? Because the title initiates these thoughts and leaves us to work through them, it checks (or performatively remonstrates against) its own efforts to conduct us by way of all it might demonstrate. In other words, it trusts and pushes us, just a bit, toward trusting ourselves, presuming we take the title's bait.

Provocation leaves readers room to think and confronts them with something to think about. The essay can do this as a rhetorical whole. Emerson's *Essays: First Series* is a case in point. In fact, the whole is so intertwined that quoting from it proves perilous. No essay stands on its own. Each belongs to a pair, which offers a kind of polarity to its partner, for example, "History" and "Self-Reliance," or "Prudence" and "Heroism." "Self-Reliance" challenges us to plumb the depths of our perception, both its voluntary and involuntary forms, and in an effort to avoid conformity. But these personal events and tasks arise on historical stages and pulsate within an "endless flight of winged facts and events" that envelops and sets our course (1996, 252). And when the two essays are set side by side, neither perspective trumps the other; if anything, it is the difference between them that is principally essayed, though those who read are left to observe that distance and, to the degree they (or we) can, measure it. Similarly, the calculations of prudence are contrasted with and contested by the demands of heroic action, but without negating prudence as a necessary capacity. Life cannot do without either, and each is haunted by the dynamics of the soul (and society) mapped in "Self-Reliance" as well as by the thought, from "History," that each "is the compend of time: . . . the correlative of nature" (1996, 254).

I could go on. The navigations of "Prudence" and "Heroism" recur in "Friendship" and "Love," though not in any scripted sense, and then again, with further variations, in "Intellect" and "Art." Taken together, these six essays navigate the personal sites opened and earmarked in "Self-Reliance" (and "Circles" for that matter), whereas other essays establish a broader, sometimes cosmic stage, namely, "Compensation" and "Spiritual Laws" (itself a contrasting pair), and "The Over Soul," which relates to "Circles" not unlike "History" relates to "Self-Reliance." The latter establishes a personal pole of activities that the cosmic events of the former suffuse without erasing. The volume thus provokes us as a rhetorical whole, at least those who greet it as unknown friends. In particular, we are called to track how the essays, in their interplay, chart the spans they name and navigate, and how they account, to the degree they do, for the topography that underwrites each point and performance.

Like You Mean It: Some writing is described as "lively." In relation to their addressees, we might term them "enlivening," or "exciting," if we recall that *citare* means "to put into motion." They infuse their readers with the energy needed to carry out whatever tasks the provocations set, perhaps with their ability to say it just so, even when they accuse or diagnose.

Some texts address the reader forthrightly, as Nietzsche does ("between you and me"), calling readers into the task at hand, sometimes binding readers to the author in contrast to those being castigated in the third person. Or they set direct exhortations into the text. "Do your work, and you shall reinforce yourself," Emerson proclaims (1996, 264). And the intimacy of a voice, particularly in the thick of complex prose (whether at the level of the sentence or the rhetorical whole), seems to suggest "we're equal to these occasions."

"There are nowadays professors of philosophy, but not philosophers," Thoreau asserts. "Yet it is admirable to profess because it was once admirable to live" (2008, 13). Ouch. But the sentences, cocksure, suggest it might again prove possible. As they compile, Thoreau's lines occasionally dispel the gloom even as they name it—their mourning occasions morning, according to Cavell. "The mass of men lead lives of quiet desperation. What is called resignation is confirmed desperation. From the desperate city you go in to the desperate country, and have to console yourself with the bravery of minks and muskrats. A stereotyped but unconscious despair is concealed even under what are called the games and amusements of mankind. There is no play in them, for this comes after work. But it is the characteristic of wisdom not to do desperate things" (Thoreau 2008, 8–9). Thoreau's exactness and concision is heartening, evidence of Emersonian scholarship. "It was dead fact; now, it is quick thought. It can stand, and it can go, it now flies, it now inspires" (Emerson 1996, 56). It flies when Thoreau names what most deny— the quiet desperation that accrues when we live to work to pay our bills. Also, when he finds it on both sides of modernity's geographical dialectic: town and country. Then there his feel for its grip on leisure, which, he notes, is only the aftershock of commercial labor. Finally, if I read it right, the passage also suggests that the spoils of the country—fur coats—further announce our desperation, whether one wears (just another trapping of wealth) or "battles" for the fur. In fact, if we think through the irony of "battles," we find the cunning of weasels in our own use of traps and snares.

Among the Pros (and Cons)

Unpopulist Views: "Everyone has their own way of experiencing everything." If only. Epiphenomenalism may be a social fact.

Holding Forth: Etymologically, "profess" involves acknowledging before others (from the Latin, *fatēri*, though also *fari*, "to speak"). And that sense of publicity remains: to declare something openly, as it does in "professional," someone publicly acknowledged as having special knowledge, training, or a skill. Professors are thus interesting birds. They have a publicly acknowledged ability (indicated by their degree and position) to publicly acknowledge a given thought as valid or true.

The professional article (or monograph) is the genre of professors. In it, the author professes that a given position is the best one going, and the terms of that acknowledgment are rendered as explicit as possible. She or he thus invites the readership to test the inferences or challenge their starting points, whether in the form of stated givens or presuppositions. In fact, the telos of the professional article (and monograph) is the public test, which, if successful, wins acknowledgment from others, say, in the form of affirmative citations.

With some exaggeration, we might say that the professional article and monograph amount to a genre of normal science. (The exaggeration lies with the absence of genuinely stable paradigms and data in philosophy.) How should we read "power" in the late Foucault? Did Rorty get Davidson right on truth, and if he got it wrong, is that a problem for Rorty or Davidson? Can pragmatists be pluralists? Are appeals to an author's intention relevant in an analysis of the artworks? I align these questions with "normal science" because their phenomenal field is more or less settled—power and the late

Foucault, truth and evidence as well as truth and meaning, pragmatism and pluralism, artworks and authorial intention. The question concerns how best to interpret these principal terms and/or their relations. "No part of the aim of normal science," Thomas Kuhn writes, "is to call forth new sorts of phenomenon; indeed those that will not fit the box are often not seen at all" (1962, 24).[48]

To be clear, the "normalcy" of the professional article (and monograph) does not preclude genuine, exciting work. Existing ways of resolving or instituting problems can be deeply criticized, and precisely because of the apparent stability of the terms they employ, including the analytic/synthetic distinction and the very idea of conceptual schemes (or paradigms for that matter). A kind of intense focus and precision seem to intensify when author and readership have a great deal in common.

In Formation: Another facet of normal science is tacit agreement about what counts as a well-formed formulation, even if formal languages are absent. Loosely speaking, the syntax (or grammar) of the professional article (or monograph) is as settled as its semantics.

In a generous and thoughtful review of my *Emerson and Self-Culture*, Corey McCall stated: "This book is written in a profoundly Emersonian Spirit," which "represents a laudable attempt to think with Emerson," and "as a provocation to think along with him, it must be judged a success" (2008). Heartening words for an author to read. I'm still grateful for them. And McCall seemed to locate the book's achievement where I had hoped, namely, in its refusal to "domesticate" Emerson's language or "back down from Emerson's provocations." And yet, the review concludes, the book is "certainly not one to recommend to scholars of philosophy who desire a basic overview of Emerson and his relevance for philosophy." Because I hadn't set out to write an overview, I only found half of this judgment odd, and precisely because I took (and still take) Emerson's relevance for philosophy to be inextricably bound to his provocations and the language in which they are delivered. My point was that "the personal," a notion introduced to name those activities that no one can do for another, for example, understand, persevere, commit, was not only *a* site for Emersonian philosophy but *the* principal site, and so a particular way of engaging Emerson was in order—what I termed "taking Emerson personally."

It may help to underscore that I did not claim that Emerson has no bearing on the remarks of Descartes and Kant (or Heidegger for that matter). Nor is it the case that he (or I) did not address recurring issues like self-knowledge, interpretation, the historicity of meaning, friendship, reform, even human action. But, such sites should not be separated from the claims they make on us, you and I, here and now. And though I did not explicitly make this argument, I hoped my text would demonstrate it nevertheless—that is, that readers would find themselves philosophically implicated in the undomesticated spirit, provocations, and language I curated, expanded, and in some cases, criticized. The end was the deed, in a sense. And my presumption was that an overview of how Emerson intersects with philosophical currents, just by being an overview, would fail to convey and demonstrate Emerson's relevance for philosophy.

I no longer find McCall's review odd, though I still find it generous (and generative). What is odd, even oblique, was my effort, under the cover of a scholarly monograph, to address professional philosophers by way of provocation and exemplification, a manner that does not exclusively address them as fellow experts and professionals. Note, I still wished to address them as philosophers, that is, as those who seek wisdom (or insight) in some general sense, and particularly in relation to the topics broached. And my goal was to do so through whatever our language could sustain in its enactment, which is irreducibly (and unavoidably) personal. But being philosophically professional, down to its genre, seems to resist (not to say "prevent") such ventures and the relations they presume.

Get Your Story Straight: Reflecting on what he takes to be the incoherence of modernity's most radical critics, Habermas observes that their texts (Nietzsche's, Heidegger's, Adorno's, Foucault's, and Derrida's) cannot be "unequivocally classified with either philosophy or science, with moral or legal theory, or with literature and art" (1987, 336). And this marks, he thinks, a regression—each has fallen behind the advances made by these discourses, advances that have partially rationalized each domain and established distinct modes of presentation.

That Habermas would prove allergic to disciplinary (and genre) confusions is unsurprising. Working to elude the paradoxes that accompany the total critique of reason, he has directed Euro-American modernity (as well as the rest of the world) toward his concept of *communicative action,* which takes its leave from "intersubjective understanding as the telos inscribed into communication in ordinary language" (1987, 311). More particularly, Habermas tries to rationalize action aimed at mutual understanding (communication), binding it to the "argumentative procedures for directly or indirectly redeeming claims to propositional truth, normative rightness, subjective truthfulness, and aesthetic harmony" (1987, 314). On this view, communication is always a matter of professing. Even in ordinary language, we are professors in training, with the exception of expressive speech acts, though even there Habermas sets us on the road to art school. Not that we will ever rationalize all the lifeworld resources on which even professional discourse rests. But doing so remains our telos according to Habermas. If we can keep our stories straight in the work of (a) predicting and controlling science as well as administration, (b) morality and law, or (c) personal, artistic expression, we should.

Habermas's disciplinary insistence sits poorly with me, even after we bracket the perspicacity of his categories of social action.[49] First, Habermas's conception of style/genre presumes a starkly classical distinction between thinking and writing. If one wishes to write for discovery and not simply in defense of validity claims, one is not going to find much space in Habermas's public sphere. Nor will one find space if one writes for secret addressees, those with whom a new "we" might emerge in the as-if of an essayistic (or poetic) venture, presuming the bottle is found, opened, and its address taken to heart. And that is what provocation often seeks. It ventures something not yet fully formulated in the hopes it might be taken up and elaborated, which likely includes being transformed. And that is also what provocation seeks even when the prose in question isn't all that radical, as in cases of pedagogical irony, where a settled thought is conveyed indirectly to unsettle the reader. The goal is to generate thought, not simply report it. Provocation thus seeks something (and someone) that a disciplinary dispatch might preclude. It is always philosophical *and* literary, therefore, and not because it remains trapped in the philosophy of the subject. (As we have seen, it is explicitly *for* an addressee, and a multiple one at that, so it evidences a concrete feel for the triadic scene of writing.)

Habermas's genre conservativism also embodies his belief that modernity has rationalized various systems out of a loosely organized lifeworld (politics, the economy, the art world, the explanatory sciences). He thus limits the texts he reads to exchanges among experts within systems or emerging systems, for example, economics or biology, even literature, where a discipline-specific, operationalized language does most of the heavy lifting. But philosophy, at least in the cases Habermas shuns, addresses people at psychosocial nodes where system and lifeworld are less differentiated, and semiosis, the whole swirl of embodied meaning-finding-and-making, proves more anarchic. The provocations of these texts thus engage and transform sensibilities more than they aim to replace one set of judgments with another. And that is why philosophers like Nietzsche, Heidegger, Adorno, Foucault, and Derrida (Habermas's targets) offer their addressees provocative exemplifications as well as claims (and arguments on their behalf). Each, and not just them, offers an example of what it might mean to inhabit history in a way that resists or even transforms the deforming currents of the age: the ascetic ideal, the metaphysics of presence, commodification, juridical power, phallogocentrism, white supremacy, somnambulant conformity, or flight from the precariousness of ordinary life. Keeping to Habermas's idiom, their texts are lifeworld gestures and actions more than they are proposals for a given position in expert cultures. For more or less ethical reasons (or matters of extramoral value, in Nietzsche's case), they combine logical-rhetorical operations from philosophy and literature and, often, venture beyond traditional genres. Are they suffering from disciplinary confusion or responding as acutely as possible to the phenomena that claim them, which includes a readership whose social psychology still operates alchemically? Habermas's discourse of modernity leaves us unable to ask this question. But those who would write deliberately should ask it in order to redress the turbulence of eco-social history—events that suffuse our intersubjective relations with collisions between system, lifeworld, the personal, and whatever enables our being-in-common.

Terms of Art: "But that's just *literature.*" And that's just unhelpful. "Literature" has more or less come to function as a residual category for those self-consciously stylized speech acts that fall outside rational systems and their communicative habits. "Literature" is thus a quick way to tell me what certain texts are not. It does not help me engage what they are. (In some contexts, it is just natural science's other, even when it is valorized.) Second, as a cultural domain, it currently lacks any serious import for life outside the production and reception of literature (or art, more generally). To term the efforts of authors like DuBois, Cixous, and Adorno "literature" is thus to deny them what they seek: a significant role in transformative learning processes. Moreover, it banishes the challenges they pose to realms of enjoyment (and thus consumption) or to a realm of formal achievement along the lines of absolute music—they are about themselves and nothing else.[50]

"Fine, but the deeper worry is sophistry. The prose you have in mind forsakes mutual understanding for manipulation." No doubt this happens, particularly in polemics. But the pursuit of transformation is not always manipulative, particularly when the changes sought result in a more alert, sensitive addressee. Moreover, do not forget that writing, even as it addresses others, has an impact on thought as well. Deliberate writing concerns both moments, and one can witness them interact in works committed to provocation and exemplification as they reach out toward secret addressees and unknown friends. (For example, what is offered by way of exemplification is precisely thought struggling with itself at its limits.) One could even say, such work seeks mutual understanding within terms that remain generative—a kind of belles lettres exchanged beneath the level of rationalized styles and genres and addressed to the inexpert; a kind of writing oriented toward a mutuality still cognizant of its roots in *mutuus*, "lent or borrowed," and always in the process of change, from *mutare*.

A: "O my friend, there are no friends."
B: "At least we've got each other."

Thinking of You: Unlike most philosophical writings, Plato's dialogues seem organized with their addressees in mind, and this holds true whether or not you believe he writes esoterically. (That just divides and further specifies the addressees.) Rich dramatic settings, erotically charged encounters, unresolved arguments, and a charismatic lead character who plays different roles at different times—it all seems quite deliberate. And not just in order to convey something. Plato's dialogues both demand and want something from their readers. Charles Kahn's emphatic insistence seems appropriate. "Plato's conception of philosophical education is not to replace false doctrines with true ones but to change radically the moral and intellectual orientation of the learner, who, like the prisoners in the cave, must be converted—turned around—in order to see the light. It is, I suggest, with this end in view that most of the early and middle dialogues were composed" (1998, xv).

Set aside, if it concerns you, whether Plato's corpus can be cut at the joints of early, middle, and late, and postpone, if you would, debates about whether dialogues like the *Crito*, *Gorgias*, or *Laches* turn us in order to see the light or to know the dimness of our mortal lot. What draws me in Kahn's account is his interpretive focus on Plato's stance toward addressees and his move away from an overarching concern with propositional content and inferential ligature. When one pauses to ask, "Why write dialogues?" the answer is in large measure pedagogical. Yes, one could satisfy the conditions for a "dialogue" and have one's chief goal be the demonstration of a doctrine. But what deliberation would lead one to elect that course? How would a dialogue further secure the validity of the conclusion reached? As Hegel observes in his anxious preface to the *Phenomenology*, staging and overcoming one's rivals does not indicate that one's position is true, even if one manages to absorb their insights and avoid their failings. We all may be mistaken, and being the best positivist around is not a badge of honor. Dialogues are attractive for those writers who seek a considered reply.

Indefinitely Yours: Dialogues (and I presume that Plato's are exemplary) can make use of the various modes of provocation already noted, for example, ambiguities and puns. Moreover, the ebb and flow of the discourse can also prove provocative in its own right—an error might go undetected or a live option be left for dead, but not, one hopes, for the reader. And such effects intensify if the dialogue fails to resolve the question at hand; the lack of conclusion forces the reader to diagnose what went wrong and to determine whether an opportunity had been missed or whether an entirely new beginning is in order. And that seems the principal goal of the dialogue—to prompt activities of interpretation, evaluation, and response (in kind), to draw one in as a participant. In fact, the dialogue should continue on with the reader (or readers), which is to say, dialogues that stay true to their bearing are, in principle, unfinished, and when effective, always incorporating new characters. Klein puts the matter nicely: "We have to be serious about the contention that a Platonic dialogue, being indeed an 'imitation of Socrates,' actually continues Socrates's work" (1965, 7).

The Windowless Monad Is the Dream of a Broken Man: You may sense a bad infinity on the horizon. Why write in a way that never comes to a close? Let me leave Plato for the moment. Isn't that the nature of anything written? It is intrinsically for another and thus awaits his or her uptake. A letter never read seems stillborn. So, too, an essay, or a dialogue, an aphorism, even a treatise. If one's text is not for another, why write at all? Or rather, why publish? (One might write to clarify, deepen, even develop one's own thought.) Second, barring the emergence of a thought capable of carrying its alpha and omega, all writing is an act of exposure with an uncertain future. (This is another side of the discovery that writing is discovery.)

Where to Begin? Like the essay, the dialogue is a rhetorical whole, not just a linear path of inferential reasoning. From his vantage point as a reader, Gadamer writes: "The real task [of reading the dialogues] can only be to activate for ourselves wholes of meaning, contexts within which a discussion moves—even where its logic offends us" (1980, 5). One thus has to think about how the beginning relates to the end, for example, and not just whether the end follows from the beginning and every step along the way. And that means, at least potentially, that everything counts. (It is also why a dialogue is in part like a work of art.) It may be, as Strauss insists, that "nothing is accidental in a Platonic dialogue; everything is necessary at the place where it occurs" (1964, 60).[51] But that is an empirical claim (or a practical maxim, or a wish). My point is more generic. The dialogue, in provoking us to think through what it, as a whole, exemplifies, renders each of its moments (whether dianoetic or mimetic), a potential vehicle for the strivings of its address. In Plato's case, what is presented (and solicited) is a recursive, affecto-discursive pursuit of the good, the true, and the beautiful. And with such goals in mind, Strauss's questions for readers serve equally well as possibilities for writers: "on what kind of men does Socrates act with his speeches? what is the age, the character, the abilities, the position in society, and the appearance of each? when and where does the action take place? does Socrates achieve what he intends? is his action voluntary or imposed on him?" (1964, 59).

As Nightingale shows, the kinds of speech or genres offered in a dialogue also present and test existential bearings.[52] And as Strauss notes, the topics covered, as a whole, help concretize what is an emerging and evolving city of speech—these are our concerns. (To my mind, provocation lurks here as well. Each act of inclusion poses the question of its exclusions. For example, wouldn't a complete corpus include a dialogue on forgiveness?)

Contesting the claim that Plato's dialogues only engage orders of thought, Paul Friedländer exclaims: "They do not philosophize about existence; they are existence, not always, but most of the time" (1969, 235). In other words, dialogues exemplify ways of being-in-the-world. More particularly, their dynamism derives from the interaction of various modes of sociality within learning processes, and this is evident in their use of (a) *character types* (tyrants, bores, the genuinely curious, dullards and bullies, the cowardly and the inventive); (b) *social roles* (priest, rhapsode, playwright, seducer and sophist, the old and the young, lover and beloved, parent and child, the native born and the foreign, slave as well as merchant and generals too); and (c) *forms of speech,* that is, ways of organizing thought in the presence of others (defining, quoting, kinds of refutation or eristics, allegory, mythic narrative, modes of inference, funeral orations, irony, and above all, *protrepsis,* the effort to draw another toward a better life). And then, each mode is enacted in possible confluences—old generals lacking courage, a bellicose sophist, an ironic seducer approaching the young, a dull-witted priest struggling with the basics of justification.

Whither Are We Going? While not quite the *Gesamtsprachwerk* of the novel (whose drama, driven by more than searching conversations, is broader in scope), the dialogue nevertheless dramatizes persons figuring out, together, terms for their being in common, what we might term "politics" in one of its most basic senses—the attempt to mediate and order our sociality with rational speech. (Codified laws are one way of organizing and preserving that speech.)

Dialogues thus exemplify a certain kind of life, one mediated and ordered by all that speech can accomplish and haunted by all that it cannot, whether in practice or principle. Near its heart, something quite particular is staged. Stanley Cavell finds Thoreau naming and enacting it in *Walden*—the passage from a mother tongue, acquired as a child, into a father tongue, a language re-authored through individuating usages that never quite follow a rule or proceed without one. A dialogue, like any repetition, replays this scene even as it dips into a prior one, a scene of address wherein something like a distinction between mother and father and their metaphorical transposition might take place. And note, this might lead us to wonder whether we want to give the latter word to a "father" given how often our so-called mother tongue gives the masculine the gift of eloquence.

Writes of Passage: In the beginning was the deed in relation, but at some point, which marks another beginning, a further deed in relation emerged, the utterance, a semiotic event designating something other than itself. But not for its own sake. Rather, it rises in and from the hope of coordinating deeds, ordering relations, and with something other than sticks and stones or even the fixed demands of ritual, family, or law. This not quite primal scene is reenacted in the dialogue, each participant conducting a kind of life shadowed by other possibilities temporarily suspended by phenomena like questions and replies, specifications and utterances offered in support of others. A possible republic is thus always underway in a dialogue. And this is why dialogues, if they wish their exemplifications to prove convincing, should situate themselves in those scenes that societies ritualistically mark: the tides of family, sex, the sacred, wealth and trade, as well as sickness and eventually death. These are vital contexts in which a primary politics arises. How shall we proceed? And as they shift, the task may as well, and one's exemplifications should keep pace. Good dramas do not simply render certain problems more accessible. They also pose them in the singularity of their occurrence.

Wrong Way Street: A dialogue adopts a very different relation to its addressees when it exclusively aims at exposing the unrealizable pretensions of rational debate, at imaging tragedy for the *zoon echon logon*. Except among the witless, fully aporetic conversations should cease, or at least arrest and convert into an image through which something quasi-Dionysian rattles the rhetorical-logical forms and character types assembled, thereby exposing that rational speech, in aiming to order our being-in-common, misses the mark. This miss may not unleash an awful upsurge of the untamed cosmos, the dead piled in a heap, but it should prove profoundly deflating nevertheless, at least according to the logic of reasoned speech. I suppose some indirect sunlight might bathe the befuddled disputants, slanting rays from whatever reasoned speech precludes. And that might disclose a truth of sorts—better to have never been born, perhaps. But, returning to deliberate writing, what would it mean to set out to open such a window, aiming at a mark that cannot be sighted?

As in a Releasing from Chains: Plato's *Lysis* engages the reader on multiple levels.[53] While its thematic topic is friendship, that concern only arises on a stage initially charged with sexual desire and encroachment on a social space reserved for youth. Catherine Zuckert reports that the palestra in which the dialogue occurs was off limits to men of Socrates's age during the Hermaea, a festival of sport taking place at the time of the dialogue (and one in which various social mores were sometimes suspended, for example, slaves might drink to the point of drunkenness). Socrates's presence there, ostensibly to help Hippothales seduce Lysis, thus draws an initial scene closer to cruising than philosophy (Zuckert 2009, 513–15). But Socrates's exchange with Hippothales takes an ironic turn when he demonstrates how to approach and win a lover by exemplifying how to exhibit *philein,* namely, by orienting another toward the good though its mutual, reciprocal pursuit. As a drama, then, the dialogue insists on the priority of philosophy to erotic conquest in the order of the good (and thus Socrates does Hippothales one turn better than the latter had initially sought).[54]

The *Lysis* champions philosophy in another way. Before Socrates, Lysis, and Menexenus can complete their exploration of friendship, the boys' brothers and family slaves interrupt and insist on taking the boys home, presumably at their family's request. Yet rather than conclude their inquiry, the trio tries to drive away their assailants. The close of the dialogue thus enacts a position developed earlier, namely, that family and king alike should defer to the wiser. (210a) Whereas the *Euthyphro* tries to open a space for philosophy between Euthyphro and his gods, the *Lysis* tries to find room between Lysis and his family for philosophy, and in the name of those who seem closest to true friends, namely, those who are akin with regard to (or have an affinity for) the pursuit of the good, or so one might conclude given the following line and the later effort to locate friendship in a kind of kinship without identity (221c–222c): "But with regard to those things in which we don't acquire good sense, no one will entrust us with permission to do what is in our opinion best concerning them; but everyone will obstruct us as much as is in his power—not merely aliens, but even our father and mother and *whatever may be more closely akin [oikeion] to us than they are*" (210bc; emphases added).

In its provocations, the dialogue operates at a meta-philosophical level, therefore; like the essay, it accounts for itself. But it does so without a personal voice vouchsafing its proceedings. For those who would deliberately provoke and prod their readers, options are thus available. The essay addresses one as an intimate companion, even in its most experimental provocations. The author of the dialogue, however, disappears in the text and leaves one in the midst of a conversation, seducing through the charisma of its characters, the excitement of its plot, and/or the depth of the questions posed. (Aphorisms have their own resources, including charm and wit, though gnomic formulations can also ignite an addressee.)

The *Lysis* also provokes thought with regard to its central topic, friendship. At times, Socrates reasons in a slippery manner. For example, in an effort to undermine the claim that "nothing which does not love in return is a friend" (212d), he identifies, without argument, *philein* across cases, for example, in the case of friends and in the case of those who love horses. And at another point, he presumes that *philein* entails a lack (215b). As readers, it is difficult to know which cases are provocations and which presuppositions, and so the dialogue is most provocative when the conversation itself runs aground—for example, when Socrates asks: "Can it be, Menexenus, . . . that we're seeking in an altogether incorrect fashion?" (213d). The question seems equally posed to the reader, who must decide whether to abandon a line of thought. The suggestion in this case holds that friendship involves reciprocity. The provocation is particularly stark given that the requirement for reciprocity was never refuted in the preceding discussion, except on the basis of the suspect analogy between the love friends share and the love one might have for horses.

The dialogue also includes moments of demonstration, which a good dialogue should. The positions mounted in a dialogue need to be credible if they are to draw the reader into the exchange. Plato's *Crito* works in part because it forces us to consider precisely what we owe the city (or the state), even as we're startled by Socrates's ability to convert his possible escape, which Crito offers, into a possible conversion of Crito into a (better) friend of the good. The *Lysis* is similar in this regard. On the stated presumption that loving another involves wishing them happiness, Socrates seems to show that one does not wish another happiness by granting them license but by exercising wisdom on their behalf, particularly when they lack it (207d–210d). Socrates also argues that those neither wholly good nor wholly bad can be friends, but only those mixed with regard to their ethical character and aware of their mixed nature (216d–218b). The *Lysis* does advance thoughts on the matter of friendship, therefore, even if it does not conclude the matter. And note, this is not because of a fallibilism that leaves all inferences open to refutation. The demonstrations of the *Lysis* are all problematic to some extent; that is, their limits are not simply possible fates in infinite inquiry; they explicitly confront the reader. Moreover, the dialogue is interrupted, leaving the task of producing even a fallible conclusion undone. A certain kind of exemplification is also operative in and through the demonstrations, therefore, particularly in the ways in which they proactively contest themselves. But the practice thereby displayed is not simply argument; friendship itself is emerging.

Even though the dialogue closes without an adequate definition of the friend, Socrates says, with apparent approval, that others will "suppose we're another's friends—for I also put myself among you" (223a). This suggests that one may put oneself among others in a way that indicates friendship, which in turn prods us to reread the dialogue with an eye on Socrates's conduct. When we do so, several features become apparent. But before we consider them, I find it significant that Socrates locates himself "among you" despite the absence of an adequate definition of friendship. This indicates, through exemplification, a kind of regard, even friendship, that binds itself to others without knowing in any thorough sense what a friend is and, thus, whether those in question are in fact "friends."[55] In other words, whatever the dialogue exemplifies by way of friendship, it does so in an intersubjective scene ruled by more than what any of the participants can discursively secure.

Socrates's actions toward Hippothales, Lysis, and Menexenus seem to have an orienting heart—how he responds to Hippothales's desire for pick-up lines. He strives to redirect an erotic ardor toward a loving regard that not only eschews flattery but also labors to orient the beloved toward the good, which, in this case, involves a deeper understanding of and feel for friendship. And not in any abstract sense. Lysis and Menexenus already have a budding friendship, which Socrates ascertains, as well as moments of rivalry (207c). Socrates's approach thus responds to their situatedness, which thickens his own exemplification—it evidences the kind of judgment needed to realize the more general point on display: friends join one another in pursuit of the good.

While Hippothales, Lysis, and Menexenus are Socrates's principal addressees, the reader remains Plato's. I recall the point because in addressing us with such an exemplification, that is, in provoking us to rethink friendship, the dialogue is also inviting us into a certain kind of friendship. We are thus not only encouraged to think along and participate but also to catch sight of the fact that by doing so we are allowing the terms of friendship to appear, at least in an incipient manner.

After staging his principal concern (and to a certain degree, Plato's), Socrates both demonstrates that and exemplifies how checking another's impulses is compatible with seeking their happiness. He checks Hippothales's predilection to approach others as sources of pleasure. And he checks (after exposing) Lysis's tendency to think about the good solely with regard his own welfare. In short, friendship, which requires that we seek another's well-being, also includes redirecting those friends when they go astray, or prodding them along even when things are going well, or protecting them from others who might undermine such pursuits, as Socrates tries to do at the close of the dialogue. And a similar commitment is manifest in Socrates's refusal to let the discussion come to a premature close, for example, when he forces the boys to wonder whether those who are good can be friends given their purported self-sufficiency (215b).[56]

Socrates also positively exercises his companion's affecto-cognitive capacities, causing them to think (and blush), suggesting that a friend not only corrects but also labors to empower. And Socrates does this in several ways, some of which are tied to the elenchus. Others are subtler, however, and reach into the boys' nondiscursive orientations. One particularly interesting effort revolves around countering Lysis's self-absorption. After his first conversation with Lysis, Socrates initially refuses to interrogate Menexenus even though Lysis requests that he do so. Not only does this again situate Lysis as the desirer rather than the desired, it also checks a petty desire. In wishing to see his friend's ignorance exposed, Lysis desires to do his friend an ill turn. But Socrates interrupts this trajectory and suggests instead that Lysis assume the Socratic role and engage Menexenus himself. This not only would require Lysis to exercise his soul more actively, it also would lead Lysis to engage Menexenus in a more beneficent (and reciprocal) manner. Sadly, Lysis declines and repeats his request. Socrates relents, making a show of his concession, thus underscoring that friends respond to the calls of others (211b; 211c). In doing so, however, he insists that Lysis must come to his aid if Menexenus proves contentious, thus repeating the point that friends help one another, not just themselves. And over time, Socrates's benevolence rubs off; Lysis and Menexenus eventually participate in the conversation, which seems to deepen their friendship, at least to the degree that friendship involves some kind of reciprocal pursuit of the good (218c).

That's Me in the Corner: Through a varied and concrete staging of human sociality, dialogues can provoke their readers toward the exercise of a basic political activity—articulating the terms that should orient our being-in-common. (Note, seeking privacy, even cultivating it, can be one of those terms, but it—the terms, the seeking, the result—remains social.) And given the complex nature of that activity and the conditions it must address, the use of characters drawn from a full range of temperamental types and social roles only enriches the likelihood that readers will find themselves drawn into the dialogue's comings and goings. Finally, such provocations need not abandon the provoked once they find themselves drawn into deeper waters. Exemplary actions are possible ways in which to accompany them, and ill-suited ones can stand as warnings (as can faulty temperaments and traits). Moreover, various demonstrations can initiate promising lines of inquiry, even if they never come to fruition on the page.

This Is Phenomenal: The task of Hegel's *Phenomenology* is to locate a gestalt or pattern of knowing in which "knowing" actually appears. The task of an educator is to organize a class in such a way that, through a kind of mutual striving on the part of teacher and students, "learning" actually appears. When deliberate writing turns toward the addressee, one should ask a similar question. What will come to pass when text and reader meet? Learning? Knowing? Insight? Transformation?

After a certain age, and in complex matters, we're not really sponges. Passive learning rarely sticks. Not that one cannot figure out how to think along with a lecture, let alone a treatise. Kant has rocked enough worlds to make the error of that presumption plain as day. But one might wish to write in a manner that prepares readers for a fresh assessment that one solicits but never concludes, leaving them to bring various things together, whether alone or with others.

Between Us: Philosophy seems anathema to guru-disciple relations. Philosophical maturity involves being able to account for oneself, including one's account and mode of accounting. However, philosophy's social life renders this presumption suspect. Many identify as, and many more function as, Kantians, Hegelians, Aristotelians, Heideggerians, Pragmatists, and so forth. It makes more sense, therefore, to say that philosophy often, even usually, moves within a guru-disciple pattern, but in a manner that could discern and counteract it.

Friedländer locates the Platonic dialogue in that contest: "Did not Plato also have, as part of his nature and as a possible danger, something of the versatility of his Sophists, even something of the clerical 'piety' of his Euthyphro?" (1969, 167). There is an exquisite power in demonstration and eloquent, just-so formulations of matters of principle. And once lodged, they become touchstones. (As Nietzsche shows in *Zarathustra*, one might try to avoid followers and end up with them anyway.) "But he also has Socrates within him," Friedländer adds, "and the decisive struggles and victories that he made public were won within himself" (1969, 167–68). Whether that is true of Plato, I do not know (though it does remind us that each genre exacts an influence on thought in its unfolding). But it seems potentially true for those who take up all that his dialogues offer.

Wanted—a Zeuxis of the Mind: It is difficult to deny the power of exquisite dialogues. Staged properly, they exemplify the life to which they are a response, and when elaborated with living types they exemplify the strivings required for the conclusions they pursue. But it seems to take a rare talent to execute such a text, though its rareness is also due to the habitus of an evolving professoriate. The must of nostalgia thus clings to any advocacy on behalf of the dialogue. But why don't we write (or cowrite) actual dialogues? Why leave it to one mouth to form the words for three? In an electronic age, writing on the same sheet is easy, at least technologically speaking. Moreover, it will avoid filling pages with tedious yes-men and dense dullards, a strategy whose politics are suspect insofar as types are summarily invited and dismissed, as with *Euthyphro* and the *Ion*, both of which seem to fail as scenes of incipient political life, and in uninteresting ways. Who needs to be shown that there are fools in the world? Finally, one's thought usually unfolds in dynamic ways when generated in the presence of another. Dialogically generated dialogues thus promise that dividend as well.

Then Came History

Current Events: Everything moves—particle, wave, and crystal, asteroids and tree limbs, money, blood, lungs, and languages. Even mountains are waves of earth, and some have yet to crest. Humans can be created and destroyed in the surge and swirl—so, too, *the human* (which is also on the move).

Is There Anybody out There? Fleeing fascism, which had laid claim to most of Europe, and facing the totalitarian devolution of Soviet politics as well as the dissolution of the proletariat as a class—that is, as an object and subject of history—Max Horkheimer sought a theoretical space from which to write on behalf of all who labor and live under the transforming traversals of capitalism: national-international, civil society–family, nature-culture, private-public, art-entertainment, individual-society, theory-practice. But in order to do so, he also needed to contradict the views and proclaimed interests of working men and women. Not all, but enough to risk vertigo. Terming the result "critical theory," he postulated—or rather imagined—intellectuals who were neither academic experts operating disinterestedly nor organic intellectuals expressing an immanently operative subjectivity. "Taken as a sociological category," he wrote, "the abstract concept of an intelligentsia that has missionary functions is, by its structure, a hypostatization of specialized science. Critical theory is neither 'deeply rooted' like totalitarian propaganda nor 'detached' like the liberal intelligentsia" (1972, 223–24; translation modified).

But who, then, was Horkheimer's addressee, and what commitments oriented his address? Taking his own activity to be part and parcel of a larger historical praxis, he obstinately held a line for what could only be an emancipatory ensemble to come—maybe. And while Derrida has shown the formal inevitability of such a bearing—for representative politics, for example—

let's focus on the empirical nature of the claim, which haunts deconstruction as much as critical theory.[57]

One need not be a Marxist to link one's writing to a general sense of the present (and thus to a foreseeable future that will become a somewhat different past). In fact, orienting one's writing toward an addressee usually involves orienting oneself toward the situation underwriting the site where text and reader meet.

Imagine an Athens where intellectuals are reviled and the basic terms of moral life unsettled. Or rather, read Thucydides, who tells us that during the plague of 430 BCE, the terms of virtue changed, even reversed, and that during the Mytilenian debate of 427 intellectuals were portrayed as vain poseurs threatening the social order. Or think of Kant for whom "critique" is not only a task for every mode of judgment he could parse—theoretical, practical, aesthetic, and teleological—but also *the* trope of enlightenment: "Our age is the age of criticism, to which everything must submit. Religion through its holiness and legislation through its majesty commonly seek to exempt themselves from it. But in this way they excite a just suspicion against themselves, and cannot lay claim to that unfeigned respect that reason grants only to that which has been able to withstand its free and public examination" (1998, 100–101, Axi).

And so forth—for many philosophers, the character of the addressee and thus of their own address is bound to the character of the historical period in which he or she writes:

    a polis in chaos (Plato),
    an enlightenment public (Kant),
    the death of God (Nietzsche),
    the consummation of the metaphysics of presence (Heidegger),
    the near totalization of the production paradigm and the eclipse of a genuine
        public (Arendt),
    the ascending, actualizing power of the proletariat (Luxembourg),
    the near totalization of the administered world (Adorno),
    juridical power and its disciplinary matrixes (Foucault),
    phallogocentrism (Irigaray),
    white supremacy (DuBois),
    somnambulant conformity (Thoreau),
    a prison industrial complex (Davis),
    heteronormativity (Rich and Warner),
    or a flight from ordinary life (Cavell).

Deliberate writing thus does more than express its situatedness. It also labors to fathom its context in order to conspire with or counter it, or more likely both. "*Geist* is liberal," Horkheimer writes, and that includes writing. "It tolerates no external coercion, no revamping of its results to suit the will of one or other power. But on the other hand, it is not cut loose from the life of society; it does not hang suspended over it" (1972, 223). And that holds for readers as well. Neither the first nor second person can free itself entirely from third-person accounts and still act deliberately (which suggests that distinctions among grammatical persons are heuristic at best and nothing like the escape hatches some philosophers take them to be).

Equal to the Moment

Keeping Current: Every relation is charged, the result of currents flowing back and forth among elements or particles interanimating one another.

Two strangers meet. One hugs the other. Both are men. Or one is a woman. No, both. No, one is a man and the other transitioning. They are in a Berlin *kneiper.* They are in the oil town, Barrow, Alaska, and on November 20. They are along the slick banks of the Amazon, also on November 20. They meet in a market in Dakar, one pale and pink, the other inky dark. They are not strangers but friends. Or they are former lovers, still bitter.

Writing has its own force fields, within and without—an exclamation point in a lyric poem, alliteration in a hypothesis, irony in a love letter, dependent clauses and parentheticals in a newspaper editorial. Add variables and the electromagnetic field adjusts. The sublime is everywhere.

For Post-Nietzscheans: God still isn't dead. You have your orders.

Playing in Traffic: In *One-Way Street* (1928), Benjamin tries to write in a manner that is equal to his moment—the right word or phrase; a given syntax, even rhythm; particular logical-rhetorical operations; this genre but not that one. Such efforts are integral to deliberate writing. Although a great deal depends on the moment one has in mind (on one's philosophy of history, which, for the present, is what ontology entails), Benjamin's considerations are instructive in a general way.

In the thick of Weimar crises, Benjamin finds typical literary performances exhausted. In fact, he believes that a reliance on such performances leaves one with sterile gestures, failed forms (or patterns) whose facticity has overrun whatever insights might appear in the course of writing, reading, and discussion. "At present," he writes, "the construction of life is far more in the power of facts than convictions, and of such facts as have scarcely ever become the basis of convictions. Under these circumstances, true literary activity cannot aspire to take place within a literary framework; this is rather the habitual expression of its sterility" (1996, 441; translation modified). I find his concern compelling, but even if you don't, that should prove significant in your own deliberations—you will find possibilities that I might regard as closed, marginal, too much buck for a bang. But let's take up his perspective and imagine writing in the face of such a foreseeable future, if only for an example of deliberate writing.

Benjamin imagines certain addressees more or less set in their ways—and this seems true of the average consumer in U.S. media markets. Each has his or her source, whether Salon.com or Fox News. (I'm reminded of the hundred or so times I've been told while traveling—"A philosopher? I have my philosophy . . ." As if the issue were simply one of having beliefs and testifying on their behalf. Not that I ignore what follows. That would be unkind, even irresponsible given the semantic weight "philosophy" still manages to carry—at least the beliefs in question are fundamental. But such beginnings are far from auspicious.)

"To convince with convictions is sterile," Benjamin writes (1996, 446). This freestanding contribution to *One-Way Street* intensifies the book's opening entry, "Filling Station," which announces the work's chief effort—to be equal to the moment with "inconspicuous forms that fit its influence in active communities better than . . . the book" (1996, 444). Entitled "For Men," Benjamin's one-liner asserts that *uberzeugen*, a verb meaning "to convince" and the basis of *Überzeugnen*, "convictions," no longer supports a future. Convictions (bound so often to slogans, even key words—liberal, conservative, socialism, capitalism, neoliberalism, terrorism, Islamism, globalization) often lead to conclusions that follow from pre-reflectively operative processes rather than premises. Addressing another through convictions thus may be *unfruchtbar*, unproductive or sterile. More precisely, trading convictions may fail to open or charge learning processes that enable one to fathom and effectively engage historical circumstance. ("I have my philosophy . . .")

A Bad Penny: The Market Place of Ideas—the metaphor's success proves its bankruptcy.

Warning: The greasepaint of populism leads to lead poisoning.

When the Going Gets Tough: I am often impatient with charges of elitism. "Elitism: the poor mind's objection," I once thought, feeling heartlessly clever. As noted, expert-level texts require folk to know things in advance (a what or two, a set of hows) and to arrive ready to work. Maligning these expectations as "elitist" mistakes reading for consumption, like a student who thinks enrollment and attendance is sufficient for learning. "Knowledge" cannot simply be made available if it's to remain knowledge.

But something else is at work in the protest, particularly when it arises in discussions about issues and texts circulating beyond expert henges. Across the globe, certainly in the United States, there is a learning gap, and one that cannot be measured by the presence of diplomas, at least not simply. The meaning of "high school graduate" depends a great deal on the high school (and the student), and so, too, on the "college" (and the student) for those who complete a four-year degree. Moreover, philosophical work takes time and energy, and neither are available to all in equal quantities. Something like *LET* (learning-energy-time) factors into all conversations.

"Yes, dumb it down, make it accessible, avoid jargon, use plain speech and plenty of examples, blah, blah, blah." Perhaps. Benjamin imagined a different course. Commenting on the short, discontinuous entries in *One-Way Street,* Adorno writes: "They do not want to stop conceptual thought so much as to shock through their enigmatic form and thereby get thought moving, because thought in its traditional conceptual form seems rigid, conventional, outmoded" (1992, 332). The question for the deliberate writer is: Will genuine thought occur when text and reader engage? One might predict that accessible content will fuel a learning process. Or . . . (or, and/or), one might make strategic use of discontinuities, hoping that breaks in the chain of thought will stimulate the desire to know and spark a lively response. So, too, puns, irony, and viscous syntax, particularly if one hopes one's texts will help generate new thoughts. What leads a mind to be lively when so much else either overwhelms or labors to preserve the lowest common denomination?

Arming the Messenger: Unlike Mandelstam's secret addressee, who has enough game to play along, Benjamin, at least in *One-Way Street,* seeks a repressed addressee, one he would awaken and mobilize. The issue is not just *LET,* therefore, but a kind of active resistance that occasionally operates pre-reflectively. How does one unlock a conviction? Neither the hoi polloi nor *oligoi* are indifferent receptors. Thought that wishes to prove incisive usually has to flow upstream.

A Mobile Counter-Army: More than an isolated belief, a conviction provides a ground for thought in the sense of a soil that generates other thoughts, questions, perhaps even a philosophical self-understanding. To unlock it, one needs to locate basic, orienting commitments, stated or not. Richard Rorty was a master at this—locating articulable turns of phrase that do most of the heavy lifting in a given position or discussion, for example, self-discovery versus self-invention in the context of self-knowledge, or "truth" at the level of sentences versus vocabularies.

The task is not exactly argument, though it can include argument. For example, in order to acknowledge and protect alterity, Levinasians resist *the other's* incorporation into orders of meaning, which always render the other within a logic of the same, usually some class to which the other presumably belongs, in whole or in part, say "woman," "human," "living being," "organic life," and so on. This commitment (alongside some of Levinas's other basic thoughts) has maintained an intuitive appeal across generations. Resist it and a counter must be found, such as: doesn't an ethical bearing require an intensification of the interpretive terms of purposive agency, and an ability to move responsibly within them? How else will we gauge, prospectively or retrospectively, the help or harm we do? These are rhetorical questions. But they specify a different sensibility and help delimit the reach of a conviction I find insufficiently ethical.

Other, complementary efforts are available, particularly if one wants to avoid the oversimplifications that Rorty-like summations often exploit. (Can one invent oneself without also discovering some of what one would refashion?) Because convictions provide broad orientations, one's counter will spark resistance. Objections should be anticipated, therefore. And without polemics, which intensify defensiveness and invite avoidance. Third, one might locate and resist one's own missteps en route, for example, the military metaphorics I've employed, which incline me toward a polemic even as I claim an aversion to it. Writing, bound to readers, is in fact a joint venture whose energies can be intensified without a body count, say, by absorbing some of the virtues of the dialogue into a prose that does not employ the full drama of the genre.

The Sweeter Science: If structural discontinuity is designed to leave room for and awaken fresh thought, short entries aim toward an accessibility that preserves the pulse of insight, though the two are designed to work in tandem, particularly when one takes *LET* into account. But what do short forms offer an age of conviction? (And note, Benjamin's entries are not only usually

short but also condensed and, thus, different than the mini-essays one finds
in revolutionary pamphlets.) I am tempted to say that Benjamin's miniatures
aim to capture and thus exemplify thought in its occurrence, except the goal
is not simply a kind of phenomenological fidelity. Rather, the task is to catch
a thought as it grasps an object in its untruth. For example, the fifth section of "Imperial Panorama" addresses the adage Poverty Disgraces No Man
(1996, 452). Benjamin claims that even if this once were true (when most
everyone was poor, for example), it no longer is. Poverty persists in large
measure because we allow it. (We may even plan for it, I would add, given
that many regard unemployment as healthy for the big picture and whoever
is invited to sit for it.) Poverty's persistence thus manifests a willful neglect of
others, which humiliates them given the telling lengths people go to secure
manicured lawns and luxury cars. But the phrase isn't just false. Its blithe
embrace of an obvious cliché, one that ignores how a basic level of poverty
is a de facto policy goal, demeans. Not that one should accept such flagrant
disrespect; Benjamin commands the reader to be "alert to every humiliation
done to him, and so discipline himself that his suffering becomes no longer
the downhill road of grief but the rising path of revolt" (1996, 452).

   At least two things are operative in this section of "Imperial Panorama."
Benjamin employs an inconspicuous form, a kind of posterlike exhortation
directing proletarians to convert grief into revolt. Second, his treatment of
the slogan Poverty Disgraces No Man exemplifies the discipline that can take
insult-added-to-injury and convert it into a diagnosis, which in turn might
fuel revolt. *One-Way Street* thus leads by example as well as provocation, and
this helps Benjamin remain true to his task: "The art of the critic in a nut-
shell: to coin slogans without betraying ideas" (1996, 460).

A Rose Is a Rose Is a Rose: In a letter to Gershom Scholem, Benjamin is re-
luctant to call what became *One-Way Street* a "book of aphorisms." Although
this reverses an earlier judgment, which terms *One-Way Street* a "slender
manuscript of aphorisms," I find the later self-understanding on point and
instructive for deliberate writers (Benjamin 1994, 302, 273). Aphorisms stand
on their own, by design, and Benjamin's various entries interact—for example, around the thought of "convictions," particularly around the epistemic
and motivating limits of convictions. Second, Benjamin's subject matter is often personal and anecdotal, whereas aphorisms generalize about classes. Yes,
these generalizations, because they stand alone, "do invite men to enquire
farther," as we've seen Bacon observe. But the aphorism's addressee (at least
as figured by the aphorists of modernity) remains generic, and Benjamin has
a more specific and varied audience in mind—activists, avant-garde artists,

intellectuals, and so forth. As a collection, then, *One-Way Street* is at once too integrated, too particular, and too pedagogically ambitious to be a collection of aphorisms. I underscore the point because deliberate writing need not conceive of its parts (or wholes) along strictly generic lines. The point is not simply to instance a form but to prove equal to the moment, and this may require leaving generic expectations unfulfilled, even among the most advanced readers.

Unequal to the Moment

Acrobatics: Realpolitik knows it's always the real world, everywhere, and that's the hell of it. Life is nowhere else. Cynicism fails to rise to the occasion. Its confidence is the residue of an evaporated fight for freedom.

Only Exits: A life without conscience departs without regrets.

The Madness of Decision: In order for writing to be equal to a moment, it must develop a feel for what is more likely than not unequal, knowing that, in every case, the least likely can still happen, and all the more so with *praxis* (as opposed to *techne*). Without those odds, all that is left is a kind of guess, though sometimes that is all we have, even with actions as common as apologizing, asking for a date, deciding which job to take. And yet, that overstates the case. In hard cases, one is not forced to guess among *all* that might be done. Certain missteps will be obvious. But there are often times when deliberation cannot find a decisive point in favor of one among a set of plausible options, though this does not remove the need to commit.

Swing and a Miss: In *One-Way Street*, Benjamin worries about what he terms the "pretentious, universal gesture of the book," but without specifying what troubles him. I don't think "gesture" is the worry, given that Lukács had already marked with approbation the essay as a kind of historical gesture or *Geste*, and *One-Way Street* is a gesture in its own way. "Universal" is more likely the source of trouble. It presumes what it should help bring about—a public, that is, a fluid, differentiated subject of communication and shared labor, one able to thematize its fate in and as moments open to even more knowledge and reform.

Benjamin also worries about the histrionics that accompany the kind of books he has in mind, namely, academic treatises that propose systematic and complete accountings. The following titles, many published in successive volumes, convey the milieu: *Logical Investigations* (Edmund Husserl, 1900, 1901), *Ethics of the Pure Will* (Herman Cohen, 1904, 1907), *Principia Mathematica* (Alfred North Whitehead and Bertrand Russell, 1910, 1911, 1912), *General Theory of Knowledge* (Moritz Schlick, 1918, 1925), *Tractatus Logico Philosophicus* (Wittgenstein, 1921), *Being and Time* (Heidegger, 1927). Even Dewey's chief text of the period carries the title *Experience and Nature* (1929). In calling attention to the heroic scope of their venture, such titles prime a learned readership for resistance and an untutored one for avoidance or deference. In *One-Way Street*, Benjamin favors inconspicuous forms, the kind that will not awaken defense mechanisms or forecast much of what lies ahead. But not for want of ambition—inconspicuous forms are subtle, even cunning. One reads along and suddenly a thought appears.

I find treatises ill formed to my moment. (In fact, they seem to eschew the moment in principle. That said, I don't see how one could declare, deliberately, that the moment for *X* is over, once and for all; unless one were writing a treatise.) John Rawls's *Theory of Justice* may be the last treatise to take a chunk of the world by storm, at least that world loosely organized by market economies and liberal states, and even he eventually pulled back from the full pretensions of that book. *LET* is one variable, even among experts who are often too busy being professionals to digest all that treatises venture. (I wonder how many who have taught and/or commented on *Theory of Justice* have read it cover to cover, and carefully.) The publishing world is also averse to large books—and we should not forget all that a moment entails. (And note that markets are not just about selling and buying. The prominence of *Theory of Justice* cannot be separated from its broad anthologization and use in courses, for example.) Finally, for decades there has been a general suspicion regarding ideal theory and totalized accounts (or metanarratives). While the sources of this incredulity are no doubt manifold, the theory of knowledge needed to underwrite a treatise has buckled under the weight of the variegated historicity of languages, the dynamism of organic and inorganic life, the logical implosion of onto-theology, and the dispersion of the subject into overlapping but acentered systems of reception and response. Even a reasonably well-schooled undergraduate will wonder whose justice, which rationality, adding when and where to their perplexity.

The treatise no longer seems a live option for those who would philosophically essay a topic. As a mode of conduct, it appears to have grown old. One might also object to such efforts on ethical grounds. Some philosophers are

outright hostile to metanarratives and the texts that might ground them because "final doctrines" seem to align with totalitarianism, colonialism, even
genocide. I find these claims overblown. Empirical in nature, they arrive with
a deductive cast, which is ironic, and a cheat. About humanism in particular,
one used to hear, with frequency: "We all know where that led . . ." But we
don't, and history would have to be immanent to its concept for us to say we
do. The moment is on the move and sublimely complex. Those who would
write deliberately need to be at once more definite and more cautious when
facing decisions and revisions that a moment might displace.

More Than One Can Chew: Claims regarding the end of philosophy always
sound like exceptions to the rule.

First Impressions: The aphorism is attractive to those who worry about
LET. Its concision can accommodate the harried reader, while its concentration allows for returns and rumination. Collections of aphorisms are
companionable, therefore, and their best efforts can burrow deeply into one's
thought and sensibility. Evagrius (345–399 AD) collected a hundred aphorisms in his *Praktikos* to focus the meditations (and thereby the souls) of desert fathers. And countless people have imagined recording their own *Pensées,*
following Pascal's example (1670), which suggests the attractiveness of short
forms outside professional enclaves, as does the success of Gracian's *Oracle*
(1647). When translated by Christopher Mauer in 1992, it was, briefly, a best
seller.

Social media seems hospitable to aphorisms. They can be tweeted or
dropped as a Facebook post. I once posted: "Philosophy begins in displacement. Wonder is just one transposition." It generated an extended conversation and led some to observe, with surprise, how thick the occasional thread
can prove.

But there are worries. In a world of short attention spans, the aphorism's
concision may enable the opposite of thought concentratedly devoted to its
object. Also, its availability, particularity when engaged in a strict alternation
between work and leisure, may reduce its pungency to ornament. In addition,
the genre's disregard for justification is troubling in a world where everyone
believes they have a right to form and maintain opinions without regard for
the inferential patterns employed or what the evidence indicates. And the
solitary voice of aphoristic thought may compound a similar tendency to not
care about what others might think. ("I have my own *Pensées . . .*") Finally,
aphorisms cannot address systematic phenomena, which is why Benjamin's

remarks on German inflation run for several pages in *One-Way Street*. I am thus drawn to texts like *One-Way Street* that try to integrate aphoristic thought within a varied, dynamic whole that is greater than the sum of its parts but less well formed. The moment, its objects, our evolving views—no genre is equal to the surfeit.

After Beauvoir

Riddle Me This: Nothing is at home in the world because the world is neither a home nor its simple absence. Animal, vegetable, mineral, shale, mushroom, shrew—each unfolds in the flying imperfect, continuous in certain currents, singular and adrift in whatever character it acquires and accrues. Writing too.

Know Thyself Is an Incomplete Instruction: Thinking about activity in general, Simone de Beauvoir argues that it "must be raised to the height of moral freedom by taking itself as an end through the disclosure of a particular content" (1976, 32). In each act, one must affirm the capacity to act, but not in the abstract. One's exemplification bears the measure. Philosophical writing knows this script. Whatever your commitments, philosophy demands that they be yours. We can philosophize together and help and/or hinder each other, and we can agree (or not). But I can neither understand nor commit for you. Philosophical endorsements on behalf of another are thus forgeries.

Over before It Began: "One can reveal the world," Beauvoir writes, "only on a basis revealed by other men," and to other men, I would add (1976, 71). Philosophical writing, even the most original, is bound to this ambiguity and this overdetermination. It therefore remains an act of inheritance, striving to establish a place where writer and addressee can meet, transformatively, and beyond "men," I hope.

Lost and Found: Suppose that in the course of writing, which includes its being read, no one learns a thing. No interesting question arises. No thesis is offered let alone defended. And the example inevitably offered never again comes to mind. Has philosophy happened? In large part, Hegel's *Phenom-*

enology concerns the many ways in which knowledge fails to appear. Philosophy may need a similar exposé.

The Narrow Is Never Straight: Recounting two years by the pond, Thoreau remarks that, "in most books, the I, or first person, is omitted, in this it will be retained," adding, two sentences later: "I should not talk so much about myself if there were any body else whom I knew as well. Unfortunately, I am confined to this narrowness of my experience" (2008, 5). Typical Thoreau: dry, a bit grating, and provocative. One may know oneself better than others but not know oneself well. Moreover, the ability to say *I* may help give oneself to oneself, but this needn't mean that the self I know better (a) appears when I say "I," or (b) is even the referent of "I." What looks like Thoreau's proximity to his own sojourn along the shore thus converts into a narrowness. "I" less secures access than marks another matter to be surveyed, or charted, or sounded like a pond fed from elsewhere.

Two-Way Street: Plato has dramatized how difficult philosophy can be. Euthyphro seems incapable of it. As philosophy begins to claim him, he turns to flee. But so, too, Crito, even in his most heartfelt arrival. By offering Socrates the opportunity to escape, Crito demonstrates how little he knows him, meaning, that for which Socrates stands. Like friendship, and even among friends, philosophy is fragile.

Authorization? The history of philosophy is not full of welcome for women. Even Beauvoir felt this keenly. Or rather, she may have felt it so keenly because she was Beauvoir—the "very circumstances that orient the woman toward creation also constitute obstacles she will often be unable to overcome" (2009, 742). The thought begins somewhere proximate to Emerson— one takes one's own fate as generalizable. But who is one to generalize? "A woman," Beauvoir writes, "could never have become Kafka: in her doubts and anxieties, she would never have recognized the anguish of Man driven from paradise" (2009, 750). Emily Dickinson provides a counter, but I feel the weight of the point. Some inner audiences conspire against those who would transformatively inherit what fate has given them to be. In fact, philosophy sometimes fails to appear because what has passed as philosophy stands in the way. And that leaves me all the more struck by how Beauvoir turned that fate into philosophy.

Sealing Wax: More muscular than the subjunctive, hope refuses the indicative yet is wiser than the imperative.

Property Is Theft

There Is a Place for Every Time: At present, "philosophy" seems a matter for academics and their charges. A small set, certainly less than fifty people, constitute the usual "public" for professional articles, particularly in print journals. Online publications draw more "hits," but who knows what kind of reading that indicates; even "download" is vague, as every student could infer who has the sense to wonder, entering a professor's office—"Have you read all these books?" Scholarly monographs from university presses, not including textbooks, usually sell modestly. If a text sells more than a thousand copies, most university presses are surprised and thrilled; five hundred is the average. Philosophy's moment is thus, for the time being, narrowly circumscribed.

Those wishing to counter such circumstances must shoot the gulf that has opened between professional discourses and the discursive habits of that vastness we often call, with too much familiarity, "everyday life." In most academic disciplines, this gap is to be expected and does not pose a problem, at least in the following way. Some may want physics and chemistry, anthropology and history to produce salable goods and services. But most are untroubled when those disciplines prove complex, even elusive. (No one says: "I have my own biochemistry . . .") Even in literary studies, many are willing to cede the province of poems to the experts. ("I'm just not a poetry person . . .") Again, they may think such knowledge useless—and that has become one meaning of "academic"—but they are unthreatened by what a Milton scholar seems to know and unsurprised if the details of Byzantine wedding rituals prove confusing. Philosophy is different.

Academic Matters: What makes an action right, a character or life good? Should we distinguish the right from the good? Given you've been wrong before, do you know what you think you know, and on what basis? When is a scientific theory "just a theory"? A man says: "You have your truth, I have mine." Is he confused? Which of nature's many patterns are really real? Any of them, all of them, or is the fact that they change all that endures? Was there a first cause? Is there a final one or set of some? Should we distinguish high from low art? What precisely is aesthetic value? There are kinds of value? Is capital punishment a legitimate form of retributive justice? What beings have moral standing? Is taxation like forced labor or a valuable ingredient in a program of distributive justice? Who precisely (or what) does a representative represent?

These queries remain significant and are broadly comprehensible. They are common in the sense of "in common," and so are the replies, that is, their speakers seem right to venture them in a way that proves absent when untutored citizens hold forth on the science of climate change. "I have my philosophy . . ." is thus an unsurprising remark, even a welcome one. Philosophy is not just a rationalized and professionalized language-game. It is in part, or rather, it has become so, but, and this is an empirical claim, it also addresses questions of general and fundamental concern, questions many currently address through the dogmas and rituals of organized religion. More than basic lifeworld resources, like ordinary language, tie philosophy to everyday life; its questions engage basic self-understandings, and the swerve of one's conduct will vary depending on one's (real) answers. Not that everyone holds explicit positions on philosophy's recurring questions. But pose them with general competence and a discussion ensues. They matter.

Faulty Footing: Almost twenty years ago, Rochelle Green, remarked in conversation: "That's because you still believe there are human beings." I did and do—though I'm still working through the thought. Does that count as evidence?

This Is Not My Beautiful House: Whatever divides academic and nonexpert discourses is a social fact, meaning, its causes are not reducible to facts about individual authors and/or readers. Could philosophers write with greater clarity and eloquence? Could nonacademic readers prove more patient as they think through the complexities that one should expect with questions that endure? Answer as you will, other issues bear on what, at present, seems a chasm—the relative distributions of *LET*, academic systems of reward, and the stimulations and numbing buzz and blink of electronic media. Our moment is thoughtless, even in those corners where genuine discoveries occur. How does one converse in a public where an antiscience stance is political capital and sound bites seem to satisfy the desire to know? Where everyone has their button words?

Inexpert Scenarios: Philosophy sits uneasily when left to experts. Not that philosophy fades from view when professors exchange and defend claims. But when left to the "experts," philosophy suffers; its ends emerge foreshortened.

On the side of the addressee, the inexpert expect to belong to the conversation—albeit one defined by the questions more than those who pose them. Many nonexperts have a stake in it. They take themselves to be potential sources of insight and wish to be recognized as such. (This is a historical-empirical claim, one that reflects a democratic turn in the kingdom of culture that was already operative in Socrates's habit of engaging a broad range of people and was vividly exemplified by texts like Emerson's essays, which are as rich as any classic, and broadly appealing, even intimately so.) Outside its (never) ivory (rarely) tower, professional philosophy appears to be hoarding what should be broadly shared. And enacted; academics also have "everyday" lives. The profession not only appears unfairly self-involved but often insincere.

"Expert" also seems like a put-on. Philosophy has never settled on the true, the good, and the beautiful. Yes, missteps are apparent and articulable, but what does it mean to be an expert of dead ends and error, even as the questions persist? Moreover, we do not know in advance who will chance on an insight and what it will portend. Philosophy lives in this exposure. Author and reader meet in it, as a presumption, and each proves philosophical by remaining true to it.

"Another call to simplicity? Availability?" Yes, in a certain sense, no, in another. Genuine difficulties cannot be shirked but they should be earned, that is, demonstrated, and developmentally, say by showing why plausible replies fall short, or by dealing sympathetically (and inclusively) with one's rivals, as if one were addressing an issue that might make fools of us all. Aristotle entertains multiple views, some held by the famous, others circulating, almost mutely, in sayings and conversations. And with a little imagination one can mark several basic self-conceptions in Hegel's *Phenomenology*. But the deeper point concerns resistance, not accepting what amounts to philosophy's exile from social life. (If I am right, people will inevitably find replies to basic philosophical questions, often without philosophy's radical reflexivity, and I would rather not leave anyone's broad, self-understanding to the currents of revealed religions or the anthropology and metaphysics of commercial exchange.)

Genuine work is accomplished when the pros philosophize. But those advances could also be set back into the conduct of life, and on both ends of the bending line that never comes full circle. This is not quite the claim: take up the questions of the day. Instead, it means binding one's concerns and proceedings to the kind of broad, basic questions I earlier specified, the questions that usually attract students to philosophy in the first place, including those who become professors. (Husserl terms this "reactivating the origins." Dewey speaks of a "method of experience." I just want to know what I'm talking about.) Yes, such questions are "introductory," but in the sense that through them philosophy is initiated.

Turning back into its inception, philosophy opens, vaguely, a novel future for what had seemed settled, perhaps obvious. Amid modest revolutions, one should anticipate prospects. "But if that is so . . ." is where minds go. I concur when Martha Nussbaum insists: "For any view you put forward . . . the next question simply has to be, 'What would the world be like if this idea were actually taken up'?" (quoted in Boynton 1999) Leaving such work to some imaginary set of plebs is no longer a satisfactory pose, methodologically or politically.

But philosophical insight also requires active reception, and that precludes its transfer through what many expect in expert cultures, something like a report of recent findings. The clarity of an argument does not guarantee its comprehension let alone its acceptance. For writer and audience, philosophy entails a struggle with oneself that expert culture presumes to resolve through the conferral of degrees. Philosophy mostly fails to appear on such stages; uncanny possibilities shade the moments to which it would prove equal.

Strange Alchemy

Untimely Expectations: Fully scripted advances rarely further the romance of philosophy, and not just because philosophy thrives in active reception. The best work is often untimely. In certain quarters, only recently has the power of Hegel been felt—after a span of almost two hundred years. Nietzsche, as he predicted, needed several decades to even begin to be heard, and the full import of his thought remains a matter of great contestation. And some whose fame and notoriety came and went have been reborn in contexts more favorable to their more radical moments: Spinoza's ontology (at least over the last thirty years), and somewhat earlier, Hume's account of moral feeling. And more recently, Schelling, particularly in his willingness to think from, not merely about, nature. And there are still other cases, say Stoicism and Adam Smith. With such fates in mind, a deliberate writer realizes that sometimes the task is less to reach a readership than to ready it. But depending on the climate of reception, such efforts can prove elusive or inhospitable. The trick—a complex one—lies with distinguishing affectation from thoughtful cultivation.

Take Notes: It is not uncommon to find certain magazines and even professional journals asking authors to work without scholarly notes. Many authors dream from time to time of writing texts without asides, digressions, and backroom arguments. (Some even succeed.) "Straight to the matter" is the wish. The presumption is twofold. Scholarly notes are unnecessary. If it's worth saying, say it in the text. Most of what falls into notes is merely academic, more a display of learning than anything integral. Second, notes interrupt the flow of reading and thus distract like clutter obscuring the lines of an exquisite design.

Worthy cautions, but an agile use of notes (and scholarship more generally) highlights what should not be forgotten but too often is in an age of digital media and commoditized social relations. Philosophical insight is a dependent affair. Invention follows listening, learning, and responding. And yet, philosophy drifts at times toward the oracular (whether through the author's voice or the searchability of documents, which allows a reader to isolate terms and claims from the whole). Under such conditions, philosophy weakens. Each thought has its all too human predecessors, and the distance it wins from them (toward some matter in common) is the mark of its advance. Notes and asides concretize one's reception and contextualize one's response. Cavell has often remarked that Wittgenstein writes as if he never read anyone whereas Heidegger writes as if he's read it all. Does a mean lie between? Our moment clings to (and longs for) executive orders (including revealed ones). A backdrop of faux necessities (genetic, economic, even eschatological) is thickening. On that stage, the relationality of thought and, more importantly, insight should not be ignored.

Philosophy also bears a history one should not bury. It may contain undiscovered presumptions or underutilized resources. And its omissions may indicate missed opportunities. Better, then, to err on Heidegger's side and keep one's reading, one's inheritances, on display. Heidegger's sustained interpretations open readers to possible double readings. Is Nietzsche really that bound to subjectivism? Isn't Schelling's account of freedom awfully close to what we find in Heidegger's own "On the Essence of Truth"? Likewise, by overtly displaying his learning, one is driven to ask about those ignored, such as Spinoza. The scholarly character of Heidegger's writing thus keeps the past open in various ways that would go missing if he opted to simply address the things themselves. Even his deference to scholarly editions reminds us that older books are often the work of editors as well as authors.

In a different way, Thoreau's broad reading exposes the complicated historicity circulating through *Walden* and testifies to the work's transhistorical and transcultural cosmopolitanism. A kind of learning was integral to his experiment at the pond, and without quotes, in their concretion, his circulations through the more than human world might have eclipsed an essential dimension of his cosmic bearing. We are in company even when the soul converses with itself.

But most importantly, and at a performative level, active scholarship (duly cited) embodies a historical bearing that strikes a counter blow to the kind of willful amnesia that the commodity form institutes. Consumers want goods in "certified frustration-free packaging," and that includes thoughts. Value, capital holds, lies exclusively on the side of demand, which translates

philosophy into the uses to which a thought can be put by the one deciding whether she or he "buys it." But such an outlook is oblivious to all it
conducts, for better and for ill, and philosophy, which cannot eschew self-
knowledge, requires a more circumspect bearing.

Current Affairs: In response to some angry mail, Adorno addressed the use
of foreign words, which he employed in a radio broadcast entitled "Short
Commentaries on Proust." (A radio broadcast on Proust? From Adorno?
Different moment.) Adorno argues that foreign words, left untranslated, are
justified when (a) the object demands it and (b) no local substitute works
as well. Testing the claim, I think "worldview" can substitute for "weltanschauung" (including its use of "view") whereas "action" doesn't really do for
"praxis." "Action" means too much, thereby losing the particular associations
of "praxis" (deliberation, commitment, not a technique), though the latter
also requires pruning.

Even as it responds to particular concerns, Adorno's essay revolves around
a particular dilemma. (His essay is thus of and beyond its moment, which any
reflective assessment and response must be, as even Lenin knew.) Adorno indicates that while the object is the primary concern of an author, the moment,
as it operates in language, remains a concern: "Even the writer who imagines
that he is going right to the subject matter itself and not to the way it is com-
municated cannot willfully ignore the historical changes language undergoes
in the process of communicative use. He has to do his formulating from the
inside and the outside at the same time, as it were" (1991, 198). I agree with the
spirit of the concluding line but the dilemma is improperly framed. Language
does not arise between a subject and an object and then enter into communication that runs like a game of telephone. We are social animals who rely on
joint action and reproduce through complex gestation periods and long, vulnerable periods of maturation. Language was most likely always communicative, therefore. The point is not incidental. Concern with the addressee is part
and parcel of linguistic competence—full stop—not some postlapsarian
fate. It thus seems mistaken to prioritize one's relation to the object over one's
relation to one's addressees and misanthropic to long for a situation in which
a speaker might only face an object. Not that one can assess the demands of
a moment in any categorical manner. I thus agree with Adorno (though not
with his translator) when I read: "It is not a linguistic *Weltanschauung*, not
an abstract pro and con, that decides on that use but a process of countless
interwoven impulses, promptings, and reflections. The limited consciousness
of the individual writer has little control over the extent to which this process
is successful. But the process cannot be avoided" (1991, 199).

Public Commitment

An Offer One Could Refuse: The modern research university presents itself as a site of inquiry, discovery, even tech transfer—in short, results. And when results prove technical, many simplify these results for laypersons. If you can, you may prove a "public scholar," one who plays the expert among the inexpert.

Philosophy awkwardly inhabits the modern research university. While the circling crises of empirical inquiry leave some room for philosophy, as do conundrums internal to certain inquiries such as self-experience in schizophrenia, these sites usually close before all that's on offer can enter. Why? Philosophy lacks results. My point is more formal than the usual handwringing over philosophy's lack of consensus. To what degree can one separate a conclusion from the process that led to it and have that conclusion maintain its character? (Would a simple assertion count as philosophy?) And does a conclusion really mark the terminus of philosophy?

Philosophy evaporates when it is reduced to belief. "God exists" means something very different in contexts like private prayer, a liturgy, or a proof fresh from possible worlds. The line becomes philosophical through the way it is offered, which invites several possible responses, including endorsement or rejection, contestation, even withdrawal. Cavell terms this way the pitch of philosophy. It attenuates if one wants the fruit without the tree (or the sun and the wind bringing clouds and rain).

For neither God nor Country: American philosophy remains honest by resolutely resisting "America." "In the name of what?" That has yet to be discovered.

Ideological Transgressions: When is one resisting? Conforming? Might one simultaneously enact both? What is to be done when one struggles to grasp what one is doing?

Purported transgressions can regress and slide into ideology, effecting repressive desublimation. In particular, logical-rhetorical operations seeking cognitive dissonance may very well effect their opposite.

I often hear that a given text "transgresses" normative orders of gender, sexuality, socioeconomic status, and ethnicity. The arguments are often nuanced and sophisticated. But what is the space of that or any transgression? And can I avoid considering the matter and still write deliberately? My concern is not unlike Adorno's worry about art, despite all he finds there. A logic of nonidentity within an artwork is nevertheless broadly trumped by the logic of identity that governs "art" in the global art market and the broader, techno-capitalist culture. Similarly, religious experiences every Sunday at eleven bind one to a cultural division of labor more often than the sacred.

Thinking of literary theory's grammatical gymnastics, Rey Chow has observed: "The revolutionary defiance of instrumentalist linguistic lucidity has transformed, in practice over time, into potentially gainful means of generating cultural as well as financial capital" (2003, 104). The remark was part of Chow's contribution to the brouhaha that surrounded the bad-writing prize flung at Judith Butler. The question it raises bears repeating, particularly since it refuses any easy distinction between symbolic and materialist politics. One needs some social-theoretical grasp of one's present if one's intervention is to do more than vent and thus play the sieve.

No Vexation without Conversation: The history behind any thought involves disagreement. An examined inheritance not only hears *why* but also *what was not affirmed.* In a moment of self-assertion when confidence men (and women) carry the vote as generals to most wills, discursive communities not only need to be able to withstand but actually embrace disagreement, and with a feel for its generative currents. Under such conditions, texts, if only for what their performance exemplifies, should model disagreement. And not just with those one opposes. Clarifying what and why one eschews a given thought, even from those one admires, sets philosophy outside (at least in part) the epic of heroes and villains (which never ends well). The conceit is as old as Plato. A kind of minimal dialogue about basic matters is a precondition for any politics that would not rely on coercion when differences that make a difference arise. In fact, what public is inaugurated by a text that never imagines any disagreement?

Neither Flee nor Fight: "Let's agree to disagree." That's no way to say goodbye. Philosophy seems bound to fighting words and to those on their verge. The trick is to get them to back down without backing off.

Propagation without Propaganda

Debutexts: If the treatise turns its back on the moment, the manifesto seems made for it. A manifesto is often a confrontation with history. It identifies prevalent forces it would expose, assault, and presumably reform. (I wouldn't find a nihilist manifesto contradictory. For the moment, it conspires with what it would eventually undo.) Embracing the present tense in order to win the future, the "manifesto is by nature a loud genre," as Ann Caws suggests (2001, xx).

The manifesto has an uneasy relation to philosophy, though as with anything, it brims with philosophical significance, and one could, no doubt, reform the genre. But a survey of examples finds programmatic assertion at the expense of reflection, declaration rather than demonstration. "It is high time," Marx and Engels write, "that Communists should openly, in the face of the whole world, publish their views, their aims their tendencies, and meet this nursery tale of the Spectre of Communism with a Manifesto of the party itself" (1992, 2). The goal is more a kind of intellectual debut than an objectification of the thought that leads one to commit to communism.

Light on justification and heavy on hortatory, the manifesto also lacks the concentrated character of the aphorism, which tries to crystalize propositional thought. Nor does the manifesto abandon itself to the experimental energy of the essay, which seeks to elude the normalizing force of systematic prose in order to generate insights that suffocate in genres like the treatise and the professional article/monograph. Manifestos, rhetorical in a more classical sense, thus lack the generative ambition that aphorisms and essays share with philosophy's more exalted, systematic presentations.

Manifestos also (usually) seek allegiance rather than a response in kind. Aphorisms call for briefs in reply—La Rochefoucauld belonged to a circle that traded in them. So, too, the essay—its ventures invite their own essay. And professional articles and monographs invite refutation. Less so the manifesto. Francis Picabia, offering a "Dada Cannibalistic Manifesto," commands "the accused" to stand, and declares that the "orator will speak to you only if you are standing," and standing as one would for a national anthem or before a flag. And even though Picabia's hectoring ironically recoils on the very modes of allegiance that it cannibalizes, it does not ultimately undermine the relation it stages with its addressees. It only displaces traditional objects of allegiance with a resplendent "nothing" that it repeats ten times over the course of eight consecutive lines. (Less maniacally, Marx and Engels call for their addressees to unite.)

Unsurprisingly, the manifesto thrived in the world of modernist art, where the putting that provided the proof was most often a work or set of works, not the manifesto. The manifesto was, rather, an effort to make space for such works, even to provide instructions for their construction. In "A Few Don'ts by an Imagiste," Pound, for example, offers ample instruction to would-be imagists. Whistler begins his manifesto on behalf of symbolism "in the character of the preacher" (Caws 2001, 3). The analogy seems right, insofar as the manifesto testifies to its commitments. The poet F. T. Marinetti's "The Founding and Manifesto of Futurism" employs several modes of testimony. Some are principled—"Except in struggle, there is no more beauty"—others aspirational, for example: "We want to hymn the man at the wheel." And some serve notice, for example, "We intend to sing the love of danger" and "We will destroy the museums, libraries, academies of every kind" (Caws 2001, 187). The manifesto is thus an expectant herald of the future it foresees rather than a possible instance of it. "A new era is beginning," writes Vicente Huidobro, closing his "Non Serviam," a manifesto on behalf of Creationism, continuing: "Opening its jasper doors, I bend one knee to the ground and salute you respectfully" (Caws 2001, 377).[58]

In one way, philosophy also defers to work to come, namely, that undertaken by an addressee who, even should she or he agree, is expected to enact the lines of thought on offer, and no one can know where that might lead. But philosophy also seeks to concretize that future within itself, whether through demonstrations or exemplifications. (Pound's manifesto is not itself an image on the terms he elaborates.) Thus even when it aims to redress its addressees en route, philosophy also offers a glimpse into that toward which the consort presumably moves.

Bit by Bit

Post-postmortem: In striving to be equal to its moment, writing includes a medium responsive, in part, to humanity's various, embodied capabilities. (The *Rubáiyát of Omar Khayyám*, published as a 17/16″ ×1¼″ manuscript and written out on vellum by B. N. Budd in 1930, remains a curiosity—its destination more likely a collection than a reader.)

The "book" has been philosophy's medium for centuries. By "book" I do not mean the idea of a totality of meaning directed by an all-seeing author, which Derrida rightly deconstructed in *Of Grammatology*. (His target, however, seems more the treatise and a certain kind of author than the book per se. Neither Plato's *Republic* nor Emerson's *Essays* is a book in the totalized sense). Nor do I take book to name the linear narrative championed by the modern novel, which lost its aura of necessity with the emergence of hypertext, as Robert Coover has observed (1992). Rather, I mean the paper codex, which includes the journal offprint, journals, and those objects that usually come to mind when one hears (or says) (or thinks) "book."

For most of my adult life, the book has been pronounced dead, and so often that our cultural coroners merit unpaid leave. That said, for the moment, there are other options, even if one more or less commits to lines of thought within linear wholes, as do most e-books, online journals, and blogs.

Building a Raft in Speech: Philosophically speaking, blogs have auspicious, etymological origins. The term abbreviates "web log," a phrase whose source domain is the log—say a ship's or captain's—and the practice of recording (or logging) notes and observations regarding matters integral to one's activity or voyage—weather, crew behavior, rations, et cetera. But log in this sense comes from *logos*, the rational speech to which Socrates hoped to subject

Athenian elites (and whomever he encountered). It also names what Aristotle sets at the absolute heart of politics and ethics—a life lived in accord with the rational speech. Philosophy in the blogosphere never abandons the manner to which it was born, therefore.

Blogs are not yet a genre, but open to multiple genres and logical rhetorical operations, which carry a good deal of the thought ventured therein. Depending on its organization, a fully hypertextual blog might lead to even greater variability. Because hypertexts invite one to proceed in a nonlinear fashion, the reader can also become an editor of sorts, click by click. Imagine establishing one's own order to Aristotle's *Ethics* or the *Tao Te Ching* (to name two canonical texts with complex editorial histories). A blogger may also install various programs that add some randomness to what comes next, thus intensifying the dispersion of the author function even as it lives on via the reader.

Whether philosophy opens into genuine, hypertextual discontinuities will (or rather should) depend on a compelling answer to *why*. What calls for it? The moment? An addressee lost to linear modes of presentation, or weakened by them? Would hypertext philosophy allow thinking to unfold in startling new ways? Would such a text intensify the cross-pollinating currents of *Beyond Good and Evil*? One could imagine an epistemology of the fragment, always addressing and changing an elusive whole, overcoming a misleading linearity by subjecting its fragments to a variety of programs that realign their order on every reading. And if one's reception is itself an addition, the program(s) could also allow for the addition of brief replies, time stamped, thereby opening hyperplanes of midrash. For the moment, however, philosophy blogs usually feature informal but more or less linear observations and reflections accompanied by occasional links to more formal (even professional) papers on the same or aligned subjects.

To their advantage, at least with regard to certain subject matters, blogs can, in ways that traditional print media cannot, "quote" sounds and images (particularly videos and film clips). Comment sections also invite a kind of dialogue among readers and/or between author and reader, even if that invitation is only occasionally accepted, and the reply rarely (in) kind. It may be that addressees are not ready for processing in public. Perhaps such sites are viewed as risky, either professionally or socially, or readers may not wish to process in public. And there are trolls, persons who undermine conversations with erroneous or inflammatory remarks, and their lurking presence may dissuade many from playing Socrates or Lysis online. Regardless, blog threads have not established, at least not effectively, virtual *peripatoi* among which folk move and post.

A Momentary Glimpse of Reason: More than other publication venues, the blog seems for the moment. It can move from creation to publication very quickly and, in the process, elude the most obvious normalizing agencies such as editors, reviewers, editorial boards, and the like. (Less obvious censors, at least at first, are self-inflicted.) With this kind of velocity, philosophy can prove responsive in ways denied writing that only winds its way toward addressees. *It's Her Factory* is a blog by Robin James. Because the field is so new, I cannot term it exemplary in either an inductive or normative sense. I offer it simply on the terms of its merits, which include vibrancy of thought and a clear proximity to other examples of philosophical writing—it is analytically acute, normatively committed, and thinks with examples in rich ways. But it is unlike the usual professional fare, and different, too, than the essay and aphorism, two alternative genres whose powers I've elaborated. It thus marks an emergent and concrete possibility for philosophy.

James's postings have a quality of promptness (which carries within it a kind of responsiveness). The semantics are conversational (though the style far from loose) and that contributes to an overall character of living address. But also, the entries seem to catch thoughts as they grip their author. One entry, from March 26, 2015, responds to an interview that also appeared that month (which James links). More particularly, it tracks tropes of race and gender in Jonathan Schecter's discussion with celebrity DJ, Diplo. James finds—and the freshness of that finding is apparent in the blog—how an apparent virtue of genre blurring and bending conducts racist, masculinist, and even neoliberal ego ideals. But the entry doesn't rest with that assessment. In its final paragraph, the blog opens the micro moment of the interview into a possible macro moment. "What I'm interested in is this," James writes. "The post-genre aesthetic that Diplo expresses in this interview is not his alone— it's a broader trend, not just in music or in art, but in how we understand and handle difference" (2015). First, I don't think one could make such a move in philosophy's prototypical print media. By the time the paper text appeared, the micro moment would have already had its moment, for author and addressee. Second, I doubt a professional publication would allow an article to close with the series of questions that close this entry in particular, even if they were stated as clearly and insightfully as they are in "Post-Genre Aesthetics, Race, and Gender."

As with any concrete social analysis, James generalizes from an example to a larger, social dynamic, but in her blog, she allows that generalization to consummate in an appropriate rhetorical operation—questions, which the micro moment generated. I say "appropriate" because the micro moment is anecdotal with regard to claims about the macro moment, and the epistemic burden of the latter should be borne in plain sight. Moreover, by leaving her analysis with such questions, she hands them off to her readers, thus provoking them, moving from her own investigation into a larger, intersubjective field of possible replies. And that brings an experimental tone to *It's Her Factory*—this is thought underway and on the way to somewhere (and someone) else, which may be all that a thought, equal to its moment, offers.

The Lesson of More: Ease of publication and the absence of scholarly review can lure online authors into blather. And most blogs—philosophical or otherwise—show little regard for what a rhetorical whole can affect and exemplify. *It's Her Factory* appreciates the value of economical writing—a particularly long analysis, for example, is extended across three entries while several others are brief, running as long as the thought they conduct. *It's her Factory*, thanks to its recurring topoi, is also something of a whole, and in a way that evidences another possibility for philosophical writing. As the entries accumulate they establish a sensibility that underwrites each entry, as is evident in several entries from 2015 that initially seem to abandon the tasks of philosophy. Following the lead of fellow blogger, Leigh Johnson, James embarks on a thirty-day song challenge in which she thinks through songs relative to occasions, changing tastes, and so forth. Though principally an exercise for James, the publication of each reflection also prods the reader into similar exercises, for example, What song do you want played at your wedding? Or, What song did you used to love but now hate? It's a fun exercise, and it creates something like an autobiographical playlist. But given the whole of *It's her Factory*, each subject—and its accompaniment—is brought before the questions and analyses ventured elsewhere. Paths of life that might otherwise elude philosophy are thereby subjected to its scrutiny—weddings, wedding songs, one's changing tastes—and that seems like a genuine (and deft) achievement for those aspiring to shoot the gulf between academia and the range of real worlds that lie outside its borders (porous as they are).

Taking Stances

After Novalis: Philosophy sickens when it's too at home.

Questioning Publication: Introducing a series of texts (he says: "the critique, the essay—call it provisionally what you will"), Lukács labors to recount his efforts in a piece titled "On the Essence and Form of the Essay" (2010, 17). It interests on several fronts, including its relation to the other texts in *Soul and Form.* (Is it akin to them, just another in the series, or something quite different?) In the context of deliberate writing, its general question is generative. "What *is* an essay? What is its intended form of expression, and what are the ways and means whereby this expression is accomplished?" (Lukács 2010, 17).[59]

In Lukács's hands, "essay" is a slippery term. It seems to refer, at least principally, to the texts that follow "On the Essence and Form of the Essay" in *Soul and Form*—readings of Rudolf Kassner, Kierkegaard, Novalis, and so on. But these studies are not essays in any paradigmatic way. Their subject is literature, not primarily their author, as with Montaigne's *Essais.* Also, they do not address universal topics along the lines of Bacon's ventures. Nor does Lukács braid these two founding efforts in the manner of Emerson's *Essays,* with the exception of "On the Essence and Form of the Essay," which commences with "My friend!" and is addressed to fellow Hungarian, Leo Popper (1886–1911).[60] Instead, he offers critical encounters with literary texts, which renders *Soul and Form* quite different than what one finds in the genre's paradigmatic proponents. But then, Lukács's studies do not offer historical (or psychological) explanations that track the origins of literary texts. They are odd, therefore, even relative to the current explanatory efforts of literary criticism. *Soul and Form* has a character of its own.

When Lukács asks, "What is an essay?" he reflects less on a traditional literary form than an emergent one. His readings aim to capture and engage phenomena that are affectively sensed within the play of a literary text but which lack designators (images, symbols, etc.) of their own. Lukács terms this emergent, elusive phenomenon "soul," a kind of existential ground principle, operative as a longing, which Lukács glosses with terms like "standpoint" or "worldview," though more to describe its function than its character, which remains literary.

The ambition and novelty of Lukács's investigations prompt him to set them somewhere outside *Wissenschaft*—a state to which literary studies might aspire as *Literaturwissenschaft*, taking "science" to involve the principled, systematic study of literary texts according to determinate judgments. It also prompts him to reflect on the proximity of his texts to art, a matter he never quite resolves in "On the Essence and Form of the Essay." Yes, literary critical essays are modeled after art, and modern art at that: "The essay has to create from within itself all the preconditions for the effectiveness and validity of its vision" (Lukács 2010, 27). And Lukács's efforts lie closer to art than science since the latter proves itself without much thought for form. But whereas artworks direct themselves toward life in order to order experience, the literary-critical essay attends to how artworks engage life in an effort to order it. Or, in Lukács's terms, literary essays concern how soul orients even as it disappears behind the form that literary works employ in addressing life experiences, say, within the social-psychological struggles of a novel's chief protagonist, to recall the developments of Lukács's 1916 essay *The Theory of the Novel*. (He terms that study a venture or *Versuch*, one meaning of the English verb "essay.") In Lukács's hands, therefore, the essay requires a form for the interplay of soul and form in a confrontation with life—an Apollonian mask for a crash of Dionysian and Apollonian currents. It may do art one better, therefore, and in an almost Hegelian manner, driving it toward greater self-consciousness.

The matter does not end here, however—the essay does not merely mirror. In acquiring a form of its own, the literary-critical essay also "becomes a worldview, a standpoint, a *Stellungsnahme* vis-à-vis the life from which it sprang: a possibility of reshaping it, of creating it anew. The critic's moment of destiny, therefore, is that moment at which things [given in life experiences] become forms—the moment when all feelings and experiences on the near or far side of form receive form, are melted down and condensed into form. It is the mystical moment of union between the outer and the inner, between soul and form" (Lukács 2010, 23). According to Lukács, a certain kind of human responsiveness and desire is thus embodied and exemplified in the form of the essay and delivered as a possibility.

Pulling up Stakes in the Essay: The metaphysics of Lukács's "essay" is intricate and dense. Soul, form, their mystical union, things, feelings, experiences, and judgments—I will neither settle this field nor trudge through its debts to Kant, Schopenhauer, and Nietzsche or its anticipations of Lukács's own turn to dialectics. And while Lukács's language is intricate, I deliberately will ignore most of what these choices carry. Not that these matters are uninteresting. But they concern Lukács—his ambitions, perplexity, and moment— more than an emergent possibility for us, and I think the latter will come into sharper relief if we risk a more general inheritance.[61]

"On the Essence and Form of the Essay" does more than conceptualize Lukács's own literary critical studies. It also invokes other texts that expand "essay" beyond Lukács's particular efforts and beyond the essay tradition as usually conceived. "I speak, of course, of Plato," Lukács writes, "the greatest essayist who ever lived or wrote, the one who wrested everything from life as it unfolded" (2010, 29). Lukács treats the essay as something like a transhistorical (if evolving) form, one that exceeds the confines of genre, and one that need not limit itself to literary-critical studies of soul and form. "Fortunately for us," he claims, "the modern essay does not always have to speak of books or poets" (2010, 31). And this opens a corridor toward philosophical writing, which can speak of books or poets but which bristles when forced to do only that. The desire not only concerns something like a birthright to address any subject matter but, also, the expectation that such an address will result in some kind of validity claim—*X* is insightful, true, violent, edifying, good, phallogocentric, prudent, right, evil, liberating, beautiful, and so on. But as the semantics of "essay" expands in my proposed inheritance, remember that the stakes are more deeply bound to the "*Stellungsnahme* vis-à-vis the life from which it sprang" and what that enables, namely, "a possibility of reshaping it, of creating it anew" (Lukács 2010, 23).

Talk Talk: Among the terms used by Lukács to recount the form of the essay, *Stellungsnahme* (unlike "standpoint" and "worldview") is the oddest. And while we might read the odd from the familiar, in this case, there is more to be had if we drive in reverse. A *Stellungsnahme* is a statement or a position, and *Stellung nehmen* means "to comment." The term underscores its own activity, therefore, which is precisely what "standpoint" and "worldview," as stand-ins for consciousness, no longer do (if they ever did). One has one's worldview, come what may. And if there are several worldviews, we may find ourselves at an epistemic endgame among monads with soundproof bay windows. Similarly, one speaks from one's standpoint—it names a site of inception with regard to speech and writing (as opposed to a project underway therein). I have mine. You have yours. But the *nehmen* in *Stellungsnahme* announces the taking underway, which, in turn, comments on and thus is responsive to whatever has already occurred. The position being taken is therefore an emergent one in a play already staged. In this sense, "form" is not a preexistent pattern like a genre but something at stake in its own responsive enactment, much like "philosophy," which also means that form cannot stand in simple opposition to content. The sense of "form" in play—its bearings if you will—is at stake in all textual operations, including its purposiveness, which Lukács codes in terms of longing, *Sehnsucht*, recalling German idealism's fascination with the erotics of reflection, its desires, even drives.

Lukács imagines that the essay apprehends, in order to comment on, life becoming form in response to extant, semiotic events. As noted, the sign in question need not be a play or poem—though it might. Ordinary language suffices—the promise, for example—as does the task of definition in its various occasions, say, Socrates and Euthyphro addressing piety in the shadow of the Athenian court. A scientific claim might come into question, though not principally in relation to its object. The concern is rather the full form of a predictive proposition. Is Horkheimer right to insist that it cannot be captured in the head of the savant, even if we tether it to an object through something like intentionality? Regardless, the trick is to not lose the responsive character of the phenomenon: human meanings in the upsurge of life, life in the grip of human meanings, writing that moves in the difference between the world we think and that with which we interact, wherever we go.[62]

A Gothic Romance: The wish to be at home everywhere, at once? Paranoia in reverse; and creepier.

Catch Me If We Can: It is at this point that I wish to bracket as much of Lukács's metaphysics as possible in order to preserve a more general scene— what we might regard as phenomenological (in Hegel's sense), and with regard to extant, semiotic patterns. The Hegelian angle is illuminating insofar as the essay, as Lukács has it, moves behind the back of a given semiotic event and tries to grasp its emergence in (and as a) response. And because it does so in order to reopen the possibility of proceeding differently, even in acceptance, the essay aspires to a kind of criticism of a given response, taking its subject as a possible pattern, say, the institution of a promise in order to better secure a future or the venture of a Platonist definition in order to insure that we'll know the good when we see it. In other words, the essay, as Lukács conceives of it (maybe less than more), affects what Dewey terms "criticism of criticism."[63]

Dewey denies that criticism is a "matter of formal treatises, published articles, or taking up important matters for consideration in a serious way." Instead, criticism "occurs whenever a moment is devoted to looking to see what sort of value is present; whenever instead of accepting a value-object wholeheartedly, being rapt by it, we raise even a shadow of a question about its worth, or modify our sense of it by even a passing estimate of its probable future." Criticism of criticism is thus a second-order reflection on extant ways of assessing issues of significance, what Dewey terms, awkwardly, "value-objects" (1981, 299).

By resisting the desire for a Platonist definition of the good, Aristotle offers, in a general way, a criticism of criticism. Rather than contesting a given definition in order to supply his own, definition itself becomes the issue, and in the context of the good life. Are such definitions likely to lead to excellence/virtue? Similarly, Dewey does not try to find new criteria to render inquiry certain but interrogates the quest for certainty and the kind of relation to self and world, that is, life, that it establishes (or conducts).

As I read Lukács, the essay is the consummate form for criticism of criticism. It confronts any and all of the ways in which we, through soul-inflected forms, address life. And by rendering them explicit, it presents them as possibilities, which prepares them for transformation (which can include renewal). Not that this renders Lukács a "pragmatist." I have no interest in the label, here or elsewhere, even if, through *pragma* back to *prasso*, one ties it to senses of "to pass over, practice, achieve." Like "postmodern," "pragmatist" currently says too much and too little. Whether embraced or assigned, it seems to demarcate schools averse to graduating students. (Such terms are more at home in polemics and manifestos.) Moreover, a good deal hinges on how one resolves disputes over the value of the "value object," and thus an alignment of Lukács and Dewey (and Hegel for that matter) leaves so much in the air that it is too soon to order school colors.

Staged Options: According to Aristotle, a tragedy presents, mimetically, an action (or two), say, Antigone's defiant piety contrasted with Creon's civic loyalty. The claim is particularly interesting given that mimesis in this sense does not unfold along the lines of a painting—the drama does not look like a single action (or two). Too much transpires on stage for that to be the case. Rather, an image of an action and the life it conducts—here ruin—arises over the course of the play through the interaction of the actors, chorus, masks, and stage relative to particular events like the fall of Oedipus and Poly-neices's attempt to take the throne from Eteocles.

In tragedy, Aristotle finds a rhetorical whole that functions as an image. Greater than the sum of its parts, it conveys a subject matter that is also more than the sum of its parts. So, too, the essay, I think (and most likely all philo-sophical writing). But without the conventions of drama, texts like the essay, the professional article, and the treatise exemplify rather than depict their bearing. (The dialogue would be closer to tragedy in this regard.) In condens-ing into a *Stellungnahme*, the essay condenses into *a* way of inhabiting life, what we might call its "positioning," if we wish to translate *Stellungnahme*. It comes to stand as a Socrates in the scenes through which it circulates, and like Socrates in the Platonic dialogues, it images philosophy, though it would be more precise to say that the dialogue, in its heteroglossia, carries the show through whatever it presents, and in the fact that, as a venture, it was elected to present all to which it aspires.

"Human character evermore publishes itself," Emerson writes. "The most fugitive deed and word, the mere air of doing a thing, the intimated purpose, expresses character. If you act, you show character; if you sit still, if you sleep, you show it" (1996, 318). So, too, our texts, which marks yet another pos-sibility for deliberate writing. Philosophical texts, through the interactions of their genre(s) and logical-rhetorical operations, present a general charac-ter. As it conducts thought, addresses interlocutors, and engages situations, philosophical writing, through exemplification, offers a way of inhabiting history, a particular way of being. "The essay is a court," Lukács writes, *ein Gericht*, a seat of judgment (thus, more than a judgment, as Anna Bostock's translation suggests). He continues: "But the essential, the value-determining thing about it is not the judgment [*Urteil*] (as with the system) but the pro-cess of passing judgment [*Richten*]" (2010, 34). To the degree the analogy with classical tragedy holds—at least as interpreted by Aristotle—this process of judging is the action imaged in philosophical writing. In how it quotes, in whether (and how) it is ironic, in its use or avoidance of polemic, in its rela-tion to genre, in its use and/or avoidance of basic forms of inference, in the care it shows with regard to the scope and intensity of its claims, in its feel for the history of its language, in its stances toward its many addressees and the situations in which they meet, in and across these occurrences, philosophi-cal writing shows philosophy at work. But not simply relative to some *eidos*, which would render the matter one of content alone, and our concern taxo-nomic. Rather, philosophical texts exemplify how philosophy inhabits the world that each of its elements bears—language, intersubjectivity, material conditions, and so forth—and offers the result to its addressees.

Character Studies

To Have or to Be? Beauvoir scripted numerous characters, including those who exist in the ambiguous currents of the human condition: the sub-man, the serious man, the passionate man, the nihilist, the adventurer, and so on. As I read *Ethics of Ambiguity*, each revolves around a particular bearing, and in the fullest sense of that word: carrying and enduring (or not) one's thrownness with a certain manner, and in particular directions, which gives birth to certain futures rather than others. So, too, one's writing.

Who Walks the Line? The most famous concept in *The Souls of Black Folk* concerns a "peculiar sensation, this double-consciousness, this sense of always looking at one's self through the eyes of others, of measuring one's soul by the tape of a world that looks on in amused contempt" (DuBois 2007, 3). But is this how *Souls* presents itself? Does it simply or even primarily exemplify a double consciousness? DuBois sets Booker T. Washington within a double consciousness, terming him the "leader not of one race but of two,—compromiser between the South, the North, and the Negro" (2007, 25). The charge is clear: Washington internalizes too much of what the white majority interjects into his ambition, both for himself and black folk in general.

But *Souls* seems to operate with a far more dynamic and multifaceted "consciousness." It gives itself over to various, distinct modes of reflection and presentation. Historical inquiry orients "Of the Dawn of Freedom," which recounts the history of the Freedmen's Bureau. Social theory propels in "Of the Sons of Man," which approaches "race contact" along a "few main lines of action and communication," such as geography, exchange relations, political relations, intellectual relations in civic-social settings, not including religion, which DuBois accords its own category. Both analyses exemplify an effort to render conspicuous how *the color line* has and continues to operate with a kind of social-objectivity. *Souls* does not limit itself to social objectivities, however. It also works its way into social-psychological sites where the color line operates, employing autobiography in "Of the Passing of the First-Born," historical fiction in "Of Alexander Crummell," fiction in "Of the Coming of John," and musicology in "The Sorrow Songs," tracking how the color line affects lives that must contend (or not) with its exclusions and refractions. *Souls* exemplifies, therefore, a polyphonic approach to language and discourse. Given the demands of its object (which includes its own latent genius), it assumes explanatory, diagnostic, rebellious, expressive, and programmatic tasks, and their interaction drives the whole address in the polyphonic company of the sorrow songs, that "music of an unhappy people, of the children of disappointment; they tell of death and suffering and unvoiced longing toward a truer world, of misty wanderings and hidden ways" (DuBois 2007, 123).

Epistemic fidelity is not DuBois's principal goal, however. He names the color line to contest and redress white supremacy, and so *Souls* offers, by way of performance, a criticism of criticisms that have hardened into pernicious habits. Its constellational discursivity thus exemplifies more than a kind of multidisciplinarity. Above all, it exemplifies the kind of bearing that DuBois feared black folk would lose if they succumbed to Washington's "triumphant commercialism." "We are training not isolated men but a living group of men,—nay, a group within a group," writes DuBois, thinking of Negro education. "And the final product of our training must be neither psychologist nor a brickmason, but a man" (2007, 42). Thought in terms of its moment, then, *Souls* exemplifies such a man at work—better yet, such a human being. Positioning itself in history, attentive to the social-psychological complexity of everything to which it must prove equal, *Souls* moves from a central, orienting term into the irreducible sites of its appearance, enlarging itself along the way, without recuperating each venture into a fixed identity. Working on and in the conduct of life—the burden of culture—it exposes in order to weaken the current of white supremacy and offers itself as proof for the claim that "we the darker ones come even now not altogether empty handed" (2007, 7).[64]

Dear Moralist: Love your neighbor as yourself? Spare me. Your neighbor.

Feedback for Reformers: Happily, some books make me feel worse about who I am. Others leave me feeling better about who I might yet be. Too many make me feel relieved about what I have not yet become.

Who Am I to You? Alongside whatever it says, a philosophical text announces, *here I am*, though not to the Other that Levinas tries to write into the very fabric of human being in the world. As Cavell suggests: "As representatives, we are educations for one another" (1990, 31). In its offers, writing's "other" is a secret addressee, its intimacy solicitous of a reading that is willing to be read in turn. Philosophy thus presumes that our linguistic resources do not reduce to a killing field for alterity. In fact, philosophical writing offers itself to another as a possible future. That which a text exemplifies might be borne in turn, or a reader might welcome the terms set forth, enact them in the space thereby cleared and preserved. But this requires trust, which something like voice might nurture. (And if not voice, what?) Moreover, it requires that one believe that another might hold the key to whoever one might become. Do we despair of this, except in sites of (presumably) shared identities? Am I not DuBois's secret addressee? Is that not me returning from his pages, and not just in differences those pages articulate and which I thereby come to (or begin to) acknowledge, reforming what keeps me from myself? Is that not also some me to be in the example? Not that one could know this ahead of time, say, through a concept of "humanity." But could one know ahead of time that such a turn of events (and persons) were impossible? The humanity exemplified by *Souls* reduces itself to neither an unconditioned subject nor a mere function of sociohistorical forces and in doing so it reaches toward an open readership. When DuBois recounts the death of his son, Burghardt Gomer, the narrative's frank despair offers a site of braided com-miseration for those forced to "grow choked and deformed with the Veil" (2007, 102). Is this not our tragedy? And the task thereby set, what *Souls* terms (and enacts as) "co-work in the kingdom of culture," is it not also mine, and in ways no one can assume for me? Must I not aspire to a kind of polyphony? Near its close, *Souls* asks: "Would America have been America without her Negro people?" (2007, 128). "No," begins a reply, followed by the effort to keep proving it, and in surprising ways.

Of the Moment: In his 1928 review of *One-Way-Street*, Ernst Bloch conceives of Benjamin's text as a cabaret. While apt in a general way, it seems to miss what the book offers when taken as a whole. German cabarets offered *Kleinkunst*, a mixture of small forms such as songs, one-act plays, jokes, and so on, and in a general way, *One-Way Street* offers a mix of small forms. Cabarets also sought to bridge the gap between elite and popular culture, and Benjamin's text, as "Filling Station" makes plain, has similar designs. But cabarets thrived on satirical exposures of hypocrisy, and *One-Way Street* offers something quite different from ironic moralism (and also something less self-possessed). Moreover, cabarets were held together by a *conférencier*, a master of ceremonies whose wit and charm kept the show rolling. But this is precisely what *One-Way Street* eschews, forcing its reader to find his or her way through its suggestions, arguments, observations, and images. Its urbanity is thus misconstrued when aligned with cabaret culture.[65] Rather, it images what it hopes is an emergent phenomenon, namely, a transformative way of inhabiting its historical present, a way that eschews universality in favor of inconspicuous, momentary gestures that seek links with reconstructive praxis.

The "book owes a lot to Paris," Benjamin writes, "being my first attempt to come to terms with this city" (1994, 25). In fact, the original cover, designed by Sascha Stone (1895–1940), focuses the reader with three street signs reading "*Einbahnstraße.*" The signs direct one to turn right along a crowded city street that runs ahead of any who would enter the book head on.

Leaving the main thoroughfare behind, the work orients without the self-legitimating gestures of systematic writing; for example, introducing settled truths, presenting axioms, or situating leading questions and claims within a current or long-standing literature. Nor does *One-Way Street* organize itself polemically, which uses the limits of its rivals to substantiate its bearings, thereby marking the political with an "us and them." The work is thus modern in an almost literal sense—it finds and elaborates its essence in the just-now of its occurrence. Not entirely. (How could it?) But what is imaged in *One-Way Street* asks to be taken on its own terms.

One-Way Street presents the reader with multiple reflective analyses, preconscious responses, and whatever unconscious forces might be objectified in dreams. It thus embodies a kind of self-regard that does not remain at the level of "convictions," what we might now term "validity claims" and whatever reasons can be employed on their behalf. Instead, it manifests a kind of self-relation wherein thought can unfold beyond the checks and balances of those conventions and possibly open a space for a renewed present. Such events are not left to speak for themselves, however. "Nothing is poorer than a truth expressed as it was thought," Benjamin declares. "Committed to writing in such a way, it is not even a bad photograph" (1996, 480). The task or activity on display is thus one of wringing objectivity out of one's subjectivity. Longings are presented as longings, which neither denies their persistence nor rationalizes them as instances of invisibly handed cunning. Dreams are set forth in a manner that preserves, even intensifies, their suggestiveness, thus underscoring how much of what befalls us remains to be interpreted. Basic commitments, pro and con, are offered aphoristically, and appropriately so, given that they orient thought rather than mark its logical terminus.

Thought unfolds in *One-Way Street* moment by moment, some brief, some extended, each haunted, in part, by what a moment might erase.

Doing Philosophy: Adorno says that *One-Way Street* earns its insights because it succumbs to its object, although, he adds, "to the point of literal extinction [*Auslöschung*] of the self" (1992, 327). I think the former observation is right, but the latter, and not just in its fierce diction (one could replace "extinction" with "snuffing out"), loses the point. In *One-Way Street*, the self unfolds in even as the performance of self-objectification, and thus it embodies what Adorno himself later valorizes in *Negative Dialectics*: "In stark contrast to the usual scientific ideal, the objectivity of dialectical cognition doesn't need less but more from the subject" (1973, 50; my translation). Yes, the prose is fearless and concentrated, and each entry follows the path of its subject matter, terminating when that relation ends. (Each entry is thus something of a one-way street.) But these characteristics, bound between two covers, should be taken as traces of a kind of (possibly) exemplary character, not of its complete self-erasure.

Turning toward its readers, *One-Way Street* does not simply presume the existence of a public able to hear and work with its presentations. Its fractured address mirrors those it addresses. A reading of several entries requires genuine concentration on particular entries (even words) as well as an imaginative, synthetic movement through the whole. In a double address, *One-Way Street* thus exercises the reader in terms of the very kind of historical existence it offers, thereby venturing a performative reconstruction of what its address presumes: a historical subject capable of encountering itself and being changed by the encounter. That venture is irreducible to authorial intent, however. Rather, it moves in and between entries in a manner that can surprise author and reader alike. *One-Way Street* thus proceeds along lines that Adorno articulates in his lectures on negative dialectics: "Thinking would require more labor and effort than Hegel's suspects, since in his discussion thought extracts only that which is already a thought" (2008, 196).

Contorted Indications: One-Way Street offers various directives, including: "There is no intact will without exact pictorial imagination" (1996, 446). The suggestion is that agents (singular and plural), which alternate between thought and action in an effort to prove equal to the moment, need concretized images of its situation. And Benjamin is insistent that the issue is principally the present. He derides fortune-tellers in order to valorize a *Geistesgegenwart*, which E. F. N. Jephcott ably translates as "presence of mind." In fact, Benjamin describes transforming a "threatening future" into a "fulfilled

now" as a "Werk leibhafter Geistesgegenwart," as "the work of a corporeally present mind" (taking *Leib* to say something more than "body," or *Kör-
per*). The claim is that the inertia of convictions that predict the future are
not equal to a moment whose contours are better apprehended in a startling
present caught in an exact, pictorial imagination—that is, a present objectified like facades and cellars, windowsills and shop fronts along a one-way
street.

Whereas *Souls* images an almost heroic humanity in the face of white supremacy (heroic in part because its humanity is evolving), the character of
One-Way Street positions itself in terms of a corporeally present mind operative through an exact, pictorial imagination. That is what it is able to muster.

According to Gerhard Richter, who moves between *One-Way Street* and
The Arcades Project, Benjamin's writings insistently preserve the "vertiginous
possibilities of referential aberration," a phrase Richter inherits from Paul de
Man even as he purports to amend it. Richter claims: "For Benjamin, then,
truth, at least the truth that is expressed in textual phenomena such as writing
and images, can only become what it is as an aberration from what presents
itself" (2006, 154). To my ear, Richter claims that figural writing preserves
truth only to the extent that it marks itself as an aberration, thus leaving its
referent, even in self-referential moments, clearly marked as exceeding what
the writing says of it.

A triadic feel for writing, wherein a speaker addresses another in a context directly or indirectly referenced, may wonder whether reference, simply
in referring, marks its distance or difference from what is thereby indicated.
The aberration is thus forgetting this, an aberration possibly preserved in
Richter's manner of redress. But the stakes are much larger for Richer, who
takes self-deconstructing referrals to initiate a politics. "The infinite deferral of a judgment as to whether these aberrations are the straight line of a
one-way street or the curvy passages of the arcades—this deferral also names
Benjamin's ethico-political hope," a "commitment that resists any premature closure of meaning and that retains its openness to a radical otherness"
(2006, 155, 156).

I pause here, and have done so for some time. It is less that Richter's analysis is mistaken than obscuring. Like the critic-philosopher Rodolphe Gasché,
I think Benjamin's analysis resists romanticism's pursuit of a wholly immanent grasp and generation of totality. And I believe that resistance orients
One-Way Street, which is why Benjamin tells Hugo Hofmannsthal that the
book's subject matter involves grasping "the actual as the reverse of the eter-
nal in history," and why he tells Max Rychner a few years later that his mate-
rialism remains theological, "namely, in accord with the Talmudic teaching

about the forty-nine levels of meaning in every passage of the Torah" (1994, 325, 372; translation of first quote modified). For Benjamin, parts indicate an interrelated whole that no part can incorporate but, qua part, must neverthe-less gesture toward—or so he suggests in his proffered clarification of objec-tive irony in German Romanticism: "The ironization of the presentational form is, as it were, the storm blast that raises the curtain on the transcen-dental order of art, disclosing this order and in it the immediate existence of the work as a mystery" (1996, 164). In other words, I think Richter is right to stress the objective irony that underwrites the presentations of *One-Way Street*, an irony that concretizes the empirical in order to intensify, in part, its self-effacement before an aspirational order toward which it gestures. *One-Way Street* opens more than a *via negativa*, however, and whatever epistemic ethos is thereby instilled. It also tries to generate an "exact pictorial imagina-tion" and diagnose how we have been deformed by history. Both moments are operative in the vivid entry "Torso" (part of a composite entry, "An-tiques"), which powerfully redirects, by overtly politicizing, the life-changing event poetized in Rilke's "Archaic Torso of Apollo": "*Torso.*—Only he who can view his own past as an abortion sprung from compulsion and need can use it to full advantage in every present. For what one has lived is at best com-parable to a beautiful statue that has had all its limbs broken off in transit, and that now yields nothing but the precious block out of which the image of one's future must be hewn" (1996, 467).

Benjamin's claim is that a sufficiently corporeal presence of mind will lead one to encounter oneself as deformed and weakened in the factual possi-bilities that compose one's personal and eco-social inheritance. One's limbs are gone, and with them, what usually passes for motility, even agency, if the latter, bound to an ablest metaphoric, is marked by the capacity to be self-moving. Now, if the goal of *One-Way Street* is to exemplify a kind of his-torical comportment, here we are told in no uncertain terms that history has deformed us and that such deformations must be felt and resisted. Moreover, if any future is to be found, it will have to be reworked, in part, from our damaged goods; that is, historical humanity is less an uncarved block than one whittled down to a nearly thinglike obstinacy.

I invoke "Torso" because its core does not revolve around the kind of self-deconstructive pathos and performance that focus Richter 's analysis. In-stead, it offers diagnoses that aim to help its readers prove equal to the mo-ment, and it does so in a rather exact manner. But given the praxical goals of *One-Way Street*—namely, to be equal to the alternating moments in which it arises—we should expect strong claims like: "And if the abolition of the bourgeoisie is not completed by an almost calculable moment in economic and technical development (a moment signaled by inflation and poison-gas warfare), all is lost" (Benjamin 1996, 470) Or, to offer an even stronger claim: in order to be equal to any moment, something more than openness to radical alterity needs to be on offer. In fact, whatever diagnoses are shared need to find traction in their historical present, and they need to be offered with the confidence that they will find traction.

Benjamin is not offering the pictorial imagination as a new form of intellectual intuition, however, as Richter rightly insists. "Technical Aid" (in a line that Richter omits, one full of Benjamin's recurring, masculinist sensuality) declares that the truth appears as a "well built" (*gesund gebaut*) concubine (*Odaliske*), "contorted" (*verstellt*) and "rattled" (*gehetzt*), "yet victorious, captivating" (1996, 480). I take the invocation of "contorted" and "rattled" to indicate that writing—the concern of the entry—does not involve transparent representations. But I do not think that Benjamin thereby undermines his sense that a certain kind of writing is able to "startle truth abruptly, at one stroke, from her self-immersion" (1996, 480). In fact, I think his thought is that such contortions allow the truth to appear in a way that more literal presentations miss, although, as we have seen, this also requires an adequate readership.

Current Will and Testament: All texts rely on assertoric content and referential concepts. *One-Way Street* is no exception: writing, inflation, "presence of mind," gifts, books, Goethe, and so on. Rather than rehearse any of Benjamin's claims in *One-Way Street*—we are no longer in Weimar Germany (I hope)—I'd rather focus on the role they play in the self-relation and intersubjective address embodied in *One-Way Street* and how that role thickens the overall *Stellungsnahme* or "positioning" of *One-Way Street*. Benjamin, like Emerson in "The American Scholar," directs our attention to the low and the common, even to the elusive (dreams, relations to animals), the anomalous (prostitutes), the inconspicuous (souvenirs, stamps), and the overlooked (the experiences of children). This renders *One-Way Street* idiosyncratic, but in a manner that reflects three, interrelated, self/world dispositions.

First, and this becomes dramatically explicit in the posthumously published theses on the philosophy of history, Benjamin's path to any whole runs through the way that whole appears in very particular parts, in phenomena that are *derivative* in a very real sense. In the language of *One-Way Street*, we could say that "the moment" to which the text and its addressees should be equal appears in concrete particulars, and to the degree that synecdoche is a genuine feature of socialization. The ephemera that draw his attention are thus openings into the larger whole he aims to unsettle, believing that reworking parts—for example, ideological slogans regarding poverty—reworks, *in part*, the whole.

Second, the marginal phenomena that lie along *One-Way Street* nevertheless reveal patterns of self/world organization; that is, they already offer objectifications of the social subject, exact images that might jar the reader into a kind of self-recognition.

Benjamin observes how giving alms to beggars manifests a mode of comportment that renders "intellect and morality, consistency and principles, miserably inadequate" (1996, 486). The point is not just that such encounters tug us toward our better selves. If we take the beggar to figure, as an exact image, a marginal event seeking our attention, such events also are loci of genuine, transformative self-encounters—a belief evidently shared by beggars (perhaps cynically), given that "no shadow of hesitation, no slightest wish or deliberation in our faces escapes their notice" (1996, 486).

A bit of strategy also leads Benjamin to fix on the seemingly marginal events of the day. Dominant symbols like flags, national monuments, and offices of state are rigorously policed by defense mechanisms that lie in wait for any who would attack them. Not so with ephemera, with what is derivative. And it is precisely because we are left unguarded in our responses to and enthusiasms for the low and common that a critic like Benjamin would focus his energies on such things. As he writes in an oft-cited line: "These are days when no one should rely unduly on his 'competence.' All the decisive blows are struck left-handed" (1996, 447).

One-Way Street offers its readers, particularly those already engaged in the transformation of social life, a way of being historical that resists and redirects the meaning and significance of dominant symbols and personal experiences. In the interaction among its entries, it also tries to stimulate the growth of those capacities required by projects of social transformation. One might say, therefore, that in a text like *One-Way Street*, the writer acts in a way that intensifies the hermeneutic activity of "active communities," thus overcoming the distinction between bourgeois intellectuals and proletarian agitators without rendering the latter thoughtless applicators of high theory. In fact, the goal is quite the opposite. The brevity of most entries allows them to be read on a bus or during a break, and their enigmatic character, particularly when read in bunches, leads them to rattle around in the brain long after the book has been set aside.

Where Do We Find Ourselves?

A Novel Situation in Common: Plato is something of an exemplar for Lukács's conception of the essay. But Plato's moment is past. "The modern essay," Lukács writes, "has lost the backdrop of life that gave Plato and the mystics their strength; nor does it any longer possess a naïve faith in the value of books and what can be said about them" (2010, 31). What was lost? Let me reply for myself (and thus to us, possibly for us), since I doubt Plato's backdrop was as integrated as Lukács supposes. (The semiotic terrain that Thucydides maps is a good deal less homogeneous than the "transcendental topography of the Greek mind" that Lukács offers in *Theory of the Novel.*)

In general, we no longer write and speak (if we or anyone ever did), with an untroubled sense that language and life occur on an ontological continuum. One can naturalize semiosis but not without losses to either its first- or second-person character, at least as many currently understand them (or understand them at all). A kind of skepticism still haunts us such that all philosophical writing moves in the gaps between sign and signified, intention and action, appearance and reality, past and future, I and me and you (and we), part and whole. Not that these gaps are wholly or even principally destructive. Philosophy seems to be born in them, emerging in and as an effort to come to terms with why they arise, what they entail, and what significance they hold for projects of knowing, the institution of positive law, human freedom and meaning—you name it. Some views try to hopelessly close these gaps (e.g., Cartesian certainty), feebly ignore them (Santayana's animal faith), or miraculously erase it (e.g., wholly externalist accounts of meaning, mind, and action). Others convert it into the basic structure of our being, for example, Dewey's transactionalism and Heidegger's fundamental ontology,

whereas Cavell writes in acknowledgment of skepticism as a recurrent possibility for beings like us, one we deny at the cost of denying ourselves.

Furthermore, and for as long as I can recall, Babel is the rule, not the exception. Our semiotic fields, within and without, are polyphonic. We write
and read amid a diversity of so-called natural languages (and their plurality
of dialects and speakers, which differ among themselves as well). The idioms of emergent systems of representation and exchange, whether in law, the
market, sacred spaces, or any number of professions, including academic
philosophy, also surround us, even drifting into so-called ordinary language.
(I think of the meme of the meme.) Philosophy thus faces the same dilemmas
that Bakhtin found facing the novel—herteroglossia, a condition intensified
by the absence (or death) of a metalanguage able to shepherd us all back (or
to) home, which, incidentally, marks the condition of the novel on Lukács
terms, "for the novel form is, like no other, an expression of this transcendental homelessness" (Bakhtin 1982; Lukács 1974, 40)

In a third twist of fate, books, whether they sell well or not, also belong to
the market, which exacts a toll on whatever can be done by way of genre and
logical-rhetorical operations on which author and reader must rely. If we add
that philosophy's "publics" are privately ordered, media ventures by some
firm or other, one can no longer proceed as if there were not a coin of the
realm. As Eddie Glaude has reminded us, echoing Dewey, a public for some
set of interlocutors (and experiences) can be eclipsed (2007).

Referential gaps, heteroglossia, the death of God, and the demands of the
market—the life that philosophy would order is a mangle. The deliberate
question is less "How far down do these influences run?" than "What should
be done when we meet them in our way?" We cannot answer except from a
turn in the conduct of life, which includes a readership that walks a circuitous
path toward every text, one that often allows them only the most oblique
approach to the kind of transparent exchange imagined by Kant when he
offered his *apologia* on behalf of the public use of reason. And while texts
like *One-Way Street* may internalize this crisis of communication and elect to
contest an unfree trade in convictions, one cannot presume that discontinuous presentations will meliorate the situation beyond providing the solace of
having refused to play along.

Writing Occasionally: It is common to hear philosophers refer to their texts
as "essays," whether in reference to a professional article, a book-length study
of a figure, or a dissertation. The part of me that thinks of Montaigne, Bacon,
and Emerson bristles when I hear "essay" bandied about in this way. But given
the scene I am recounting, contemporary philosophy is bound to the essay,

and in the following sense: "The title of every essay is preceded by invisible letters, by the words 'Thoughts occasioned by . . .'" (2010, 31—translation modified). Here the ellipses, which Lukács employs, are precise. We don't know the full occasion that informs our thought or follows from it. Philosophical writing relies on more than can be made explicit, let alone recounted whenever it ventures forth. Each . . . is a stair in a winding series whose origin and terminus elude our reflective grasp, to recall the opening of Emerson's "Experience." Philosophical writing is thus occasional in a very fundamental sense, a fact that Hegel tries to bury with a sneer toward edification in paragraph 9 of *The Phenomnology*. Philosophy thus remains up for grabs in its execution, as Lukács says regarding the modern essay (which he distinguishes from the "icy perfection of philosophy," thinking of the treatise). To be clear, the limit on which this realization turns is not some unfathomable hinge in a scheme-content distinction. The culprit, rather, is what we might term our dynamic partiality. We know enough to know that we belong to a larger, dynamic whole whose charges exceed, even as they flow through and thereby change us, recurrently.

Bear with Me: Unwilling to remain vexed, I have imagined a topography. Philosophical writing (or writing more generally) is bound to and has an impact on three relations worth distinguishing in an analytic sense, if only to render us more conscientious.

Modes of writing influence, in part, how one's thought develops, and thus one chief area of concern is *thought's self-relation*. Aphorisms require great concentration with regard to a universal topic (friendship, self-deception, vanity, the press, etc.) and concision, namely, the abandonment of justification. The essay, however, admits of expansion, although that expansion need not be systematic; that is, one's starting point need not be secured through demonstrations of its place on axiomatic grounds or within an extant literature (as it would in the treatise and professional article, respectively). Justifications may be offered, but they obviously beg questions that can only be indicated, and so the essay always has a fragmentary quality, particularly since it need not conclude with clear results. Instead, it can experiment with questions, replies, terms, and phrases, and not only end in irresolution but also draw its reader therein. Not that genre marks the only issue of concern. Translation, explicit quotation, and the employment of examples all establish conditions to which one's thought must respond. For example, thinking with a quotation, responding to its syntax and key terms, letting everything one quotes count, offers a different scene and trajectory for thought than citing schools or sketching paradigmatic commitments for views held by the likes of enemies or friends. (One might also explore what I term "thinking through examples," which exceeds the mere mention example just given in order to concretize thought, to push against the instancing tendency of discursive thought with something that moves between instance and singularity.)

Writing also adopts a stance, a posture, comports itself *toward addressees*. Dialogues presumably invite the reader into the fray, although this depends on the dialogue, both with regard to its explicit doctrinal content and with regard to the kind and depth of fray it enacts. (*The Republic* seems not only to lead one into an unresolved thematic fray regarding the nature of the soul, the proper course of education, and of course, the nature of justice but also to confront us with its own status as a "city in speech," and one with a mimetic cast no less, thus raising the question of its own *poesis*. Can we say the same about Berkeley?) In a different way, Emerson's essays offer their readers provocations aimed to jump-start trains of thought that only crescendo in the reader's self-reliant elaborations and contestations. But what about the professional article, which seems oriented toward what we might term a "contribution" to a conversation among experts? It seems to be an enlightenment genre par excellence adding to a perpetually revised encyclopedia. Regardless, note that a stance toward one's addressee is somewhat formal (the expert, the general reader, beginning students, workers of the world, etc.) as well as concrete (whoever is likely to read this given its presuppositions, vocabulary, language, medium, etc.). But again, the issue isn't just one of genre. Examples seem particularly inviting to addressees, whereas indirect citation, whether it jars or not, seems designed for an audience in the know. Irony is often celebrated in this context because it seems to nudge readers into a mode of thinking against their initial grasp of things, and one might employ it to that end, that is, pedagogically.

Thought unfolds into an address, souls conversing, but never between, or just between, you and me. *Historical situations* always stage communication. This is the moment to which Benjamin's *One-Way Street* would prove equal, one characterized, on his view, by a crisis of experience under the tyranny of convictions. Along oddly similar lines, Bacon was drawn to the aphorism because he thought its concentrated observations could break through scholastic habits of mind. (But what keeps an aphorism from becoming a slogan, particularly in age of executive summaries, which are genres of extreme self-preservation?) Of course, the matter at hand also concerns where one publishes. And at the level of component, matters like who one cites and in what way also prove germane. If the world of U.S. scholarship is white supremacist, what kind of world should one reflect in one's footnotes and bibliography? Or, should one employ footnotes at all? Will that dissuade the general reader?

But what if this aversion arises out of an anti-intellectual disposition and a transposition of the priesthood of all believers into epistemic matters that cannot be resolved by what one knows in one's heart?

I note these spheres of concern because each gathers issues facing those who wish to write deliberately. And while I find it useful to parse them in deliberation, I also think it important to bind them back together such that they announce something like a mode of historical bearing. I have committed to the term "bearing" because it gathers so many moments integral to writing: (a) a general bearing or manner—for example, ironic, experimental, or systematic; (b) the end toward which the writing bears (as one might bear north), say a post-theological culture, or, god help us, a post-secular one; (c) that which we bear when we write, as in carry, eco-social semiotic fields, such that writing is inevitably a struggle with multiple inheritances, some of which our thought (d) might not be able to bear, in the sense of endure. (I have been and to a degree remain that white supremacist citer, and a masculinist one at that.) Even in the absence of illocutionary effects, perlocutionary ones result, and thus, (e) like it or not, writing bears, like a child, futures within which it is a variable.

As I prepare to write, I think: How will my thought unfold in this genre and in these logical-rhetorical operations? What kind of relation will this establish with my addressees? And how is this likely to function in the material-semiotic of the present as well as the near and foreseeable future? And how do the likely consequences at each turn, to the degree I can fathom them, relate to the ends I seek? And then, more generally, how am I, here and now—this moment in multiple we's—inhabiting history, conducting a world I aim to transform? Praxis is always, in part, the creation of the world to come. What and who would I and you, and so we, like to meet?

Acknowledgments

Gratitude should flow with joy. It is a boon to need and rely in a life of replies.

Richard Lee and Michael Sullivan read a nearly final draft. I benefited from their suggestions and needed their reassurance that this was not sheer folly. (They let me know I could ditch the "sheer.") My wife, Hilary Hart, brings me genuine happiness, and that has not left my voice unchanged.

The American Philosophical Forum allows presentations that philosophize in unusual ways. I never would have written this book if that organization had never existed. Thanks to John Stuhr, its organizer, and all who make it such a rich venue, particularly Vincent Colapietro, Megan Craig, Bob Innis, Eduardo Mendieta, and Emily Zakin.

The *Journal of Speculative Philosophy* published two papers venturing thoughts recurring here: "Writing as Praxis" and "Giving Voice to Philosophy." Each has been reworked and dispersed, but I thank that journal for its support and the permission to rework what they initially published.

Some of the aphorisms included here also appeared in a short collection of aphorisms titled "Footholds: An Annual Philosophy," though most have been modified to some extent. The set was published in *Minima: A Journal of Intellectual Micro-Genres*, edited by Mikhail Epstein. That initial support was and remains much appreciated, as was the collegiality of Walt Reed and Marshall Duke, who, shortly after my arrival at Emory, invited me to participate in a group of scholars thinking about genre and writing.

These essays and experiments notwithstanding, the extended project grew out of an essay on Benjamin's *One-Way Street*: "Being Equal to the Moment: Form as Historical Praxis." When *Philosophy and Literature* elected to publish it (then edited by Gary Hagberg), I thought "just maybe." It, too, has been reworked and dispersed.

Tony Leyh and Ben Davis helped me assemble the bibliography and index. Thanks to both. Thanks also to my graduate seminar on writing and form in philosophy. They were game to read everything from Evagrius to Benjamin. Jessica Locke took the bait and her dissertation on the Lojong Tradition in Tibetan Buddhism was an inducement to keep pursuing my project, as was Ellie Anderson's paper on clarity.

Various colleagues were vital interlocutors along the way. Andrew Mitchell generously listened to initial descriptions and helped me find my way. Lynne Huffer and Don Verene were sincerely helpful with irony. Several conversations with Fred Marcus (Hegel, Wittgenstein, Kant, Thoreau) also gave me food for thought. Marta Jimenez, Rob Metcalf, Jeremy Bell, and Chris Long helped me navigate Greek texts as well as avoid overt pratfalls. (I hope.) Ongoing conversations with Todd Cronan, Kevin Karnes, Andrew Mitchell, and Carla Oeler were an education. Carla was a particularly wonderful interlocutor as we worked through Lukács and Bahktin on the novel. Finally, an invite from Emory's Institute for the Liberal Arts to discuss the project over lunch led me to articulate the whole that was taking shape. Angelika Bammer, thank you for that opportunity, and thanks to my colleague, Tom Flynn, for attending.

A year at Emory's Fox Center for Humanistic Inquiry allowed me to finish this project free from the unwelcome hassles of the academic year. (Some of those hassles are more than welcome, but I was mostly free of those as well.) Thanks to those who run the center (Tina, Keith, Collette, and Amy) as well as to my fellow Fellows.

Emory's College of Arts and Science generously supported this project with research funds that allowed me to hire Tony and Ben and chase down books as the project grew. Subvention funds from the college as well as from the Laney Graduate School have also underwritten the publication of this book in order to make it more affordable. Thank you, Carla Freeman and Rosemary Hynes as well Michael Elliott and Lisa Tedesco.

Notes

1. Amélie Oskenberg Rorty has made a similar set of observations, which I found through Eduardo Mendieta's discussion of autobiography and diaries (Rorty 1998; Mendieta 2014a).

2. "Style" receives broad and diverse treatment in *The Concept of Style*, edited by Berel Lang. As Lang notes in the postface to a second, enlarged edition, there not only is a diverse history of styles, but that concept also has a diverse history, which is one of the reasons I have elected to avoid it. ([1979] 1987) That said, I agree with Lang's argument in *The Anatomy of Philosophical Style* that matters of genre and what I term logical-rhetorical operations (instead of "style," which is Lang's term), are not incidental to philosophical writing, an argument also forwarded by Lawrence M. Hinman (Lang 1990; Hinman 1980). The spirit of what follows is thus akin to Lang's analyses even as it avoids one chief letter.

3. In "Reception and Impact: The First Decade of Nietzsche in Germany," Adrian Del Caro reports that Nietzsche was often damned by praise for his style, which led him to be classified as a poet rather than a philosopher, for example, by Joseph Diner and Johannes Schlaf (Del Caro 1982, 40–41). Based on the material that Del Caro reviews, I would add that those who championed Nietzsche's "philosophy" often did so at the expense of his writing, as if it were, almost literally, an afterthought.

4. This view has been ventured by many in many ways, but I initially found my way to it in conversation with Peter Warnek and Chris Long, though also Jill Gordon, whom I met at a conference on philosophy and literature, kindly convened by the faculty at Cal State Fullerton. Each has developed their reading in their own ways, and to our benefit. See Gordon (1999); Warnek (2005); Long (2014).

5. Note that the commitments behind particular dialogues cover many fields of philosophy, including ethics (toward what do dialogues aim?) and philosophical psychology (what capacities are activated by dialogical exchanges?), even ontology, as Sean Kirkland has argued (2012).

6. This is not the place to explore Nietzsche's novel and provocative thoughts on truth. I thus rely on a gloss that captures, I think, the phenomenological feel of the movement from novelty to truth—from what is surprising toward what one cannot imagine being otherwise—and I take that feel to be what Nietzsche has in mind in the final section of *Beyond Good and Evil*.

7. My path to this position was cleared in part by exchanges with Marta Jimenez, Christopher

Long, and Robert Metcalf. Thank you to each and for more various conversations regarding the
Greek texts I discuss.

8. My summary relies on passages in *Nicomachean Ethics* 4.4, 1040a, *Metaphysics* 1.1, 981b,
and 7.7, 1032b. I have also relied on Joseph Dunne's *Back to the Rough Ground* (Dunne 1993) and
benefited from the thoughts of my colleague, Marta Jimenez.

9. The following discussion recasts remarks from "The Nature of Aims," chap. 19 of *Human
Nature and Conduct* (Dewey 1983, 154–63).

10. This point was made independently at a talk that Kathryn Gines delivered at Emory
University and in conversation by Tommy Curry. To my knowledge, Gines has not yet made the
point in print, whereas it will appear in a forthcoming book chapter of Curry's: "Towards a Black
Criticus: Culturalogics, Epistemic Schemas, and the Activity of Archive in Black Philosophy."

11. Locke is also writing in the context of colonial war and expansion, including the dispossession of native lands in North America. In "Logics of Violence and Vulnerability," a manuscript still in preparation (consulted September 20, 2017), Falguni Sheth argues that Locke's
conceptions of property and theft are driven in part by his need to protect colonial govern-
ments from the charge that they were unduly imposing state power over sovereign indigenous
populations.

12. In the passage I cited earlier, Bacon accentuates the genre's negative force: "Discourse
of illustration is cut off; recitals of example are cut off; discourse of connexion and order is cut
off; descriptions of examples are cut off" (1868, 172). Somewhat naively, he seems to think that
these excisions only leave room for "some good quantity of observation," which strikes those
whose understanding is "sound and grounded" (1868, 172). I find this naive because the topics
themselves and the space allotted institute inevitable partialities. In other words, I think it a
mistake to look past the ways in which the topical nature and brevity of the aphorism positively
directs thought.

13. Even among the aphorisms attributed to Hippocrates, one finds terms combining in
suggestive ways, for example: "Desperate cases need the most desperate remedies" (1950, 207).
While these early aphorisms—the collection gives us the term—seem principally concerned
with preserving medical information in a memorable manner, thinking's self-relation is nevertheless being cast in a determinate manner.

14. For an instructive, learned, and philosophically rich reading of Montaigne's engagement
with and transformations of Aristotelian philosophy, see Ann Hartle's *Montaigne and the Origins of Modern Philosophy* (2013) as well as *Michel de Montaigne: Accidental Philosopher* (2007).

15. These meanings remain current from Webster's 1828 edition into the current, 11th edition. The *Oxford English Dictionary* reports a 1484 instance in which a squire is said to essay
(as in "test the worthiness of") his wife, as well as a 1593 instance in which the prodigal son of
Christian scripture is said to "essay the world," which I take to mean, test the value of what it
has to offer.

16. Benjamin's prose lies in wait for the *Müßiggänger*, the idler, though he takes the notion
of idleness or indolence in a less pejorative manner than does Emerson, I think, since Benjamin fears the industrious are more prone to cling to and thus protect their convictions. And
this leads one to wonder how the idle reader of *One-Way Street* relates to and contrasts with
the flaneur, the not-quite-idle stroller among the Paris arcades, who moves "ostensibly to look
around, but in truth to find a buyer" (Benjamin 1999, 10). And then it is difficult to not also
think of the leisure that purportedly enables philosophy, thus giving us yet another scene in
which quotation, as an act of thought, might unfold. But so many redirections threaten to lead

me too far astray, and so I will leave it at that, but not before noting what even an endnote can do for thinking.

17. I would distinguish quotation in order to think with an author from (a) quotation as ornament, where we say what we mean and then have the words of another simply echo the thought—thereby setting ourselves in good company—and (b) quotation as substitute thinking, where we simply let the quoted words stand for the thought we wish to make. For an elegantly written, learned, and insightful study of the use of quotes, quotation anthologies, and the historical travails of oft-quoted material, see Morson (2011).

18. Lyotard announces this in his introduction (1984, xxv).

19. It is worth noting that Lyotard's report is also an intervention. Qua philosophy, which Lyotard aligns with the question, *The Postmodern Condition* interrogates the spreading hegemony that his empirical survey uncovers. It thus refrains from a theory that might address knowledge or inquiry as a totality in order to recall us to the "heteromorphous nature of all language games," and in the name of justice, no less (1984, 66). This leads me to ask, in an open manner, whether Dewey's theory of inquiry can interrupt this hegemony, presuming that Lyotard's sense of his present was accurate and still portrays ours.

20. I should note that Harvey's concern lies as much with how examples are themselves classified—usually within a universal-particular dichotomy—as it is with how they function in discourse.

21. I am summarizing observations offered at the beginning of "The Origin of the Work of Art" (Heidegger 1993). In doing so, I am excising Heidegger's commitment to "great art," if only because it seems to weaken the charge he gives himself in the study's early stages.

22. Gregory Vlastos sketches the evolution of *eironeia* and various cognates in *Socrates: Ironist and Moral Philosopher* (1991), arguing that after and because of Plato's depictions of Socrates, irony shed an initial sense of deception in favor of a kind of indirect communication and provocation. For a thematic recounting of various kinds of irony, see Colebrook (2003).

23. I am not defending de Man's view, though this is not a sly way to say—"of course we know this is bunk." Deconstruction remains a cluster of texts and thoughts that call for careful thinking, and to the point that there is no way around it; one has to work through it, and perhaps remain at its limits. My point is just that de Manian irony, in expanding to the figure of the "absolute" thereby becomes part of the fabric of the cosmos that define the situatedness of praxical subjects. "More clearly even than allegory, the rhetorical mode of irony takes us back to the predicament of the conscious subject; this consciousness is clearly an unhappy one that strives to move beyond and outside itself" (de Man 1983, 222).

24. My gloss draws from bk. 6.16 and bk. 9.44–46.

25. My use of "covert" draws from Wayne Booth's account in *A Rhetoric of Irony*, albeit in a looser way than he intends (1974, 5–6). Booth is primarily interested in what he terms stable ironies, namely, those whose covert meaning can be reconstructed—one can get it and show why. I am less interested in the specifics of his taxonomy, however, than the simply felicity of the term "covert." For me, then, "covert" only indicates that something other than the overt meaning is intended, and it is the reader's job to think it through. At *Republic* 337e, Socrates addresses Thrasymachus as "you best of men." I am confident that Thrasymachus is not the best of men (the overt meaning), but he is probably not the worst either, and so the covert meaning is somewhat unstable. In fact, the point may be more provocative than assertoric, that is, the address is a way of asking the reader: Why is he not the best of men?

26. All citations from the *Republic* will rely on Bloom's translation (1991). To allow readers to

consult whatever translation they have, or to check Bloom's Greek, I will refer to the Stephanus numbers that run along the margins of many versions of the *Republic*.

27. Shortly thereafter, Thrasymachus refers to Socrates's "usual trick; he'll not answer himself, and when someone else has answered he gets hold of the argument and refutes it" (337e).

28. Deborah Nails helpfully characterizes these figures and many more (2002).

29. Not only Socrates gave rise to the concerns voiced by Thrasymachus. Thucydides reports that, in the Mytilenian debate (427 BCE), Cleon heaped ridicule on the notion of public debate about matters of law and civic duty. In particular, he was scornful of sophisticated arguments that ran counter to or undermined what he took to be evident sense, and he suggested that those who love to participate in such debates are keener on speaking and outwitting one another than on prudently steering the polis (3.38).

30. I am not only thinking of Socrates's declarations of ignorance, which seem partly true and false (and thus complex, as Vlastos claims [1991, 31–32]). His tongue-in-cheek estimations of his interlocutors also come to mind. After being accused of refusing to give his own account, Socrates's replies: "That is because you are wise, Thrasymachus" (337a). Socrates also tells Euthyphro, after the latter claims "exact knowledge" about "divine laws" that "the best thing for me, my admirable Euthyphro, is to become your pupil" (5a). One is driven to hear these remarks ironically because we cannot believe that Socrates means what he says, given the evident limits of Thrasymachus and Euthyphro. As Quintilian would have it, we sense that these words are out of keeping with the character of Socrates (8.6.54–55). Socrates seems sufficiently canny to recognize a bully and a blowhard when he meets one.

31. The prevalent view is that Socrates's "habitual irony" is not a skeptical posture (let alone a vain one) but an ethical one. As Jonathan Lear puts it, to be Socratic is "*to be* ironic in the service of helping oneself and one's readers to move in the direction of virtue" (2011, xi).

32. Besides Socrates, one might also think of Rorty's pragmatic relation to terms that drift toward truth with a capital T (e.g., nature or reality), or the good with a capital G (e.g., rights). One affirms them because they are useful, not because they connect one to things in themselves or the moral fabric of nature. See Rorty (1989).

33. I take it Lear would concur, given his remark that "ironic existence does not imply that one is occasioning ironic experiences all the time. Ironic existence is rather the ability to live well all the time with the *possibility* of ironic experience. This requires practical wisdom about when [and how, I presume] it is appropriate to deploy irony" (2011, 30).

34. I am retelling in my own way the reading Charles Scott offers in *Language of Difference* (1987).

35. To appreciate how far Nietzsche takes his perspectivalism, consider the last line of section 22: "Providing that this also is only interpretation—you will be keen enough to object? Well, all the better" (1966, 31).

36. Though I am uneasy with this use of "rights," I otherwise concur with Foucault's claim that "the polemicist . . . proceeds encased in the privileges that he possesses in advance and will never agree to question. On principle, he possesses rights authorizing him to wage war and making that struggle a just undertaking; the person he confronts is not a partner in the search for the truth but an adversary, an enemy who is wrong, who is harmful, and whose very existence constitutes a threat. For him, then, the game consists not of recognizing this person as a subject having the right to speak but of abolishing him, as interlocutor, from any possible dialogue" (1997, 112).

37. A larger argument lurks. I've offered it in "Essaying America," published in *After Emerson* (2017).

38. Luther's translation of John 1:1 reads: "Im Anfang war das Wort." Faust, meditating on the translation (lines 1224–37), and focusing on *logos*, settles on "Im Anfang war die Tat," offering "deed" after considering and setting aside "word" (*Wort*), "meaning" (*Sinn*), and "power" (*Kraft*). "It is not possible for me to set the word so high," he says. "I must translate it [*logos*] differently" (Goethe [1808] 2008, 54; my translations).

39. Since doing is responsive, it is clearly derivative of the relation to which it responds. But if that relation involves the sedimented deeds of our own making and those with whom we live, it seems impossible to locate a site where one unfolds without the other. But this is not a genuine resolution of the question. Better then to note it, mark the problem, and recall another line from Wittgenstein's notebooks, this one gathered into *On Certainty*: "It is so difficult to find the beginning [*Anfang*]. Or, better: it is difficult to begin at the beginning. And not try to go further back" (1969, 62e).

40. Albert William Levi offers a genealogy of professionalism in philosophy that reaches back to Descartes and culminates in G. E. Moore, in whom an "enthusiasm for the perfection of tools and techniques, the employment of a division of labor which narrows interest and limits the area of legitimate professional concern, and a strong consciousness of purely professional commitment expressed in the professional association and increased reliance on the purely professional media of communication become decisive for the philosophic task" (1974, 251). While I agree that professionalism in philosophy has narrowed the scope and avenues of its conduct, deliberate writing needs a more refined approach than Levi's genealogy allows. Even if "method" becomes paramount in a tradition that runs from Descartes through Kant to Moore (and I'm uncertain it does), each author relates so differently to genre and logical-rhetorical operation that "method" obscures more than it illuminates when we search for possibilities. Moreover, academic professionals who eschew method nevertheless limit their address to expert cultures, and thus "method" may not be decisive for those looking to step outside of expert modes of address.

41. Melzer's text (2014) is explicitly for readers, not writers, but in recalling various examples, it offers possibilities to the latter.

42. Melzer locates four reasons for esoteric writing, two negative, two positive. The two negative reasons are the same I offer, and they are rather obvious. However, his two positive reasons (political reform and/or education of elites) do not seem to require esoteric writing, whereas the negative reasons do, and so the positive reasons seem less important for those deliberating about whether to write esoterically.

43. Culler explores Cavell's *The Claim of Reason* and tries to make room for "this stylish, mannered prose designed to capture attention" and prod one to think for oneself precisely through its occasional tedium (2003, 55). Butler offers a similar point: "Part of my point will be that to pass through what is difficult and unfamiliar is an essential part of critical thinking" (2003, 199).

44. My performative emphases are just one way of hearing this lucid summation by Robert Bernasconi:

> Locke, Kant and Hegel did not simply reflect the prejudices of their time. They reinvented those prejudices by giving racism new forms. Locke played a role in formulating the principle that masters have absolute power and authority over the Negro slaves at a time when the form of North American slavery was far from having been decided. Kant was the first to offer a scientific definition of race, and he himself appealed to this idea of race in order to legitimate prejudices against race mixing. Hegel was a *precursor*

of the mid-nineteenth-century tendency to construct philosophies of history organized around the concept of race, such as we find in Robert Knox and Gobineau. The fact that Locke, Kant and Hegel also played a role in formulating emancipatory ideas constitutes the problem I am concerned with. It does not make it disappear. This is because the annunciation of fine principles—the philosopher's stock in trade—is no guarantee that one is not at the same time undermining or negating those principles. (2003, 37)

45. Paul Taylor made the remark in a recent conference presentation, "Jazz, Standards," redirecting an analogous point from his "Race Problems, Unknown Publics, Paralysis, and Faith"—large scale social injustice gnaws at the roots of social trust and the endurance, even hope that trust underwrites (2007, 135–51).

46. This is not to say that Kant's manner of philosophizing never functions as an example. To the degree that critique culminates in transcendental arguments, the latter do exemplify philosophy in what Kant terms, at least in a footnote, the age of critique, but only in a very general and possibly academicized manner.

47. I prefer "demonstration" to "instruction" because I have philosophical writing in mind, which usually binds knowledge claims to justifications, whereas instruction in a more general sense may just involve the transmission of dogma.

48. Because philosophy rarely has anything as stable as a paradigm in place, the invocation of normal science is a stretch in this context, though not, I think, wholly unwarranted.

49. In *You Must Change Your Life*, I argued that Habermas's three modes of action do not account for the basic ways in which we are in-the-world (2002).

50. This is not to suggest that literature proper, which I would align, porously, with various genres built around paradigmatic examples, fails to contribute to transformative learning processes. But that is a matter for another time, although I have begun to sketch such a view (Lysaker 2015).

51. Friedländer suggests something similar when he draws Plato's dialogues into the vicinity of artworks (1969, 158). But as Klein shows, this view is already found in Schleiermacher (1965, 3–4).

52. Nightingale writes: "Plato uses intertextuality as a vehicle for criticizing traditional genres of discourse and, what is more important, for introducing and defining a radically different discourse, which he calls 'philosophy'" (1995, 5).

53. I will quote from Bolotin's translation (1979). I have also benefited from Bolotin's interpretation, as I have from Zuckert's *Plato's Philosophers* (2009), Kahn's *Plato and the Socratic Dialogue* (1996), and Gadamer's *Dialogue and Dialectic* (1980).

54. Though the dialogue is initiated by Hippothales's request, he is more or less abandoned a third of the way through after Socrates catches "sight of him in agony and disturbed by what had been said," adding: "And I recalled that though he was standing near Lysis he wished to escape his notice" (2102–11a). It is difficult to interpret Hippothales's response. It might indicate that he is ashamed by Socrates's beneficence, or it might indicate that he knows he can never address a handsome youth in so dispassionate a manner and so he cowers, flush with disappointment. Or he might be terrified that Socrates is stealing his prospective date. Regardless, Hippothales is not taken up into whatever progress follows, nor is he among those with whom Socrates associates himself at the dialogue's close.

55. My reading falls between Bolotin and Zuckert on this score. Zuckert somewhat overstates the case when she claims that that Socrates says that he and the boys have become friends, whereas Bolotin understates the matter when he insists that Socrates clearly refrains from pre-

senting himself as the boys' friend (Zuckert 2009, 22; Bolotin 1979, 199). While Socrates only reports that others will term "the trio friends," he nevertheless acknowledges that he, too, puts himself among them, that is, these two who regard themselves as friends. That acknowledgment must be accounted for, and precisely because it persists despite its lack of categorical knowledge. (In fact, it is this dissonance between conceptual knowledge and self-understanding that renders the trio ridiculous, according to Socrates, but all the more tender, at least to me.)

56. Gadamer takes the boys' limits to indicate that "what friendship is can indeed be asked only of those who are older" (Gadamer 1980, 8). Perhaps, but most of the other dialogues like the *Lysis*, which focus on Socratic interrogation, suggest that adults aren't very cogent with regard to matters of virtue, even when they have enacted it over the course of their lives, e.g., Nicias and Laches with regard to manliness/courage.

57. I have in mind the kind of deliberations operative in the following remark, which Derrida offered in response to a question concerning the relative necessity of an encounter with materialist thought:

> There is what you call this "encounter," which has seemed to me indeed, for a long time, absolutely necessary. You may well imagine that I was not completely unconscious of it. That being granted, *I persist in believing that there is no benefit, theoretical or political,* to be derived from pursuing the contacts or the articulations as long as their conditions are not rigorously elucidated. In the long run that could only result in dogmatism, confusion, opportunism. To impose such prudence upon oneself is to take seriously the Marxist text, its difficulty, its heterogeneity as well as *the decisive importance of what is at stake historically.* (Derrida and Houdebine 1973, 33; emphasis added)

58. My emphasis on the preparatory nature of the manifesto runs counter to Caws's claim that it is "not, generally, a prefatory pre-appendage to something else" (2001, xxv).

59. On the whole, I follow Bostock's translation, and where I don't, I will underscore the deviation. For example, she translates *Wesen* as "nature," but *Wesen*, particularly after Hegel, is *the* term for "essence." That valence should not be softened. The essay's fundamental character is at issue in Lukács's opening gambit. Moreover, nature is nearly hopelessly ambiguous and too easily an answer to the question *Wesen* poses.

60. By addressing "On the Essence and Form of the Essay" to his friend, Lukács underscores and individuates his address and performatively poses the question of its form. Does the opening "My friend!" locate his genre-defining piece outside the genre form he wishes to define and to which the other essays in *Soul and Form* aspire?

61. For example, the "moment" or *Augenblick* of the essay is not simply temporal for Lukács's but also a kind of seizing in suddenness, and thus the "moment" of the critic's destiny involves an objectivity laced with subjectivity. One might also explore how the condensing or *verdichten* that form accomplishes is churned with a kind of poetizing, the *dichten* of *verdichten* and, thus, also of making—from *poesis*—as opposed to nonhuman nature or *physis*, which only further complicates the objectivity of the essay without effacing it. For a particularly intriguing reading of "On the Essence and Form of the Essay" in terms of Kant's distinction between determinate and reflective judgment, see Huhn (1999). I am inclined to also find Hegelian motifs at work, particularly with regard to the term "form," but Huhn's analysis is illuminating.

62. Melvin Rogers finds something like a *Stellungsnahme* operating in Billie Holiday's performance of "Strange Fruit," which he then sets into a dramatic and instructive context of democratic practice in the likes of Jefferson and Whitman. I first encountered "Race and the

Democratic Aesthetic: Whitman Meets Billie Holiday" in a lecture delivered at Emory University. It later appeared as a chapter in an edited volume called *Radical Future Pasts* (Rogers 2014).

63. My inheritance inches toward Adorno's characterization, which holds that the "essay has something like an aesthetic autonomy that is easily accused of being simply derived from art, although it is distinguished from art by its medium, concepts, and by its claim to a truth devoid of aesthetic semblance" (1991). And yet, Adorno goes too far in insisting that the essay aspires to validity in a manner completely devoid of aesthetic semblance. Precisely through their work with concepts (and the limits of concepts), essays exemplify what concepts can only designate.

64. For an analysis of literary techniques in *Souls,* see Brodwin (1972). A more general analysis of DuBois's literary achievements, including but not limited to *Souls,* can be found in: Rampersad (1979). A collection edited by Dolan Hubbard (2003) explores many of the ways in which *Souls* exemplifies an emerging black consciousness in the early twentieth century. Nearer to my reading lies Cheryl Butler's suggestion that *Souls,* as an ensemble of essays, exemplifies a kind of soul that, continuous with social systems, underlies subjectivity (2003). And Robert Gooding-Williams has explored *Souls* in terms of an Afro-modern style of political thought (2009). For a reading that brings *Souls* into conversation with Walter Benjamin, see Frankowski (2014).

65. My account of German cabaret culture relies on Alan Lareau's historical review (1991) and John Houchin's account of its French predecessor, *cabaret artistique* (1984). More generally, the analogy also disconcerts given the ways in which Weimar cabaret culture (and French cabaret culture after 1900) was principally a commercial venture, or so Houchin and Lareau argue. In other words, in most cases, *Kleinkunst* was a concession to a paying crowd in search of something just above light entertainment. I take it that Benjamin's stylistic choice is precisely not a concession but an attempt to prove "equal to the moment."

References

Adorno, Theodor. 1973. *Negative Dialektic*. Vol. 6 of *Gesammelte Schriften*. Frankfurt am Main: Suhrkamp.

———. 1991. *Notes to Literature*. Vol. 1. Edited by Rolf Tiedemann. Translated by Shierry Weber Nicholson. New York: Columbia University Press.

———. 1992. *Notes to Literature*. Vol. 2. Edited by Rolf Tiedemann. Translated by Shierry Weber Nicholson. New York: Columbia University Press.

———. 2008. *Lectures on Negative Dialectics*. Malden, MA: Polity Press.

Agamben. Giorgio. 1999. *The Man without Content*. Translated by Georgia Albert. Stanford, CA: Stanford University Press.

Appiah, Kwame Anthony. 1992. *In My Father's House: Africa in the Philosophy of Culture*. Oxford: Oxford University Press.

Aristotle. 1991. *Rhetoric*. Translated by George A. Kennedy. Oxford: Oxford University Press.

———. 2002a. *Nicomachean Ethics*. Translated Joe Sachs. Newbury, MA: Focus Publishers.

———. 2002b. *Metaphysics*. Translated by Joe Sachs. Santa Fe, NM: Green Lion Press.

Bacon, Francis. 1868. *The Advancement of Learning*. 5th ed. Edited by W. A. Wright. Oxford: Oxford University Press.

———. 1996. *Francis Bacon: A Critical Edition of the Major Works*. Edited by Brian Vickers. Oxford: Oxford University Press.

———. 1994. *Novum Organum*. Translated and edited by Peter Urbach and John Gibson. Chicago: Open Court Publishing Company.

Bakhtin, M. M. 1982. *The Dialogic Imagination*. Austin: University of Texas Press.

Baldwin, James. 2010. *The Cross of Redemption: Uncollected Writings*. Edited by Randall Kean. New York: Random House.

Barthes, Roland. 1977. *Image, Music, Text*. Translated by Stephen Heath. New York: Farrar, Straus and Giroux.

Beauvoir, Simone de. 1976. *The Ethics of Ambiguity*. Translated by Bernard Frechtman. New York: Kensington Publishing Corporation.

———. 2009. *The Second Sex*. Translated by Constance Borde and Shelia Malovany-Chevallier. New York: Random House.

Benjamin, Walter. 1994. *The Correspondence of Walter Benjamin: 1910–1940*. Chicago: Chicago University Press.

———. 1996. *Selected Writings*. Vol. 1, *1913–1926*. Edited by Marcus Bullock and Michael W. Jennings. Cambridge, MA: Belknap Press of Harvard University.

———. 1999. *The Arcades Project*. Translated by Howard Eiland. Cambridge, MA: Harvard University Press.

———. 2003. *Selected Writings*. Vol. 3, *1938–1940*. Edited by Marcus Bullock and Michael W. Jennings. Cambridge, MA: Belknap Press of Harvard University.

Bernasconi, Robert. 2003. "Hegel's Racism: A Reply to McCarney." *Radical Philosophy* 119:35–37.

Blanshard, Brand. 1954. *On Philosophical Style*. Bloomington: Indiana University Press.

Bolotin, David. 1979. *Plato's Dialogue on Friendship: An Interpretation of the Lysis, with a New Translation*. Ithaca, NY: Cornell University Press.

Booth, Wayne. 1974. *A Rhetoric of Irony*. Chicago: University of Chicago Press.

Brodwin, Stanley. 1972. "The Veil Transcended: Form and Meaning in W.E.B. Du Bois' *The Souls of Black Folk*." *Journal of Black Studies* 2, no. 3 (March): 303–21.

Boynton, Robert. 1999. "Who Needs Philosophy?" *New York Times Magazine*. November 21.

Buber, Martin. 1970. *I and Thou*. Translated by Walter Kaufmann. New York: Charles Scribner's Sons.

Butler, Cheryl Blanche. 2003. *The Art of the Black Essay: From Mediation to Transcendence*. New York: Routledge Publishing.

Butler, Judith. 1999. "A 'Bad Writer' Bites Back." *New York Times*. March 20.

———. 2003. "Values of Difficulty." In *Just Being Difficult? Academic Writing in the Public Arena*, edited by Jonathan Culler and Kevin Lamb, 195–215. Stanford, CA: Stanford University Press.

———. 2005. *Giving an Account of Oneself*. New York: Fordham University Press.

Carson, Anne. 1995. *Glass, Irony, and God*. New York: New Directions Publishing Company.

Casey, Ed. 2010. "Finding (Your Own) Philosophical Voice." *Proceedings and Addresses of the American Philosophical Association* 84, no. 2 (November): 27–44.

Cavarero, Adriana. 2005. *Toward a Philosophy of Vocal Expression*. Translated by Paul A. Kottman. Stanford, CA: Stanford University Press.

Cavell, Stanley. 1988. *In Quest of the Ordinary: Lines of Skepticism and Romanticism*. Chicago: University of Chicago Press.

———. 1990. *Conditions Handsome and Unhandsome: The Constitution of Emersonian Perfectionism*. Chicago: University of Chicago Press.

———. 2003. *Emerson's Transcendental Etudes*. Stanford, CA: Stanford University Press.

———. 2005. *Philosophy the Day after Tomorrow*. Cambridge, MA: Harvard University Press.

Caws, Mary Ann. 2001. *Manifesto: A Century of Isms*. Lincoln: University of Nebraska Press.

Celan, Paul. 1986. *Collected Prose*. Translated by Rosmarie Waldrop. New York: Routledge.

———. 2001. *Selected Poems and Prose of Paul Celan*. Translated by John Felstiner. New York: W. W. Norton.

Rey Chow. 2003. "The Resistance of Theory; or, The Worth of Agony." In *Just Being Difficult? Academic Writing in the Public Arena*, edited by Jonathan Culler and Kevin Lamb, 95–105. Stanford, CA: Stanford University Press.

Cixous, Hélène. 1993. *Three Steps on the Ladder of Writing*. New York: Columbia University Press.

Colebrook, Claire. 2003. *Irony*. New York: Routledge Publishing.

Cooper, Anna Julia. 2016. *A Turn in the South*. Mineola, New York: Dover Publications, Inc.

Coover, Robert. 1992. "The End of Books." *New York Times*. June 21.

Culler, Jonathan. 2003. "Bad Writing and Good Philosophy." In *Just Being Difficult? Academic Writing in the Public Arena*, edited by Jonathan Culler and Kevin Lamb, 43–57. Stanford, CA: Stanford University Press.

Curry, Tommy. J. Forthcoming. "Towards a Black Criticus: Culturalogics, Epistemic Schemas, and the Activity of Archive in Black Philosophy." In *Contemporary African American Philosophy: Where Do We Go from Here?* Edited by Daw-Nay Evans and Tommy J. Curry. London: Bloomsbury Publishing.

Davidson, Donald. 1984. *Inquiries into Truth and Interpretation*. Oxford: Oxford University Press.

de Man, Paul. 1983. *Blindness and Insight: Essays in the Rhetoric of Contemporary Criticism*. New York: Routledge Publishing.

De Morgan, Augustus. 1847. *The Calculus of Inference, Necessary and Probable*. London: Taylor & Walton.

Del Caro, Adrian. 1982. "Reception and Impact: The First Decade of Nietzsche in Germany." *Orbis Litterarum* 37:32–46.

Dennett, Daniel. 1995. *Darwin's Dangerous Idea: Evolution and the Meaning of Life*. New York: Simon and Schuster.

Derrida, Jacques. 1982. *Margins of Philosophy*. Translated by Allan Bass. Chicago: University of Chicago Press.

———. 1995. *On the Name*. Edited by Thomas Dutoit. Translated by David Wood. Stanford, CA: Stanford University Press.

———. 2005. *Sovereignties in Question: Poetics of Paul Celan*. Edited by Thomas Dutoit and Outi Pasanen. New York: Fordham University Press.

Derrida, Jacques, and J. L. Houdebine. 1973. "Interview: Jacques Derrida." *Diacritics* 3, no. 1 (Spring): 33–46.

Dewey, John. 1981. *The Later Works of John Dewey, 1925–1953*. Vol. 1, *Experience and Nature*. Edited by Jo Ann Boydston. Carbondale: Southern Illinois University Press.

———. 1983. *The Middle Works of John Dewey*. Vol. 14, *1899–1924*. Edited by Jo Ann Boydston. Carbondale: Southern Illinois University Press.

DuBois, W. E. B. 2007. *The Souls of Black Folk*. Oxford: Oxford University Press.

Dutton, Denis. 1999. "Language Crimes: A Lesson in How Not to Write, Courtesy of the Professoriate." *Wall Street Journal*. February 5.

Emerson, Ralph Waldo. 1969. *The Journals and Miscellaneous Notebooks of Ralph Waldo Emerson*. Vol. 7, *1838–1842*. Edited by William H. Gillman et al. Cambridge, MA: Harvard University Press.

———. 1973. *The Journals and Miscellaneous Notebooks of Ralph Waldo Emerson*. Vol. 10, *1847–1848*. Edited by William H. Gillman et al. Cambridge, MA: Harvard University Press.

———. 1996. *Essays and Poems*. New York: Library of America.

Frankowski, Alfred. 2014. "Sorrow as the Longest Memory of Neglect." *Journal of Speculative Philosophy* 28, no. 2: 154–68.

Friedländer, Paul. 1969. *Plato: An Introduction*. 2nd ed. Princeton, NJ: Princeton University Press.

Foucault, Michel. 1997. *Ethics: Subjectivity and Truth*. Translated by Robert Hurley. New York: New Press Publishing.

Fulton, Alice. 1999. *Feeling as a Foreign Language: The Good Strangeness of Poetry.* St. Paul, MN: Graywolf Press.

Gadamer, Hans-Georg. 1980. *Dialogue and Dialectic: Eight Hermeneutical Studies of Plato.* Translated by P. Christopher Smith. New Haven, CT: Yale University Press.

———. 1997. *Gadamer on Celan: "Who am I and Who are you?" and Other Essays.* Translated and edited by Richard Heinemann and Bruce Krajewski. Albany: SUNY Press.

Glaude, Eddie. 2007. *In a Shade of Blue.* Chicago: University of Chicago Press.

———. 2011. "On Prophecy and Critical Intelligence." *American Journal of Theology and Philosophy* 32. no. 2: 105–21.

———. 2017. "James Baldwin and #BlackLivesMatter." In *The Political Companion to James Baldwin.* Edited by Susan McWilliams. Lexington: University Press of Kentucky.

Goethe, Johann Wolfgang von. [1808] 2008. *Faust. Eine Tragödie.* Edited by Karl Heinrich Hucke. Münster: Verlag Aschendorf.

Gooding-Williams, Robert. 2009. *In the Shadow of Du Bois: Afro-Modern Political Thought in America.* Cambridge, MA: Harvard University Press.

Gordon, Jill. 1999. *Turning toward Philosophy: Literary Device and Dramatic Structure in Plato's Dialogues.* State College, PA: Penn State University Press.

Habermas, Jürgen. 1987. *Philosophical Discourse of Modernity.* Translated by Frederick Lawrence. Cambridge, MA: MIT Press.

Hanssen, Beatrice. 2006. *Walter Benjamin and the Arcades Project.* London: Continuum International Publishing Group.

Hartle, Ann. 2007. *Michel de Montaigne: Accidental Philosopher.* Cambridge: Cambridge University Press.

———. 2013. *Montaigne and the Origins of Modern Philosophy.* Evanston, IL: Northwestern University Press.

Harvey, Irene. 2002. *Labyrinths of Exemplarity.* Albany: SUNY Press.

Heidegger, Martin. 1993. *Basic Writings.* Edited by David Farrell Krell. New York: Harper Collins Publishers.

———. 2009. *Basic Concepts of Aristotelian Philosophy.* Translated by R. Metcalf and M. Tanzer. Bloomington: Indiana University Press.

Hickman, Larry. 2007. *Pragmatism as Post-Postmodernism.* New York: Fordham University Press.

Hinman, Lawrence M. 1980. "The Style of Philosophy." *Monist* 63, no. 4 (October): 417–24.

Hippocrates. 1950. *Hippocratic Writings.* Edited by G. E. R. Lloyd. New York: Penguin Books.

Horkheimer, Max. 1972. *Critical Theory.* Translated by Matthew J. O'Connell, et al. New York: Herder and Herder.

Horkheimer, Max, and Theodor Adorno. 2002. *Dialectic of Enlightenment.* Edited by Gunzelin Noeri. Translated by Edmund Jephcott. Stanford, CA: Stanford University Press.

Houchin, John. 1984. "The Origins of the 'Cabaret Artistique.'" *Drama Review* 28, no. 1 (Spring): 5–14.

Hubbard, Donald, ed. 2003. *The Souls of Black Folk One-Hundred Years Later.* Columbia: University of Missouri Press.

Huffer, Lynne. 2012. "Foucault and Sedgwick: The Repressive Hypothesis Revisited." *Foucault Studies* 14:20–40.

Huhn, Tom. 1999. "Lukács and the Essay Form." *New German Critique* 78:183–92.

James, Robin. 2015. "Post-Genre Aesthetics, Race, and Gender." *It's Her Factory* (blog), March 26. https://www.its-her-factory.com/2015/03/post-genre-aesthetics-race-gender/.

Kahn, Charles. 1998. *Plato and the Socratic Dialogue: The Philosophical Use of a Literary Form.* Cambridge: Cambridge University Press.

Kant, Immanuel. 1996. *Practical Philosophy.* Translated and edited by Mary J. Gregor. Cambridge: Cambridge University Press.

———. 1998. *The Critique of Pure Reason.* Translated by Paul Guyer and Allen W. Wood. Cambridge: Cambridge University Press.

Kirkland, Sean. 2012. *The Ontology of Socratic Questioning in Plato's Early Dialogues.* Albany: SUNY Press.

Klein, Jacob. 1965. *A Commentary on Plato's "Meno."* Chapel Hill: University of North Carolina Press.

Kraus, Karl. 1965. *Beim Wort Genommen.* Munich: Kösel-Verlag.

———. 1986. *Half-Truths and One-and-a-Half Truths.* Translated by Harry Zohn. Manchester: Carcanet Press Ltd.

———. 2001. *Dicta and Contradicta.* Translated by Jonathan McVity. Urbana: University of Illinois Press.

Kuhn, Thomas. 1962. *The Structure of Scientific Revolutions.* Chicago: University of Chicago Press.

La Bruyère, Jean de. 1929. *The Characters of Jean de La Bruyère.* Translated by Henri van Laun. Ann Arbor, MI: G. Routledge & Sons Ltd.

Lang, Berel, ed. [1979] 1987. *The Concept of Style.* Ithaca, NY: Cornell University Press.

———. 1990. *The Anatomy of Philosophical Style.* Oxford: Basil Blackwell Ltd.

Lareau, Alan. 1991. "The German Cabaret Movement during the Weimar Republic." *Theater Journal* 43, no. 4: 471–90.

Lear, Jonathan. 2011. *A Case for Irony.* Cambridge, MA: Harvard University Press.

Levi, William Albert. 1974. *Philosophy as Social Expression.* Chicago: University of Chicago Press.

Locke, John. 1988. *Two Treatises of Government.* Student Edition. Edited by Peter Laslett. Cambridge: Cambridge University Press.

Long, Christopher P. 2014. *Socratic and Platonic Political Philosophy: Practicing a Politics of Reading.* Cambridge: Cambridge University Press.

Lukács, György. 1974. *Theory of the Novel.* Translated by Anna Bostock. Cambridge, MA: MIT Press.

———. 2010. *Soul and Form.* Edited by John T. Sanders and Katie Terezakis. Translated by Anna Bostock. New York: Columbia University Press.

Lyotard. Jean-François. 1984. *The Postmodern Condition: A Report on Knowledge.* Translated by Geoff Bennington and Brian Massumi. Minneapolis: University of Minnesota Press.

Lysaker, John. 2002. *You Must Change Your Life: Poetry, Philosophy, and the Birth of Sense.* University Park, PA: Penn State University Press.

———. 2015. "Finding Our Bearings with Art." *Nonsite*, no. 16. June 22. http://nonsite.org/article/finding-our-bearings-with-art.

———. 2017. *After Emerson.* Bloomington: Indiana University Press.

Mandelstam, Osip. 1979. *The Complete Critical Prose and Letters.* Translated by Jane Gary Harris and Constance Link. Edited by Jane Gary Harris. Ann Arbor, MI: Ardis.

Marx, Karl, and Friedrich Engels. 1992. *The Communist Manifesto.* Edited by David McLellan. Oxford: Oxford University Press.

McCall, Corey. 2008. Review of *Emerson and Self-Culture,* by John Lysaker. *Notre Dame Philosophical Reviews,* November 17. https://ndpr.nd.edu/news/23852- emerson-and-self-culture/.

Melzer, Arthur. 2014. *Philosophy between the Lines: The Lost History of Esoteric Writing.* Chicago: University of Chicago Press.

Mendieta, Eduardo. 2014a. "Philosophy's Parlipomena: Diaries, Notebooks, and Letters." *Journal of Speculative Philosophy* 28, no. 4: 413–21.

———. 2014b. "The Sound of Race: The Prosody of Affect" *Radical Philosophy Review* 17, no. 1: 109–31.

Mikkelsen, Jon. 2013. *Kant and the Concept of Race.* Albany: SUNY Press.

Montaigne, Michel de. 1948. *Selections from the Essays.* Translated by Donald M. Frame. Wheeling, IL: Harlan Davidson Inc.

Morson, Gary Saul. 2011. *The Words of Others: From Quotations to Culture.* New Haven, CT: Yale University Press.

Nails, Debra. 2002. *The People of Plato: A Prosopography of Plato and Other Socratics.* Indianapolis: Hackett Publishing.

Nancy, Jean-Luc. 1991. *The Inoperative Community.* Minneapolis: University of Minnesota Press.

———. 1993. *The Birth to Presence.* Stanford, CA: Stanford University Press.

Nietzsche, Friedrich. 1966. *Beyond Good and Evil: Prelude to a Philosophy of the Future.* Translated by Walter Kaufmann. New York: Random House.

Nightingale, Andrea Wilson. 1995. *Genres in Dialogue: Plato and the Construct of Philosophy.* Cambridge: Cambridge University Press.

Nussbaum, Martha. 1999. "The Professor of Parody." *New Republic.* February 22.

Plato. 1991. *The Republic.* Translated by Allan Bloom. New York: Basic Books.

Quintilian. 2001. *The Orator's Education.* 5 vols. Edited and translated by Donald A. Russell. Cambridge, MA: Harvard University Press.

Rampersad, Arnold. 1979. "W.E.B. Du Bois as a Man of Literature." *American Literature* 51, no. 1 (March): 50–68.

Richter, Gerhard. 2006. "A Matter of Distance: Benjamin's *One-Way Street* through *The Arcades.*" *Walter Benjamin and the Arcades Project.* Edited by Beatrice Hannssen. 132–156. London: Continuum International Publishing Group.

Rogers, Melvin. 2014. "Race and the Democratic Aesthetic: Whitman Meets Billie Holiday." In *Radical Future Pasts: Untimely Political Theory*, edited by Romand Coles, Mark Reinhardt, and George Schulman, 249–82. Lexington: University Press of Kentucky.

Rorty, Amélie Oskenberg. 1998. "Witnessing Philosophers," *Philosophy and Literature* 22, no. 2: 319–20.

Rorty, Richard. 1989. *Contingency, Irony, and Solidarity.* Cambridge: Cambridge University Press.

Schlegel, Friedrich von. 1967. *Kritische Ausgabe Seiner Werke.* Vol. 2. Munich: Verlag Ferdinand Schönigh.

Scott, Charles. 1987. *Language of Difference.* Atlantic Highlands, NJ: Humanities International Press.

Stevens, Wallace. 1971. *The Palm at the End of the Mind.* New York: Alfred A. Knopf.

Strauss, Leo. 1964. *The City and the Man.* Chicago: Chicago University Press.

Taylor, Paul C. 2007. "Race Problems, Unknown Publics, Paralysis, and Faith." In *Race and Epistemologies of Ignorance*, edited by Shannon Sullivan and Nancy Tuana, 135–52. Albany: State University of New Work Press.

Thoreau, Henry David. 2008. *"Walden," "Civil Disobedience," and Other Writings.* Edited by William Rossi. New York: W. W. Norton.

Union of Concerned Scientists. 2014. "Why Clean Cars?" http://www.ucsusa.org/clean-vehicles #.Vt3Y7BpsNBw.

Vlastos, Gregory. 1991. *Socrates: Ironist and Moral Philosopher*. Ithaca, NY: Cornell University Press.

Warnek, Peter. 2005. *Descent of Socrates: Self-Knowledge and Cryptic Nature in the Platonic Dialogues*. Bloomington: Indiana University Press.

Warner, Michael. 2002. *Publics and Counterpublics*. New York: Zone Books.

Wittgenstein, Ludwig. 1969. *On Certainty*. Edited by G. E. M. Anscombe and G. H. von Wright. Translated by Denis Paul and G. E. M. Anscombe. Oxford: Basil Blackwell Publishing.

———. 1980. *Culture and Value*. Translated by Peter Winch. Chicago: University of Chicago Press.

———. 2001. *Philosophical Investigations*. 3rd ed. Translated by G. E. M Anscombe, P. M. S. Hacker, and Joachim Schulte. Malden, MA: Blackwell Publishing Ltd.

Zack, Naomi. 2005. *Thinking about Race*. 2nd ed. Belmont, CA: Wadsworth Publishing.

Zuckert, Catherine. 2009. *Plato's Philosophers: The Coherence of the Dialogues*. Chicago: University of Chicago Press.

Index